ALONE AMONG FRIENDS
A Biography of W. Robert Parks

As President of ISU, Dr. Parks fostered a recognized collegial spirit throughout the university staff.
—MARVIN AND JULIA ANDERSON

I always think of Dr. Parks as a true friend to the students. He respected them as much as they respected him.
—BARBARA T. BROWN

Bob and Ellen Parks were very special people. The twenty years they devoted to a rapidly growing university well earned them the distinction of having the university library named after them.
—BOB AND BARBARA EDDY

Bob Parks had the respect and admiration of the entire university community throughout his tenure. He broadened the dimensions of ISU and took us to new heights.
—BARBARA E. FORKER

W. Robert Parks: The right president during the best and the worst of times at Iowa State University.
—PILAR A. GARCIA

At his inauguration, Dr. Parks said, "Iowa State University has been a highly technical university and I feel we should move towards a more broad-based university." Well, he did it. Iowa State went from six colleges to nine under his leadership and he paved the way for future presidents to build on this foundation.
—SAM HAMILTON

Dr. Parks gave me the inspiration for a lifelong involvement in politics in none other than Government 315.
—CHARLES T. MANATT

At his first convocation as president, Dr. Parks clearly laid out his vision to broaden and deepen the academic foundations of Iowa State, and he worked his plan. To the consternation of some of the previously favored, there was to be no free ride, yet he assured us that the whole university community would advance. We are what we are today as a result of Dr. Parks's vision over three decades ago.
—JOHN PESEK

We propose a toast to President W. Robert Parks for his support and dedication to the university library.
—PETER A. AND SARA R. PETERSON

Dr. W. Robert Parks and his wife, Ellen, gave dignified, inspired leadership to ISU. Their character, integrity and vision enhanced the greatness of our University.
—DUANE AND ALPHA SANDAGE

Dr. Parks's early leadership and foresight as an advocate for conservation of our outdoor resources is noteworthy.
—RALPH SCHLENKER

Thanks, Bob, for your constant friendly support during the seventeen years that I was a member of your administrative team.
—DAN ZAFFARANO

Dr. Parks merged the humanities and science into the Land Grant culture at Iowa State University in a way which permanently broadened the experience and perspectives of Iowa State students.
—STEVEN E. ZUMBACH

W. Robert Parks, president of Iowa State University, 1965–1986.

ALONE
AMONG FRIENDS
A Biography of W. Robert Parks

Robert Underhill

IOWA STATE UNIVERSITY PRESS   AMES

ROBERT UNDERHILL is Professor Emeritus of English and Speech at Iowa State University. He served as a U.S. Air Force officer in World War II and the Korean War and earned his M.A. and Ph.D. from Northwestern University in Evanston, Illinois. In 1947 he began teaching at Iowa State and later became chairman of the Department of Speech. He had a distinguished career in administration and teaching and is the author of a number of scholarly articles and books, including *The Truman Persuasions, The Bully Pulpit,* and *FDR and Harry: Unparalleled Lives.*

Text designed by Kathy J. Walker
Jacket designed by Nicholas E. Tann
Jacket image from portrait of W. Robert Parks painted by Peter Egeli and reprinted with permission
Photographs, unless otherwise indicated, courtesy of the Parks family

©1999 Iowa State University Press
All rights reserved

Iowa State University Press
2121 South State Avenue, Ames, Iowa 50014

Orders: 1-800-862-6657
Office: 1-515-292-0140
Fax: 1-515-292-3348
Web site: www.isupress.edu

Authorization to photocopy items for internal or personal use, or the internal or personal use of specific clients, is granted by Iowa State University Press, provided that the base fee of $.10 per copy is paid directly to the Copyright Clearance Center, 222 Rosewood Drive, Danvers, MA 01923. For those organizations that have been granted a photocopy license by CCC, a separate system of payments has been arranged. The fee code for users of the Transactional Reporting Service is 0-8138-1759-5/99 $.10.

∞ Printed on acid-free paper in the United States of America

First edition, 1999

Library of Congress Cataloging-in-Publication Data

Underhill, Robert.
    Alone among friends: a biography of W. Robert Parks / Robert Underhill.—1st ed.
        p. cm.
    Includes bibliographical references (p.   ) and index.
    ISBN 0-8138-1759-5
    1. Parks, W. Robert (William Robert).   2. Iowa State University—Presidents Biography.   3. Iowa State University—History.   I. Title
LD2547.U63   1999
278.1'11—dc21
[B]   99-40810

10 9 8 7 6 5 4 3 2 1

*For two special alumnae of Iowa State—
my daughters Sue and Sandy*

Contents

Foreword *by Robert D. Ray* — xi
Preface *by Martin C. Jischke* — xiii
Acknowledgments — xv

1. Iowa State University: Its Beginning — 3
2. A Boy and His Family, 1915–1938 — 15
3. Intermittent Years, 1938–1958 — 35
4. Prelude Years, 1958–1965 — 59
5. Outset of the Parks Presidency — 75
6. The Vietnam Issue — 117
7. Race Relations at Iowa State University — 149
8. Parks and ISU Extension — 173
9. Parks and Intercollegiate Athletics — 199
10. Building and Funding Iowa State University, 1965–1986 — 229
11. W. Robert Parks: A Reckoning — 251

Chronology: The Presidency of W. Robert Parks, 1965–1986 — 265
Notes — 287
Bibliography — 297
Index — 303

Foreword

The theme of this book, *Alone Among Friends,* authored by Dr. Robert Underhill, enriches the reader with the history of W. Robert Parks and Iowa State University—and to understand either, the records of both have to be examined. However, while the theme focuses on Iowa State University and its leader of twenty-one years, the author exposes the reader to much more.

For instance, if you're a history buff—or even if you're not—you will be fascinated with an era when Iowa legislators and the governor represented their constituents well by planning for a "state agricultural college" at the same time the country was being split apart over slavery. Congress established the Land-Grant Act, and the college at Ames, Iowa, became the first land-grant college in the United States.

Or, if you're especially interested in education—or even if you're not—you'll enjoy how the author traces the growth of this school to its current role as one of the world's great institutes of higher learning.

Or, if you wish to learn about a leader, educational or otherwise—or even if you think you're not interested—you'll learn about style, perseverance, and success: the kind of leadership that has had a profound effect on the lives of a great many people, especially students, motivating them to become productive contributors in agriculture, engineering, education, and so many other careers.

Or, if you would just like to know how a person can grow personally, professionally, intellectually, and happily by marrying a wonderful partner and parenting a family with strong values, then you'll certainly want to read this inspiring story about W. Robert Parks.

I would be remiss if I did not mention a personal reference about Bob Parks. I was honored to serve as Iowa's governor during fourteen years of President Parks's tenure as president of Iowa State University. I observed his style and effectiveness in his role as president of this top-level school of higher learning, and I worked with him on many occasions. He was a strong advocate for whatever his cause, and he would always make a compelling case for funding and advancing ISU—but he also was civil when it was not possible to meet all of his requests.

This book makes reference to what some of us call "the campus arrest era," the most difficult period during my governorship. Students grew extremely restless during the Vietnam War. They were being called on to risk their lives during a very unpopular war without, to them, a logical reason. Riots broke out all over the country. Students were gunned down by the National Guard at Kent State and tension ran high. Parents were demanding safety for their sons and daughters, and legislators were involved, which threatened academic freedom. It was the leadership on our campuses and the Board of Regents that prevented a catastrophe. Bob Parks was one cool-headed, sane arbiter of differences. He proved himself a true leader.

By reading this book, you are given a rare opportunity to understand how a person can prepare to be a leader and then be that leader. In Bob Parks's case, he took a good school and developed it into a great first-class university of excellence, one of pride for us Iowans—and to him we say, thank you!

Robert D. Ray
GOVERNOR OF IOWA, 1969–1983

Preface

W. Robert Parks was president of Iowa State University for more than twenty years during a difficult time in our nation's history—from 1965 to 1986. Bob was a remarkably savvy leader as well as an adept political scientist, able to use the skills of his discipline—political science—in the arena of real world leadership. The late 1960s and early 1970s saw great national debates on civil rights, equal rights, and the Vietnam War. University campuses were caught up in student protests on these issues and more general protests about student rights and responsibilities. Bob demonstrated great diplomacy, great humanity, and, above all, great skill in meeting anywhere and anytime with students, giving them a very sympathetic ear for their concerns, and maintaining the critical roles of the university and its relationship to the people of Iowa. Few universities and fewer university presidents negotiated these difficult times as well as ISU and he did. The result of his efforts for over two decades was an Iowa State University very different from the institution that existed when he assumed the presidency.

The accomplishments of President Parks were many and significant. He raised the visibility of the humanities within the College of Science and Humanities, now the College of Liberal Arts and Sciences, thus helping ISU become a broader and more complete institution. He took the dream that President James Hilton left him, and oversaw the construction and completion of the Iowa

State Center—the "crown jewel" of the university. It is difficult for me to imagine our university without the Iowa State Center: the cultural offerings—theater, music, comedy—in C.Y. Stevens Auditorium and Fisher Theater; the continuing education programs, meetings, and conferences in the Scheman Building; and, of course, Cyclone athletics in Hilton Coliseum.

Bob Parks also met the challenges posed by the baby boom generation. He led the university through a period of dramatic expansion—new residence halls; new classroom buildings; thousands of new students; many new faculty, programs, and courses; and the support services to accommodate the growing university. As the nation's first land-grant institution, ISU has a commitment to accessibility to and opportunity for public education. The expansion during the Parks presidency helped ensure access and opportunity for that generation and for future generations of Iowans.

Therefore, as the current president of Iowa State University, I am very appreciative of the tremendous vision and leadership that W. Robert Parks gave to Iowa State and of the absolutely remarkable institution—faculty, staff, and students—that he left to his successors. Iowa State University is one of our nation's greatest institutions of higher education, and we all owe a great deal to Bob Parks who helped make so much of it possible.

Martin C. Jischke
PRESIDENT, IOWA STATE UNIVERSITY

Acknowledgments

There is no heroic poem in the world but is at bottom a biography, the life of a man; also, it may be said, there is no life of a man, faithfully recorded, but is a heroic poem of its sort, rhymed or unrhymed.

Thomas Carlyle
Sir Walter Scott, 1838

In the spring of 1858 the Iowa General Assembly passed an act authorizing a "State Agricultural College and Model Farm." The original small college created by this act lies near the center of Iowa and today has swelled into a modern university—a meeting ground for ideas of growing intensity and importance. Men and women from Iowa State University have pushed their works into the consciousness of the world like huge weather fronts that sweep in from seas and over all inhabited lands.

A comprehensive history of the institution has not been written since Earle D. Ross's *A History of Iowa State College of Agriculture and Mechanic Arts* was published in 1942. *Alone Among Friends* includes the more recent story of the university and gives glimpses of persons who helped burnish the school's reputation during the latter half of the twentieth century.

An account of Iowa State University could not be written now without including considerable details from the life of William Robert Parks, for his career and the history of the institution have become inseparable. He was the school's eleventh president, serving for an unprecedented twenty-one years (1965–1986)—a period that saw major disruptions and unrest on college campuses across the nation. Many capable university presidents were swept away in this undertow of unrest, but President W. Robert Parks emerged from it with distinction and even greater honors.

The decision to write his biography was distilled through nearly four decades of teaching at Iowa State, even though my actual writing did not begin until the spring of 1997. A book of this sort could not be published without assistance from many persons. My primary obligation is to Parks himself, not only for his years of dedicated service but also for his willingness to share experiences and beliefs. Throughout our numerous discussions he and members of his immediate family, including his gracious wife, Ellen, were generous in giving their time and answers to my probings.

Moreover, I am indebted to innumerable faculty colleagues and former students in Ames or elsewhere who have served in institutions of higher education and have contributed interviews, letters, or testimonies pertaining to their associations with Robert Parks.

This book's publication also results from cooperative efforts of several other parties led by Murray Blackwelder, vice president for External Affairs at Iowa State University. Along with energetic colleagues in the Iowa State University Foundation and selected members of the Iowa State Alumni Association, Murray helped bring my efforts into print by raising funds from close friends of Robert Parks and supporters of the university. To each of these generous donors I offer sincere thanks:

Marvin A. and Julia Faltinson Anderson
Robert W. and Roberta Boeke
Barbara T. Brown
Maxine Burch
George C. Christensen
Reid W. Crawford

Bob and Barbara Eddy
Barbara E. Forker
Richard H. and Charlotte L. Forsythe
Pilar A. Garcia
Dale Grosvenor
Marion and Deane Gunderson

ACKNOWLEDGMENTS xvii

Samuel C. Hamilton
Warren and Beverly Madden
Charles T. Manatt
Wayne R. Moore
John Pesek
Peter A. and Sara R. Peterson
Stanley Redeker

Duane and Alpha Sandage
Warren and Velma Sargent
Ralph Schlenker
Bill and Toni Whitman
Daniel and Suzanne Zaffarano
Steven E. Zumbach

I would be remiss if I did not call attention to Robert D. Ray, who was governor of the State of Iowa during most years of the Parks presidency. Ray's endorsement of my work is genuinely appreciated. Also, Stanley Redeker, long-time president of the Board of Regents, along with Willard "Sandy" Boyd, president emeritus of the University of Iowa, granted lengthy interviews and, therefore, deserve my special thanks.

In addition, I am grateful to numerous persons on the staff of the William Robert and Ellen Sorge Parks Library for their assistance throughout the time I was doing research. Joan Mueller was particularly helpful in providing a secure place for study and storage of my materials. In the Documents and Special Collections Section of the library, Becky Jordan, Betty Erickson, and Judy Casey were knowledgeable and courteous. Moreover, Linda Speth, former director of the Iowa State University Press, was always supportive. I appreciate her discernment as well as her judgments and those of my editors Jane Zaring, Lynne Bishop, and Betsy Hovey.

Finally, my two daughters, Susan Mills and Sandy Ryan, were constant in their interest in the project; without their encouragement, the book would not have been written.

Robert Underhill
PROFESSOR EMERITUS OF ENGLISH AND SPEECH

ALONE AMONG FRIENDS
A Biography of W. Robert Parks

CHAPTER 1

Iowa State University: Its Beginning

There is a history in all men's lives,
Figuring the nature of the times deceas'd,
The which observ'd, a man may prophesy,
With a near aim, of the main chance of things
As yet not come to life, which in their seeds
And weak beginnings lie intreasured.

William Shakespeare
King Henry IV, Part II

"Either that basket's six inches too low or I'm jumping higher than I used to."

The backboard with hoop and net had been put up so that the owner's twelve-year-old son could practice, and the gray-haired man from next door had come over to give it a first test. He had dunked it easily, and his judgment, quickly confirmed by means of a ladder and a carpenter's folding yardstick, would not be surprising if it had not come from a university president just beyond sixty years of age. However, there are many surprises in the career of W. Robert Parks.

The life of Robert Parks cannot be separated from the history of Iowa State University. We would do well, therefore, to take a quick glance at the institution's very beginning on the Iowa prairie.

In 1858, while Stephen Douglas and Abraham Lincoln were conducting their epochal debates throughout neighboring Illinois, citizens in the twelve-year-old state of Iowa, recognizing that technically trained experts were needed to develop its natural resources, were agitating for a state agricultural college.

Benjamin F. Gue of Scott County was a member of the Iowa General Assembly at the time, and one day in the legislature he rose to proclaim in the florid style of the nineteenth century:

> Young men sorely felt the meager equipments which poverty had entailed upon them as they attempted to meet in debate the educated professional gentlemen, lawyers skilled by long practice in public speaking, with all the advantages of a college education; and it raised the inquiry, why should land grants and money endowment be given to enable the wealthy to choose the so-called learned professions, to get all the inestimable benefits of a university education while the sons and daughters of the mechanics, farmers, and all grades of workers were deprived by virtue of scanty incomes from participation in the benefits of a higher education?[1]

That was the nub of the argument: the need for agricultural and technical education was no less than the need of training for other professions. The efforts of Gue and other pioneers for technical education paid off with the chartering of the Iowa Agricultural College. A resultant bill authorizing the charter was passed by the General Assembly of Iowa and duly signed by the governor on March 22, 1858. This momentous act, providing for a "State Agricultural College and Model Farm, to be connected with the entire Agricultural Interests of the State," marks the actual founding of what would become Iowa State University.

There was spirited controversy in the Iowa legislature as to where such a "State Agricultural College" should be located, and in the summer of 1859, after considerable balloting, a farm of 648 acres in the western portion of Story County was selected. The site at the time was one of extreme isolation, which Gue described as nothing but a great prairie farm, wild, but beautiful in its wilderness, remote from railroad, river, cities or towns, it seemed far better adapted for the quiet retreat of some pioneer farmer and backwoods hunter, than for a site upon which to erect a College for the children of the farmers and mechanics of a great State.[2]

The only settlement in the region then was a hamlet called New Philadelphia, which later became the southern part of Ontario. The "Agricultural College" enterprise begun on this prairie land undoubtedly helped attract new settlers, and within a decade the village of Ames was founded nearby. This village, which would grow and become the home of Iowa State, prospered to the extent that by 1869 it could boast 650 souls and business establishments, including four general stores, three family groceries, a hardware store, two druggists, three milliners, two dealers in grain and agricultural implements, two lumberyards, two blacksmiths, a wagon shop, a paint shop, two coopers, two furniture manufacturers, two jewelers, three cobblers, two harness shops, a livery stable, two hotels, two land agencies, two attorneys, and five physicians.[3]

Arguments over education persisted even during the critical Civil War period, and the contention that higher education should be made more practical and available to more people was not confined to Iowa. In Washington, D.C., Congress also was debating the issue. One of the driving forces there was Representative (later Senator) Justin Smith Morrill of Vermont. He had introduced a bill in 1857 that called for the granting of public lands in order to establish educational institutions, but it wasn't until five years later that Congress passed such enabling legislation.

Southerners, led by Senator James M. Mason of Virginia, argued that accepting Morrill's bill would mean substituting the New England school system for that of the South. Northerners replied that southern spokesmen were opposed to educational advances for the masses. The act was no shoo-in, and by 1862 the nation was embroiled in civil strife. President Lincoln, just beginning his second year in office, was under attack by members of his own party, and although Republicans controlled Congress, the party was badly split over the slavery issue and the lack of military successes won by Union forces under the command of General George McClellan. In both Senate and House, Republican legislators divided along sectional lines, with Easterners opposing Westerners. On few economic issues was division more apparent than on the Land-Grant Act.

The outcome was that when the Land-Grant Act was passed in 1862, it was named after its chief sponsor, Representative Justin Smith Morrill of Vermont. The Land-Grant Act paved the way for many of the country's best-known universities today—Purdue, Wisconsin, Massachusetts Institute of Technology, Cornell, Texas A&M, to name a few, and, of course, Iowa State University.

The initial Morrill Act (a second one providing direct appropriations to member colleges that could show that race and color were not admissions criteria was passed in 1890) called for the federal government to provide each state with a grant of land that could be sold to finance a college, hence the name "land-grant." The amount of public land so designated was thirty thousand acres for each senator and each representative that the state had under the apportionment of 1860. Proceeds from the sale of land so chosen were to be invested in U.S. bonds or other safe stocks yielding no less than 5 percent and thus would constitute a "permanent endowment" for at least one college where the leading object should be to teach, "without excluding other scientific and classical studies," branches of learning that were related to agriculture and the mechanic arts.

Two other pieces of federal legislation, both of which had origins at Iowa State, helped define the mission of land-grant colleges. The Hatch Act of 1887 created the agricultural experiment station program, which enabled colleges to conduct agricultural research and to uncover scientific knowledge that could be shared with students and farmers. The Smith-Lever Act of 1914 extended the concept of service to the community by creating the federal Cooperative Extension Service. The concept of helping the community was unique to land-grant colleges, and the focus early ones put on agriculture is understandable because they came into existence at a time when half the U.S. population lived on farms and another 10 percent was employed in agriculture.

Iowa was the first state to act upon provisions of the Land-Grant Act. The state rushed ahead with its plans for an agricultural school, and in ensuing years the resultant institution could take justifiable pride in the fact that it was the nation's oldest land-grant university. Other states, however, followed in quick order, and within eight years, thirty-seven states had authorized some type of educational institution dependent upon the seminal Morrill Act of 1862. The growth continued, and by the time the twentieth century neared its end, the number of land-grant colleges and universities throughout the nation and in U.S. territories such as Guam and the Virgin Islands had swollen to over 105.[4]

Iowa's quick action on the Land-Grant Act of 1862 by no means ended controversy over the name of the hoped-for agricultural college or its main offerings. There continued to be hot rivalry over its location, and there were related disputes about buildings, curricula, and accountability.

Even if such an institution were to be funded, should it be at the primitive "Agricultural College" near New Philadelphia, where premature celebrations had taken place? Or should it be operated within the university already started in Iowa City?

The State University had been opened in 1856, and its supporters claimed that its very existence would be threatened if a separate institution were to be created. An agricultural college, they argued, should not be another institution but should be "attached" to the State University. Moneys derived from the sale of public lands would be given to the university, which in turn would create within its confines an "Agricultural College and Model Farm."

Opposed to that idea were proponents for a separate institution. These spokesmen, led by Suel Foster, a horticulturist from Muscatine, William Duane Wilson, editor of the influential *Iowa Farmer,* and the redoubtable Benjamin F. Gue, argued that a working class college "must be entirely independent of ordinary colleges and universities where theories are taught without practical illustrations."

Gue and his class-conscious enthusiasts, who dominated a joint committee appointed by the general assembly, jabbed at opponents and tried to ridicule the idea that a farm could be run from an urban campus. The committee report asked:

> Does any reflecting person believe that these most important provisions of the system of agricultural education can be connected with the State University, located in the heart of a populous city, where no experimental farm can be connected with it, with no suitable boarding house where young boys can be under the care and control of a suitable person who would look to their welfare? They would be turned loose after school hours, to all the enticements, vice, and corrupting influences of a city.[5]

Immediately upon the heels of chartering a "State Agricultural College and Model Farm" in 1858, the Iowa legislature created a governing board of trustees charged with overseeing the enterprise. During the first decade of its existence, the new college was more hope than reality, and it was not until 1869 that the trustees were able to secure funding for a president and a beginning faculty.

The board set the intended curriculum and chose Adonijah Strong Welch, then serving as a U.S. senator from Florida, as the institution's first president. Welch and his family came to Iowa in October of 1868, and in March of the following year his formal inauguration took place. Three men as well as a matron and teachers of sideline subjects like music, French, and German already had been chosen for a faculty.

A class of ninety-three students—seventy-seven men and sixteen women—also arrived in 1869. With its enrollment of women, the Iowa Agricultural College was the first land-grant institution to be truly coeducational from the beginning. The enterprise on the prairie was not yet impressive, and one freshman wrote his parents that the college was nothing more than a "fenced-in" farm.

Thus Adonijah Strong Welch was Iowa State's first president; there would be ninety-six years and nine more presidents before

Robert Parks of Tennessee, Wisconsin, Washington, D.C., and Ames took the post.

The near-century that elapsed between the inaugurations of Welch and Parks was not without controversy over the college's primary purpose and its curricula. Indeed, the name of the institution was frequently a point of contention. Children may chant that names will never hurt, but more experienced persons realize that adage simply isn't true. Language has a queer kind of sorcery, as if it were a guarantee of reality, and words can fix identities for good or ill.

When Iowans began their "Agricultural College and Model Farm" there was no agreement on what it should be called. As early as 1879 some supporters were saying that "agricultural college" was a misnomer. One suggestion was to rename it "National School of Science," a designation already used by the Bureau of Education. President Welch didn't like that choice but recognized the restrictions implied in "agricultural college." He paid tribute to the dominance of agricultural interests but wanted to add "industrial" to the college's name. Various other names were bandied around before 1896, when a new name, "Iowa State College of Agriculture and Mechanic Arts," was adopted by the board of trustees.

This name did not end confusion and controversy, however. In 1898 the legislature passed appropriations for the "Iowa State Agriculture College," yet the heading on the particular bill read: "State College of Agriculture and Mechanic Arts." Some agricultural leaders were not pleased and were less so when people began referring to the institution only as the "State College." That designation, they maintained, lacked recognition of the state's greatest strength. Moreover, there was frequent confusion with two other educational institutions: the University of Iowa in Iowa City and Iowa State Teachers College in Cedar Falls.

In truth, many names were being used for the Ames school. Students and most journalists at the time called it simply "Ames" or "Ames College." One history of Story County published in 1890 showed references to the "Industrial College," the "Iowa Agricultural College," and the "Iowa State Agricultural College." Hoping to create a more proper identity, the board of trustees in June 1898 gave official sanction to a college name, motto, and insignia by adopting an impressive seal with the inscription "Iowa State College of Agriculture and Mechanic Arts—Science with Practice."[6]

The name issue remained more or less dormant for the next fifty years, until the post–World War II era when returning GIs and a more mobile population combined to explode enrollments at all institutions of higher education. Expanded enrollments meant new courses at Iowa State and broader services to communities.

Again, protests arose over limitations implied in the name "Iowa State College of Agriculture and Mechanic Arts." To most people the word "college" had come to signify a school that granted only bachelor degrees or to a division within a university. In contrast, a "university" denoted an institution of higher learning—with teaching and research facilities—made up of an undergraduate division, which awarded bachelor's degrees, and a graduate school and professional schools, which awarded master's degrees and doctorates.

After World War II there was little dispute that in practice Iowa State was meeting the ordinary definition of a university. It had a flourishing graduate college and professional school and was authorized to grant master's and doctoral degrees. Iowa State was a university in every way except for its outdated name. Sentiment for adopting the name "university" was strong among faculty, alumni, and students. Michigan State and several other schools already had done it, so it was an obvious change.

Yet there was opposition to the name change, too, and one of the most influential of the opponents was Dr. Virgil Hancher, president of the University of Iowa. President Hancher regarded Iowa State as a technical institute. He had come into his presidency after a successful stint as a corporate lawyer in Chicago, and upon occasion said that he felt handicapped among educators because he "was not of the cloth." Careful observers would not agree with his modest assessment and more accurately judged him as a brilliant administrator and excellent public speaker.

Hancher marshalled lobbyists in the legislature and tried to convince many alumni of the University of Iowa that according university status to Iowa State would be a mistake. President Hancher expressed his philosophy clearly even when he came to Ames and participated in a Founders' Day Convocation on March 22, 1958. In the speech he gave as part of that day's celebration, the president of Iowa State's sister institution said:

> In the context of higher education in Iowa, it is the function of the three publicly-supported institutions of higher learning to complement, rather than supplant, the other institutions in the state. Our three institutions attempt to provide a coordinated plan of education—with teacher training predominant at the Iowa State Teachers College; with the liberal arts and sciences, graduate study, and certain professions at the State University; with science and technology, the allied applied arts and sciences, graduate study, and certain other professions at the Iowa State College.[7]

Thus the name issue was already on the front burner in 1958, when Robert Parks was appointed dean of instruction. He unhesitatingly joined with those agitating for a change to university status. Soon he had reason to wonder if he had made the right decision to return to Iowa State.

> When I came back from Wisconsin, Jim Hilton was the main person who brought me back. That was my good feeling about the whole brouhaha over names, but I was so discouraged. In one of the first dean seminars we had— before the name was changed to a university—President Hilton had taken the view that we really didn't need to change the name. Iowa State College was a great name.
> We had just been admitted to the National Association of State Universities—AAU—which was a prestigious organization, and we were the only college in its membership. Then to say that the name wasn't that important really discouraged me. I thought, "Gee, I just can't put up with this." But Hilton went around the room, and the people who needed most to say it said it outright.

Floyd Andre, Dean of Agriculture, and Helen LeBaron, Dean of Home Economics, and Merchant, Dean of Veterinary Medicine, they all said, "No, you're wrong, Mr. President. We've got to go to a university."

I know Jim Hilton expected those people to agree with his position, but to a person they didn't. That settled it, and a big, big decision was made.[8]

President Hilton, recognizing that his most dependable administrators were unanimous in support of a change to university status, agreed to present the proposal to the regents and fight for it if necessary. James Hilton, notwithstanding all his admirable qualities of leadership—integrity, organization, and vision among others—did not like verbal sparring. His strength and preference lay in one-to-one encounters, where he was able to use his prestige, personal warmth, and considerable insights.

On the other hand, Hilton's counterpart at the University of Iowa, President Virgil Hancher, was never reticent about engaging in public debate; he particularly enjoyed rebuttal and verbal ripostes. A superb public speaker, Hancher had taken a rigid view of the state's institutions of higher education: there should be one university, one technical institute, and one place primarily for training elementary and secondary teachers, so he vigorously opposed naming Iowa State a university and was able to persuade several lobbyists in the legislature to side with him.

The arguments of President Hancher and his supporters, however, failed to win much support in the general assembly and won none from the Board of Regents. It's impossible to measure the extent or the means by which Hilton and Parks won approval to rename the institution, but in reality there was less public opposition than either had expected.

The name change occurred in two steps. First, at its meeting on March 12–13, 1959, the Board of Regents approved a change of names for the five existing divisions at Iowa State College. The new official titles were College of Agriculture, College of Engineering,

College of Home Economics, College of Sciences and Humanities, and College of Veterinary Medicine.

At that meeting President Hilton presented the recommendation, written in its final form by Robert Parks, that the name of the institution be changed; however, the board carried that specific item over until its next public meeting. Then in April at its monthly meeting, the board's president reported that the regents had met in an executive session and voted (with one abstention) to accept the recommendation and file a request with the state legislature that the name of the college be so changed. Accordingly, the shift from college to university status was ratified by Iowa's Fifty-Eighth General Assembly, and on July 4, 1959, Iowa State College of Agriculture and Mechanic Arts officially became Iowa State University of Science and Technology.[9]

CHAPTER 2

A Boy and His Family, 1915–1938

Ah! Happy years! Once more who would not be a boy?

Lord Byron
Childe Harold

From Mulberry, Tennessee, where Robert Parks was born, to Chicago is a distance of 533 road miles, and another 355 from that metropolis to Ames, Iowa, where he spent most of his adult life and garnered the bulk of his laurels. The world turned around twenty-six thousand times in the years between his birth and 1986, when he retired from the presidency of Iowa State University; social, political, and economic changes that occurred during that span of seventy-one years are even more remarkable than any measurements of distance or time. Governments disappeared and were replaced by newer ones, national boundaries were redrawn, and miracles of communication and transportation made the world a smaller place in which to live.

In the interval between Robert Parks's birth and his retirement, American society underwent a revolution in manners and morals. Usually the revolution was led by shock troops first formed on college campuses.

During Parks's lifetime Americans became mobile. The automobile changed from being a luxury for a few to a necessity for all. At a time when he was still a very young boy, two women in Muncie, Indiana, spoke their minds to investigators gathering data for a seminal study entitled *Middletown*. Said one, "We'd rather do without food than give up our car." And another housewife, responding to a comment on the fact that her family owned a car but no bathtub, explained, "Why, you can't go to town in a bathtub!"

Robert Parks would see his country suffer its most severe depression, and he would witness its unprecedented prosperity along with huge improvements in the comforts of daily life. It likewise was a period during which his country fought three major wars, enjoyed incredible technological advances, and eradicated polio and small pox.

Changes in education were equally dramatic, and Parks was a leader in many of them. Fewer than 200,000 students graduated from high school in the year 1915, and only 1 out of every 50 went to college. By contrast, in the year he left his presidential office at Iowa State University, more than 2,609,000 seniors graduated from the nation's high schools, and in many school districts 3 out of every 4 graduates were going on to higher education.

Increased mobility and widespread education along with other changes had profound effects upon American communities and personal lives. Lives were not recast overnight, but they were extraordinarily altered, often with startling social effects. Let's begin slowly and turn back the calendar as we take a closer look into the life of a man who for more than three-quarters of the twentieth century was both witness and participant in some of these epochal changes.

The Year Robert Parks Was Born

At a banquet and in response to a toast in honor of babies, Mark Twain, America's unparalleled and uninhibited commentator on wisdoms and follies, reminded listeners of an obvious but often forgotten truth. "We have not all been generals, or poets, or statesmen," he said, "but when the toast works down to the babies we stand on common ground."[1]

In late autumn the gently rolling, fertile, blue-grass country of middle Tennessee is at its best. On the southern edge of this area, twenty miles from the Alabama border, lies Mulberry, the settlement nearest the farm where William Robert Parks was born. The year he entered this world, the unincorporated village had three churches, a general store, a blacksmith shop that later became a filling station, and a school that went through the tenth grade.

Mulberry is seventy-five miles due south of Nashville, and the nearest town of any size is Fayetteville, eight miles distant. The entire area is rich in history. Thirty-five miles northeast of Mulberry is Murfreesboro, which was the capital of Tennessee from 1819 to 1825 and was where Andrew Jackson and Thomas Hart Benton once practiced law. The Civil War battle of Murfreesboro (Stones River) was fought there December 31, 1862 to January 2, 1863, and today the Stones River National Military Park commemorates the site.

On the thirteenth day of October 1915, William Robert Parks—the seventh and last child of Benjamin Newton Parks and his wife Minnie Angeline (nee Taylor) Parks—was born. The newborn's arrival on the 130-acre farm two miles from Mulberry did not attract much attention beyond members of his immediate family and a few close friends and neighbors; other events were capturing the nation's interest.

It was a time when Woodrow Wilson, who had won election with a campaign promising New Freedoms, was completing his third year in the White House. Most Americans were reading about events in Europe, where in the previous year (July 28, 1914) Austria-Hungary had declared war on Serbia for presumably harboring the terrorist organization responsible for assassinating Archduke Franz Ferdinand. Germany backed her ally Austria, and Russia quickly mobilized in order to protect her small ally Serbia. Germany promptly declared war on Russia and France. Next, armies of the kaiser overran Belgium and Luxembourg preparatory to crossing into France. Britain, honoring her pledge to defend Belgium neutrality, declared war on Germany. Thus was launched what historians, with ominous prescience, termed World War I.

Initial American reaction was horror and determination to keep war from U.S. shores. At the outset, most working people across the forty-eight states were both neutral and pacifist. The famed industrialist Henry Ford, undeterred by derision from critics, particularly members of the Eastern press, chartered a steamship, filled it with preachers, pacifists, and assorted reformers, and sailed to Europe hoping to persuade combatants to "get the boys out of the trenches by Christmas."

A crisis for the Wilson administration came on May 7, 1915. On that date a German submarine fired a torpedo into the Cunard liner *Lusitania,* which went down in eighteen minutes, drowning 1198 people, including 128 Americans. Most Americans were incensed, but only a small minority jeered when President Wilson declared on May 10: "There is such a thing as a nation being so right that it does not need to convince others by force. ... There is such a thing as a man being too proud to fight."

Yet in the ensuing diplomatic notes to Germany, Wilson took a different position, virtually demanding that Germany end its submarine blockade. His secretary of state, William Jennings Bryan—a man Robert Parks's father admired very much—resigned in protest rather than go along with what he considered his chief's bellicose stance.

Articles on the front page of the *New York Times* on Wednesday, October 13, 1915—the day on which William Robert Parks was born—suggest the mood and concerns of Americans over the expanding war in Europe. The major headline was "Russia Sends an Army to Serbia's Aid," and an adjoining smaller article was introduced by "Bulgaria's Sudden Entrance into the War a Serious Blow to Allied Hopes." On the far side of page one was a boxed caption regarding a speech Theodore Roosevelt had given to a New York chapter of the Knights of Columbus: "Roosevelt Bars the Hyphenated!" Jingoism was spreading rapidly, and the former president fanned it further by declaring there was "no room in this country for dual nationality."

In 1915 the names of General John (Blackjack) Pershing, Eddie Rickenbacker, Alvin York, and other heroes of the "war to save democracy" were not well-known. Alvin York—later Sergeant York, the most decorated man to come out of that war—was twenty-eight years old, living a backwoods life a hundred miles north of Robert Parks's birthplace.

Calvin Coolidge had forsaken his law practice in Northampton, Massachusetts, in order to become a member of that state's senate. Warren G. Harding was in Washington, D.C., as a U.S. senator after his affable personality had won him support from Ohio's political leaders in the off-year congressional races of 1914. Dwight Eisenhower, a twenty-five-year-old graduate of the military academy at West Point, was in Texas completing his first post. Another future president, Lyndon B. Johnson, was seven years old, growing up on the banks of the Pedernales River in the parched environs of the Lone Star State.

Two other persons destined to live in the White House were only two years old in 1915: Richard Nixon was in Whittier, California, toddling around in the small grocery store owned by his parents, and Leslie L. King (Gerald Ford had been christened Leslie L. King but later was renamed after being officially adopted by his stepfather) was living with his mother in Omaha, Nebraska. In northern Illinois, Ronald W. Reagan was a chubby four-year-old whose father upon seeing his son for the first time remarked, "Why, he looks like a fat little Dutchman." The nickname Dutch stuck with Reagan up through his college years.

John F. Kennedy would not be born until another two years had passed, and it would not be until 1924 that Jimmy Carter and George Bush would make their entrances into the world.

Ancestry

By 1915 the name Parks was far from unknown in the middle Atlantic states. One of Robert's ancestors, Thomas Parks, had migrated from England to the colony of Virginia during the first quarter of the eighteenth century. In the 1750s this Thomas Parks moved to Albemarle County, Virginia, and at his death it was learned he had bequeathed all his "worldly stock and substance unto my best beloved son Thomas Parks likewise I do make and constitute him to be my sole heir and executor." To his other sons, John, Samuel, and Charles, as well as to daughters Martha Russell, Mary Bond, and Elizabeth Hutchins, he left one shilling each.[2]

Thomas Parks, Jr., moved to North Carolina, and among items in his will accepted by the court in January 1791 were (1) to wife, Priscila (*sic*), "one negro girl Ivy and the land and plantation whereon I now dwell," (2) to "daughter Peggy one negro girl named Hannah to her and her heirs forever the said negro to be delivered to her at the time of the rest of my estate being divided or at the day of her marriage," (3) to son Reuben, "All the land whereon I now live as low down as the middle branch after the demise of his mother," (4) to son Ambrose, "my Island land," (5) also to wife, Priscila, "the use of all my moveable Estate only as before directed during her natural life and then to be equally divided among children, namely, Ambrose, John, Thomas, Reuben, Aaron, Mary Johnson, and William."[3]

The North Carolina state census of 1787 lists Aaron and his brother Ambrose as living on adjacent farms. It was a period of extensive migration from that state to the newly opened lands of Tennessee, and Aaron Parks was among those making the move. Carrying with them their household belongings and some livestock, Aaron's family settled into a wild area near East Norris Creek about midway between the future villages of Fayetteville and Mulberry.

It was truly a frontier region then, with heavily timbered hills and dense canebrakes along the streams. No Indians inhabited the area, but several tribes were using it as hunting grounds. They were hostile to white intruders, but by 1809, the year Lincoln County was created, the Indians had surrendered their claims to the region.

William Parks was the oldest child of Aaron and Oney Parks. He was active in buying and selling land in the Norris Creek area for more than three decades. He and his wife Mary (nee Thurston) had ten children, one of whom was Benjamin Thurston Parks, who would become Robert Parks's great grandfather.

Around the middle of his lifetime, Benjamin Thurston Parks planned to leave Tennessee in favor of a move to Texas, but he became ill and had to cancel those plans. He survived his illness, however, and in 1856 purchased 515 acres of land near Mulberry Creek. The price was $20,620. At the time of his death in 1857, his will directed (1) amounts of $10,500 and $4,510 were to be paid to Willis Holman (the man from whom he had purchased the 515 acres), (2) his wife was to receive the entire estate for life or during her widowhood (after her death or remarriage the estate was to be divided among their five children), and (3) "If any Negroes belonging to the estate should prove disobedient or uncontrollable, they could be sold and the money put in interest for the benefit of the family."[4]

It is not known how many slaves Great Grandfather Benjamin Thurston Parks owned. His account book, now in the possession of Joe Parks, lists the names and dates of birth of twenty-three, dating from 1839 to 1862. A hundred and fifty years later, W. Robert Parks of Iowa State said this about his great grandfather:

> My brother, Joe, had a ledger ... a kind of record my great grandfather kept—a mishmash sort of thing telling what he had bought or sold—and it had a list of twenty-three black people at different times. He just had the dates with their names, and the date they were born. ... He wasn't a large slave owner; I don't know how many he had, but he owned some. ... My sister and I didn't like to go to his son's (my grandfather) house because it was kind of a gloomy old place and just no fun. Anyway, in those early days the most fun for us was going to a little cabin on my grandfather's place where two inhabitants were Uncle Louis and Aunt Rose Parks. They were descendants of slaves; there was no doubt about that, and they were real fun to be with. They always had nice stories or a little something to show us.[5]

Benjamin Thurston Parks's wife Martha (nee Thomison) died in 1880, and pursuant to the will of her husband, she left each of their five children approximately one hundred acres of the original estate.

The oldest of these five children was Elisha Thomison Parks, paternal grandfather of W. Robert Parks.

Although a Confederate state, Tennessee was not among those fervently advocating secession; in fact, it was the last state to secede and the very first one to come back into the Union. Most military historians surmise that it might have remained neutral like Kentucky and Maryland except for its location. The state was long if measured east to west, and it so happened that the blue-uniformed soldiers, to do any good, first had to come right straight through Tennessee, so battles were brought to the state.

During the Civil War, Elisha Parks served in the Eighth Tennessee Regiment, and Robert Parks related an account of his grandfather's military career:

> My Grandfather Parks was a Confederate soldier in a Tennessee regiment. I don't think his regiment ever got out of the state, but he was injured in the Battle of Murfreesboro, also called the Battle of Stones River. You know those old muzzle-loading guns— you shot once and then had to load them. The usual procedure was to put the stock of the gun on your knee while reloading. Well, my grandfather shot and then cocked his knee up to rest his gun on it while reloading. Some Yankee shot him in the knee, and so he was crippled the rest of his life.[6]

Elisha Parks and his wife, Mary, had four children, the oldest of whom was Benjamin Newton Parks, father of Robert Parks. Benjamin married Minnie Angeline Taylor on St. Valentine's Day, 1895. The couple would have seven children, with Robert being their youngest.

Minnie Angeline Taylor, Robert's mother, also had ancestors with distinguished histories. About the middle of the 1600s, James Taylor of Carlisle, England, landed in colonial Virginia. To family and friends he became known as "James the First," and some genealogists claim to have traced his ancestry back to Rowland Taylor of Madleigh, England, who was burned at the stake in 1555, a year in the early reign of Queen Mary, later called "Bloody Mary."

A BOY AND HIS FAMILY, 1915–1938

James the First married twice, and his unions produced eleven children in all. One daughter, Frances, married Ambrose Madison, a large landowner on the shores of the Chesapeake Bay and the grandfather of James Madison, fourth president of the United States.

A later U.S. president also descended from the line of James Taylor. One of James the First's grandsons was an early Zachary Taylor, who had a son appropriately named Zachary Taylor II. This son in turn was grandfather of the better known Zachary Taylor—Louisiana planter, general in the Mexican War, and twelfth president of the United States.

William Blanton Taylor, Robert's maternal grandfather, was born in 1838, and at the age of twenty he married a neighbor's daughter, Angeline Scott. Angeline's father had died, and the young girl, not yet fifteen, was living with her mother close to William Taylor's home. A year and half after their marriage, their first child was born; eleven others would follow. The tenth was Minnie Angeline, destined to become the mother of Robert Parks.[7]

When talking about his ancestry, Robert Parks described his grandfather William Taylor:

> Neither my mother's nor my father's side of the family was particularly illustrious, but the Taylor side must have had more status than the Parks side. They came over earlier. When my maternal grandfather and grandmother met, he was quite an operator. He had six boys and six girls, and when he died, he left something to each of them—some money. And my mother got some of that. He started absolutely from nothing, settled down, and got capitalistic notions, inventions, all that, and was good at business. He was outstanding and successful; how well he was liked in the community, I don't know. I do remember my father didn't like him very well, for I recall him saying, "Your mother's father [William Taylor] sometimes makes me so mad I can hardly stand it." So I think he probably was a snob.[8]

William Taylor's daughter, Minnie Angeline, married Benjamin Newton Parks when she was nineteen, and their first child was

Mary Badgett. Mary Badgett was like a second mother to young Robert Parks. When she was twenty-four years old, she married Floyd Farrar, a teacher in the Tennessee public schools, and they spent most of their wedded life in Nashville. Unlike her mother, Mary Badgett would bear only one child.

The first son born to Benjamin and Minnie was Elisha Taylor. Everyone called him Taylor, and he became a hero and role model for his brother Robert. The latter described their relationship:

> He [Taylor] meant a great, great deal to me. As a young adult he went to Texas, where he had a rich aunt and the best luck in the world—trying to farm a place that simply wasn't farmable. However, the land was in the heart of a rich oil field, and this aunt got wealthy overnight. Well, she did something really important for the family. She took Taylor out there and got him started in real estate or something like that. He made it big and moved to Shreveport, but the interesting thing about him was that he was totally unhappy. He was an academic for sure. So he ditched it all when he was twenty-six years old, came back to college, got his Ph.D. in six years. He was my major professor at Berea College.[9]

Early Years

Benjamin and Minnie Parks already had six children when their youngest one arrived in 1915. Elisha Taylor Parks, the first boy in the family, was two years younger than Mary. The second boy was named Claude Alexander and was the only boy from Benjamin's family who did not choose to make his mark in the field of education. Instead, Claude went into business with the Southwestern Gas & Electric Company in Shreveport, Louisiana.

Born in 1903, the third son was Joseph Howard, who, like older brother Taylor, got a Ph.D. in history. Joe would become a distinguished professor at the University of Georgia.

Another son, Horace Newton, arrived in 1903, and he, too, became a teacher. Horace was forty-six years old at the time of his death and was serving then as the supervisor of vocational agriculture for Middle Tennessee College at nearby Murfreesboro.

Four years before the birth of Robert Parks, Benjamin and Minnie had a second daughter—Minnie Lorraine. Lorraine would marry James Hatcher and move farther south to Mobile—Alabama's tiny portion of land on the shore of the Gulf of Mexico.

Days on a hardscrabble farm in middle Tennessee began early for the Benjamin Parks family. Keeping a large family afloat during lean times and on marginal land meant work and lots of it. From all reports Robert Parks, the youngest in the family, was more sheltered than his siblings, yet from the time he started school, he, like every other member in the family, had responsibilities.

According to Parks, his father was an unsung hero. In addition to trying to eke out a living for a large family, Benjamin Parks had a job delivering rural mail—a job he kept for more than thirty years. There were three rural mail routes around Mulberry, and Benjamin drew the worst one. It was strictly hill country with rocky, rough roads and was often tough going—blistering sun in summer, sometimes pounding rain, lightning, and in winter snow or sleet. Benjamin carried mail with his horse and buggy—a buggy that had little curtains on the sides—for twenty-five years before he was able to use a car and bounce his way along the washboard route.

The farm itself wasn't much. In later life whenever Robert Parks would describe it, he'd say:

> Our "farm"—I hate to use that word because it has a connotation which doesn't really fit—was a subsistence farm, but when you talk about subsistence, you're usually talking about poor people. We weren't in that category. My father had a job. ... But the farm gave all the kids a place to work. We really lived on a cash income from my father's job ... that was our dependable source of income.[10]

Robert Parks started school in Mulberry when he was six years old. The Parks children had a horse and buggy of their own, and during the day their horse, along with those of other pupils, was kept in the stable just behind the school itself. Horace, who was eighteen the year Robert started school, usually hitched up the horse and drove, but he also helped eleven-year-old Lorraine watch over the baby of the family. It was a big thing for Robert to climb into the buggy and go off to school with his sister and brother. These three usually went together, but as Robert grew older he often walked by himself. The two miles each way, he said, "wasn't much for a healthy kid."

He liked to dawdle on the way to and from school, examining new weeds or flowers and throwing stones at whatever struck his fancy. He was eager to play catch with his bigger brothers but wouldn't throw baseballs until his teen and young adult years.

The first three grades of the Mulberry school were lumped together; the next seven met separately. Robert said he liked school from the very beginning and "could hardly wait to get there." Years later, his daughter Andrea gave a slightly different version, saying her grandmother told her that in his earliest years Robert wasn't much interested in schoolwork. His interest didn't develop until he took up sports and only then because he wanted to be sure he was eligible for baseball and basketball.

Asked about his earliest remembrances of the little school in Mulberry, Parks said:

> I do remember one thing. My mother had bought me a lunch basket—a little thing, not very substantial. I took my lunch in that, but I soon saw that my playmates in the first grade were bringing paper sacks. I got into a fight about that once, just a friendly fight, but it broke my basket, and from that point on I carried a sack like the rest of them.[11]

Robert's parents always took keen interest in their children's schooling. Benjamin was chairman of the Mulberry school board and led community efforts to get the school there enlarged. However, the state legislature passed a school consolidation measure that allowed only three four-year high schools in Lincoln County, so Benjamin and his cohorts were disappointed.

Despite its small size and limited funds, the Mulberry school maintained good standards. Parks remembered Era Mae Richardson, who taught seventh grade, as one of the best teachers he ever had. "She was a spinster but married later," he said, "and she was tough, especially on grammar and language—that sort of thing."

If Miss Richardson and her colleagues were tough, it must have been only during school hours, for according to Parks he and five or six of his buddies "loafed like crazy" at Mulberry. They thought it was "real cool" not to have to study or take books home—an attitude that worried his parents.

There weren't a lot of books in the Parks home when Robert was very young, although several monthly magazines were always lying around. One was a general farm magazine called *Home Comfort,* and his mother subscribed to *Cosmopolitan* and *Ladies Home Journal,* both of which he read regularly. It was not unusual for the boy to get a book for birthdays or Christmas. Parks didn't recall that any of the books were very "intellectual" but said he doted on the Horatio Alger series. Alger's story was always the same, namely, a young boy who through honesty and hard work would strive and succeed. Critics claimed he wrote his first book, *Ragged Dick,* and then rewrote it thirty-two times under titles such as *Onward and Upward, Bob the Bootblack, Sam at the Sawmill, Tom the Tailor,* and *Dan the Draper.*

Benjamin and Minnie Angeline Parks were religious enough to attend their Baptist church nearly every Sunday, and children living at home were expected to accompany them. From all reports, however, the home Benjamin and Minnie Angeline established was an open, liberal one, tolerant of any view. Religion in the home wasn't rigid, but the parents didn't want their children to forget it either.

Lessons learned at Sunday school during childhood stayed with Robert Parks all his life. For example, Iowa State University had a tradition of a ceremonial lighting of a Christmas tree on the central campus long before Parks became president of the institution. In remarks at the lighting ceremony one year, he reminisced that in Sunday school his teacher always wanted students to learn the Bible, so when she called a student's name, he or she couldn't just answer "here." The answer had to be a verse from the Bible. Parks complained whimsically that with his name so far down the alphabet, by the time the teacher got to him the other kids had used up all the short verses like "Jesus wept" or "God is Love."

Benjamin Parks's home was a friendly environment enriched by close family ties. Robert remembered sitting in a semicircle in front of the fireplace in the living room and listening to his parents and older brothers and sisters discuss current topics. Among those was the sensational Scopes trial, which took place in nearby Dayton.

In 1925 the state of Tennessee passed a statute that prohibited public schools from teaching any theories of evolution contrary to the one of divine creation as related in the Bible. John T. Scopes, a biology teacher, was indicted and tried on charges of teaching the Darwinian theory of evolution. The proceedings captured the nation's interest, and the little town of Dayton was delighted with the circus atmosphere that took over as reporters and observers poured in from all over the country. Clarence Darrow and other distinguished attorneys appeared in Scopes's defense, and William Jennings Bryan was chosen to lead the prosecution. Robert Parks recalled that his father, Benjamin, believed unreservedly in Bryan's arguments and thought Darrow and his cohorts were "scum." Scopes was convicted but later released on a legal technicality. The law remained on the state's books, although the outcry over the case undoubtedly discouraged enactment of similar legislation in other states.

Robert also recalled when Charles A. Lindbergh astounded the world in 1927 by landing in Paris after flying solo in his tiny monoplane, *The Spirit of St. Louis,* across the Atlantic. Parks was going on twelve years old then, and every member of his family thought Lindbergh's feat was "big, really big," likely to have a greater impact than even Robert Fulton's steamboat, invented more than a century earlier.

Parks didn't recall any discussion about a local industry that would become nationally known: the Jack Daniel's Distillery. It was located in Lynchburg, just seven miles up the road from Mulberry. Liquor wasn't kept in the Parks home, or if it was, the children weren't aware of it. Benjamin Parks and his wife were good Democrats, but Mulberry was a very dry hamlet. Benjamin and Minnie Angeline supported Franklin Roosevelt and didn't like Al Smith because he was a "wet" and wanted to repeal Prohibition. Nevertheless, Robert suspected that his father "might have liked a little nip every once in awhile if it had been handy."

By the late 1920s, Robert Parks could occasionally go to a movie in nearby Fayetteville, although his parents were careful about the films he was permitted to see. They didn't think movies were a very good thing. Nor did they really approve of card playing; cards, they thought, were not good for young people and often led to worse pastimes.

Behavior standards in the Parks home were neither strict nor harsh. When the children needed disciplining, either parent might administer punishment, but when the mother did it, she did it not by using a stick or switch but in her own way—assigning another chore or taking away an expected pleasure. Parks, however, stressed that his father was always fair and treated all the children equally.

> There was one, however, who didn't get the message. That was Joe—in some ways the most successful of us boys. Joe was twelve years older than I, so I never witnessed it, but he was a hard one to live with. He and my father must have been at loggerheads. I remember Joe ran away from home one time, but he came back and turned out to be one of the most loyal and home-loving persons of us all.[12]

By the time Robert Parks was ten years old, sports had become a consuming passion. Helping stoke that fire was admiration for the athleticism of his older brothers, Taylor, Joe, Claude, and Horace. All were then about six feet tall—as tall as their father, who was putting on more weight. Young Robert was shooting upward, too. Already he was playing basketball with the freshman and sophomore boys at the Mulberry school. In those days, basketball rules called for a jump at center court after every basket, so a tall boy who could play center was always a team standout.

Robert had other advantages. Not only was he tall and agile, his brother Joe was a high school teacher and athletics coach. Brother Horace also was a teacher and assistant coach at another school, so between them they supplied Robert with a basketball, football, or baseball and bat. He was always well equipped for sports.

Sports were a primary motivation during his last two years of high school. A good school bus system had been established by then, and at first he tried riding that bus into Fayetteville. However, there was a problem because the school bus would load up rural kids as soon as classes for the day were over. Basketball practice began then, so most farm boys couldn't stay for it. Brother Joe came to the rescue and arranged for Robert to stay with a cousin right there in town.

During his two years of high school in Fayetteville, Robert Parks was a skinny six-foot kid weighing less than 145 pounds. The Lincoln County High School basketball team with him at center was good enough to win the county tournament. His team was playing in the district tourney when he first heard of the oncoming depression. The news hit hard when the coach told the boys there was no money to get them home—the school had run out of funds. Some players had a little pocket money, and by pooling that collection the team got back to Fayetteville. It was the end of the season anyway.

Throughout the Great Depression, life on the farm of Benjamin Parks was not too bad by community standards. Banks closed all around them, but since the Parks family had no money in a bank, the impact was indirect. Benjamin and Minnie Angeline were scared, but so was everybody else. At least he had his job as a mail carrier, so they had a regular income—something most of their neighbors did not.

As weighed on most scales, the cruelest year of the Great Depression was 1932, when somewhere between 12 and 13 million people were out of work—the figures varied according to whose scales were being used. Two years later when Parks graduated from high school, some of the political momentum that had swept Franklin Roosevelt into the White House had ebbed.

The precedent-breaking legislation passed during FDR's remarkable First Hundred Days was credited for a quick upsurge in business. Proponents of that belief liked to point to the Federal Reserve Board's Adjusted Index of Industrial Production, which had risen all the way from 59 in March 1933, when he took office, to 100 in July. Then in August a setback began: the index receded from 100 to 91. In September it slipped to 84, in October to 76, and by November it had reached 72. Critics began to ask if the New Deal recovery was just a flash in the pan.

As the winter of 1933–1934 set in, the New Deal's once solid support started to fragment. Admittedly, unemployment figures were lower, but many liberals were unsatisfied with what they considered the snail's pace of the Roosevelt program. Farmers were angry at the failure of the Agricultural Adjustment Act (Triple A) to bring better prices for their crops, and labor unions complained that the National Industrial Recovery Act, which stated that "employees shall have the right to organize and bargain collectively ... shall be free from the interference, coercion, or restraint of employers ... or their agents," was not being enforced. Instead, charged labor leaders, the NRA (as it was popularly called) had been captured by employers who were using it to their great advantage.

One New Deal measure extremely popular in the region where Robert Parks spent his boyhood was the Tennessee Valley Authority, which Congress approved in May 1933. The act that created the agency provided for federal operation of an existing dam at Muscle Shoals, Alabama, but even more important, it included an ambitious plan for development of the whole Tennessee Valley through the building of other federal dams, through the sale of power from them at low prices, and through federal subsidizing of conservation measures throughout the valley. There were no electric lights on the farm while Robert was growing up, and shortly after he started college, his parents moved into nearby Mulberry.

Not many high school graduates went on to college during those depression years, but the Parks boys were exceptional. Strongly encouraged by their parents, four of the five boys would go into some branch of education, and three would earn Ph.D.s. In 1934, when Robert graduated from high school, Taylor, Joe, and Horace already were teaching. There was no question in young Robert's mind; he intended to follow the path taken by these brothers.

In high school Robert's academic record had developed rather late, but by the spring of 1934, it had grown enough to put him very near the top of his class. Taylor, the oldest brother in the family, was teaching at Berea College, fifty miles south of Lexington, Kentucky, and undoubtedly he helped steer Robert there.

Berea was modeled after Oberlin College in Ohio. The latter was chartered in 1834 by two missionaries as an institute combining educational philosophy and manual labor. The school was a pioneer in coeducation, having given degrees to women in 1837, and during the Civil War era was a strong abolitionist center.

John G. Fee, founder of Berea College, had graduated from Oberlin and believed implicitly in that school's system. Oberlin had been among the first of American colleges to admit blacks, and when Fee secured the charter for Berea in 1855, he followed the Oberlin creed.

Berea's announced mission was to further the education of able southern mountain boys and girls who needed financial help. By the time Parks arrived, the school had a comparatively liberal environment and wherever possible was encouraging the joint education of blacks and whites. Parks summarized his reasons for choosing Berea:

> Berea took the bulk of their students, 90 percent of them, from mountain counties. I was not from a mountain area; Lincoln County is not mountainous, but 10 percent came in on their high school record and their entrance examinations. And I did well on those. I don't think my brother Taylor had anything at all to do with my acceptance other than maybe he himself was well thought of there. It was the school most available to me at the time. I'd rather have gone to Vanderbilt or something like that but had no chance of doing it.[13]

Among crafts taught at Berea College were woodworking, baking, iron mongering, weaving, mechanics, and broom making. Products from such endeavors were later sold. Every student had to have a labor assignment, and to abet that assignment, the college owned several businesses, including the town's utilities, a press, a tavern, and several other manufactories. The tavern, according to Robert, wasn't much—just a "hanging out" place; most of the town was "dry as a bone."

While at Berea, Robert worked in the college press, which among other contracts printed the weekly county newspaper. The paper consisted largely of jobs or job applications, for there was still a lot of unemployment in that Kentucky county. He was mainly a proofreader, putting into practice some of the language skills that had been honed by his mother. Minnie Angeline was ever alert to her children's grammar, and Robert said that he and she often would try to catch one another in grammatical errors.

Berea College had 734 students enrolled the year Parks started there, and the town itself numbered 1510 persons. Because he wanted so badly to be like his older brothers, all three of whom had established strong academic records, Parks put a damper on his athletic ambitions. He played on the freshman basketball and baseball teams at Berea but didn't go out for the varsity, which then was limited to the upper three years. By the time he started his second year at Berea, he had made up his mind what he wanted in a career, and that future didn't lie in sports.

By going to school throughout the summer months, he was able to graduate in three years. His favorite courses there were literature, history, and political science. Early in college he thought about law and for a short while had dreams of being an attorney—a Clarence Darrow type—but when he found out more about law courses, he abandoned the idea. He just didn't relish spending so much time with wills, mergers, deeds, and contracts.

He liked the way political science was presented by one professor, but he wasn't sure of job opportunities in it—a huge consideration for a kid coming out of the Great Depression era. Of one thing he was certain: he wanted an academic career like his brothers.

CHAPTER 3

Intermittent Years, 1938–1958

People wish to be settled; only as far as they are unsettled is there any hope for them.

Ralph Waldo Emerson
"Circles," *Essays: First Series*

Robert Parks enrolled at Berea College in the fall of 1934, and by going to classes throughout the torrid summers of 1935 and 1936, he was able to complete his undergraduate degree in 1937. Eager to match the educational records of his older brothers, he immediately started graduate study at Kentucky University in Lexington, fifty miles farther north. The state university with its student body of corduroy-clad young men and women decked out in saddle shoes, bobby socks, and pleated skirts was quite a transition for the young man from a small town in southern Tennessee.

Parks wasn't yet sure about his future but knew he wanted to work somewhere in the social sciences. He chose, therefore, to major in political science at the University of Kentucky. A favorite professor taught political science, however, and further honed his interest in political systems and philosophies. Studying politics, current political topics, and politicians soon was more enticing than the field of history. Although still interested in history, he couldn't forget the

Great Depression, when so many people were unable to find employment; moreover, he thought there would be better jobs in political science than in history, where there were no possibilities except in teaching. By contrast, political science held opportunities in government positions, city managerships, and a broad spectrum of other endeavors.

At the University of Kentucky a master's thesis was required for political science majors, and Parks chose to do his on the justice of peace system, established in England in 1630. These justices, selected from the gentry, had large administrative and police authority; they represented royal authority to local government, especially in rural areas of the British Isles. The JP system was set up in the American colonies, but by the nineteenth century it had become relegated to a minor role in both England and the United States. "The Squire in England," Parks said, "really amounted to something. He was the head honcho."

Upon receiving his master's degree, Parks was ready to move into a Ph.D. program. He didn't give much thought to undertaking it there at Kentucky because even though advanced graduate study in political science was offered, the doctoral program was not considered near the quality of ones at Wisconsin, Michigan, Minnesota, Indiana, or several other states. Parks later gave his reasons for choosing Wisconsin:

> I remember only two Ph.D. students in political science at Kentucky while I was there. The program was very small, and even my professors didn't encourage me to stay; instead they urged me to go to Wisconsin. One of my best teachers had a Ph.D. in political science from Wisconsin, and he was instrumental in encouraging me to go to Madison. Furthermore, I got a good teaching assistantship, which, of course, was a great inducement.[1]

Accordingly, in the fall of 1938 Parks and a friend, who had taken his master's degree in mathematics at Kentucky the same period that Parks had earned his in political science, went to Wisconsin University together. The trip took him farther from home than he had ever been before and into a region where he faced both environmental and cultural shocks.

He had seen occasional light snows before but nothing like the deep blankets of it in Wisconsin. Despite an early purchase of a long, heavy winter overcoat, he thought the weather was "frightfully and intolerably cold."

Furthermore, Wisconsin introduced Parks to landscape different from what he had been used to. Lakes or rivers mark most of the state's boundaries: to the east is Lake Michigan, to the north Lake Superior, and the Mississippi River separates much of Wisconsin from Iowa and Minnesota. Within the state, too, are several sizable lakes and countless smaller ones that accent its verdant forests and have made the area attractive to homesteaders and tourists alike.

As a young graduate student in 1938, Parks discovered that along with environmental changes from Lexington to Madison came cultural shocks. Admitted to the Union in 1848 as its thirtieth state, Wisconsin had gained a reputation for progressivism. The state was among the first to establish a free public school system ranging up and through the university level. Abolitionist groups in Wisconsin helped in the early formation of the Republican Party. During the 1880s and 1890s, distress of farmers in Wisconsin helped set off fierce opposition to eastern railroad companies, which were being fattened by enormous land grants. The trend in the state toward liberal political views, already strong, was given additional impetus in 1906, when the crusading Robert M. La Follette undertook his first term as a U.S. senator. Joined by other leaders, La Follette, who ran for president of the United States in 1924 on the Progressive ticket, succeeded in keeping Wisconsin in the forefront of most liberal legislation.

As a political scientist Robert Parks was keenly interested in the careers of public figures as well as federal and state legislation, particularly that which concerned agriculture. Politics in Wisconsin was exciting to him, therefore, because it was different and innovative.

Throughout his life he would follow political events very closely. Once he became an administrator, he was increasingly careful about separating his personal leanings from professional judgments or decisions. Wayne Cole, a friend of the Robert Parks family while they lived in Ames, recalled a discussion that illustrated in part Robert's political orientation:

> Both Bob and Ellen Parks were liberal Democrats, and both reflected Wisconsin's progressivism. A specific episode comes to mind revealing their value systems. In the midst of the McCarthy era I was bemoaning McCarthyism and expressing fear that it could be pointing toward some form of fascism in the United States. Bob, who abhorred McCarthyism as much as I did, took a more hopeful, even optimistic, view. He said he had more confidence than I had in the good sense and decency of the American people. He thought McCarthy would go too far and in doing so would alienate the American sense of decency. At the time I said I hoped he was right but feared that he was wrong. Of course, in the turn of events he was right and I was wrong.[2]

Another change Robert Parks encountered when he arrived on the Wisconsin campus was that he found himself thrust into a wider group of nationalities than he had known in rural Tennessee or Kentucky. The diversity of cultures in Wisconsin is traceable to the middle of the nineteenth century, during the decade between 1850 and 1860, when the population of the United States increased by more than a third, from 23 million to over 31 million.

English, French, Italians, Scandinavians, Poles, and Hollanders were among the immigrants; the majority, however, came from two ethnic stocks: Irish and German. In Ireland, special reasons like widespread poverty caused by the Industrial Revolution, famines resulting from failure of the potato crop, and dislike of English rule were largely responsible for emigration, but it was the collapse of liberal revolutions in Germany that sent a flood of immigrants from there to America. A great many of this latter group, having little money, chose to move westward where land was cheaper and more plentiful than near the eastern seaboards. Wisconsin as a young state offered unusual opportunities for foreign-born arrivals to become farmers or business owners in a new setting.

It took a little orientation for Parks, therefore, to get used to a society where speech, habits, and everything seemed more forthright than in the South. One of his early opinions about the Badger State was touched off by an incident that occurred a few days after his arrival in Madison.

> Other things, too, in the environmental change from Lexington to Madison, my impression was that people were pretty rude in Madison. I remember one occasion on which I was sort of strolling down the street, in no big hurry, and some woman came up behind me and stepped on my heel. Then she said, "You deserve that. You should have been walking faster." I said to myself, "No one would have done that down South, maybe privately but certainly never publicly."[3]

Parks also believed that Wisconsinites had another unenviable trait:

> I thought people in Wisconsin were terribly boastful; I still think so. They're always bragging about their state. The Green Bay Packers is just one example.* I characterize them as kind of frozen Texans.[4]

Parks did not find everyone in Wisconsin unattractive, however, for it was there that he met Ellen Sorge. Ellen had been born in the town of Reedsburg, forty-five miles northwest of Madison. She had been an outstanding student throughout her elementary and high school years, and when she was a teenager, her parents had moved to Madison so that their talented daughter could go to college. Upon receiving her high school diploma, Ellen Sorge promptly enrolled at the university, and by 1937 was a graduate student in political science.

That was the same year Robert Parks left Berea College and

---

*The Green Bay Packers had just won the 1997 Superbowl at the time this interview took place.

started his master's study at Kentucky University. In those days, the few college scholarships available were based entirely upon academic records, and Ellen, who could present Phi Beta Kappa honors, had won one from the political science department at Wisconsin.

The first meeting of Robert Parks and Ellen Sorge has become a family joke with the advantage usually going to the one who's telling it. Robert gives the following version:

> When I got to Wisconsin I wasn't sure how things worked, so the first thing I did was to report to the political science department, which was in South Hall of an old building. The first person I ran into was a little kid walking about as fast as she could down the hall. She looked like she belonged there, so I introduced myself. She said her name was Ellen Sorge. I figured she must be a secretary because I didn't think a woman like her could be a graduate student, which she turned out to be. So she says, and I usually agree, that I married the first woman I saw at Wisconsin. That wasn't quite true but almost, and it was the best decision I ever made.[5]

Parks had come to Wisconsin with a guarantee of a teaching assistantship, and when he met his major professor for the first time, that worthy welcomed him, described his duties, and assigned him an office. Graduate instructors had to share offices, and by coincidence Parks had drawn Ellen Sorge as an office mate. His professor wasn't above needling his newest graduate assistant and said to Parks, "She's the smartest student in the department—even smarter than you."

When asked if she recalled their first meeting, Ellen said, "The first time we met I thought he was very thin. He was a little over six feet, and all I saw was a tall, skinny kid—a real beanpole."[6]

Robert had his teaching assistantship, and Ellen retained her departmental scholarship for the next two years as they studied together and often took the same courses. They quizzed one another in the two languages required for the Ph.D. Robert said that French was easy for him, but German proved more difficult. Another requirement that he thought was "pretty hard for those of us on the humanities side" was a course in statistics.

By the opening of 1940 he and Ellen had fulfilled their residence requirements and were ready for preliminary examinations. Those were scheduled for the spring of that year. The exams took about a week, and according to Parks were "really tough." Nevertheless, both he and Ellen passed them the first time.

Other events made it an exciting time. He and Ellen had begun "going steady" but found opportunities to gather with fellow students to talk about such topics as the U.S. Census report that the country's population had reached 131 million, President Franklin Roosevelt's decision to run for an unprecedented third term, and the nation's first-ever peacetime draft. The war, which had broken out in Europe the preceding September, seemed to be worsening with each passing week. Allied troops, defeated by a German blitzkrieg, were dramatically evacuated from Dunkirk, and forces of the Wehrmacht entered Scandinavia. Winston Churchill was named prime minister of England, and the British Royal Air Force bombed Berlin to the astonishment of Reichsmarshal Hermann Goering, who had proclaimed the capital unassailable.

As graduate students, Robert and Ellen had little time or money to spend on purely social affairs. When they went out together, it usually was to a college function or to a local movie where they could see stars like Carole Lombard, Katharine Hepburn, Clark Gable, Bing Crosby and Bob Hope, or Humphrey Bogart. They watched a new movie entitled *The Grapes of Wrath,* starring Henry Fonda, and later went to a college malt shop where they lingered over Cokes.

Despite college pressures and gloom generated by threats of war, it was a happy time for the ambitious young couple. They liked their studies, were in love, and were planning to marry in the coming summer. That ceremony took place on July 1, 1940, in Reedsburg, Wisconsin, in the same Methodist Church where Ellen's mother and father had married. According to Parks it was a small, intimate affair attended by only Ellen's parents and some of her relatives who lived nearby.

It wasn't a big wedding; I can tell you that. We couldn't afford anything more. Ellen's mother was never too free with her money; she had grown up in exceedingly hard times, and I recall asking her how much I should pay the minister. She said five dollars would be enough, and at the time that suited me just fine.

Ellen wore a pink sort of dress; I don't remember much more about it, but I had an old gabardine suit, which was my best suit. I thought the whole affair went off very well, and the knot must have been tight enough because it has held for more than half a century.[7]

There should be no wonder that Robert's brothers took pleasure in needling him, insisting that the only thing that saved him from being a nonentity was the fact that the talented Ellen had condescended to accept his name. Ellen contributed to their marriage partnership a wide range of talents, constant awareness of current events, and a limitless supply of common sense.

In most universities, the president's wife is like the first lady of a state—watched and compared with predecessors to see if she is traditional or more avant-garde. In either case, she is not apt to find her situation always comfortable. As a spouse she is expected to be a partner who gives psychological support and counsel to the important executive, and she must also fulfil the sometimes belittled responsibilities of homemaker. If the president's wife takes an active role in campus matters, some critics will charge her with overstepping her position even at a time when others claim she is not doing enough.

A scholar by nature and training, Ellen soon put aside her academic honors, and after her husband moved into high-level administration, she avoided any role other than that of mother, wife, confidante, and hostess. When asked if Ellen ever expressed regret over moving away from her profession as a political scientist, her longtime friend Jean Peterson replied:

Not at all [emphasis as spoken]. In fact, if you asked Ellen that question, I'm sure her answer would be that the important things in life are the family—the children and her husband. She wanted her daughters to have Ph.D.s, too. She wanted her daughters to have that scholarship and that kind of background, and she saw to it that they did. But she had her priorities, and her family came above all else.[8]

As years went by it became apparent that Ellen was the perfect complement to her husband, performing the duties of a "First Lady" in her own way, with a sincerity that collected friends and respectful admirers. In large social gatherings she was friendly and gracious, but with intimate groups she did not shirk from entering into spirited discussions. More outspoken in her political beliefs than her husband, she never hesitated to identify herself as a liberal Democrat and often said that she was "more feisty than Bob" when the talk turned to politics.

Ellen had long been impressed by the brief span of life, and she was frank in admitting that she was mainly concerned with the safety and welfare of her family. In 1943, for example, when daughter Andrea was only four months old, Ellen had gone back to work but could hardly wait until the time came to go home. Years later when asked if she ever regretted giving up her career as a political scientist, she answered,

> I never saw death until 1961, when my grandmother, who was 86 years old, died. I had got the feeling much before that time and still have it that there is a terrible fragility to life, how short it really is. So in 1943 I went back to work but could hardly stand it until I got home to be with that baby. I thought the best way I could savor life was to spend as much time as possible with our children, and that's what I tried to do—never with any regrets.[9]

Thus Ellen, with the same background and orientation of her husband, was happy to put aside the career for which she had planned and take over the roles of wife and mother. A devoted and solicitous mother, she continued to read widely and remained extremely well-informed on political issues.

Wayne Cole observed,

> We were always impressed that Ellen, who also had her Ph.D. from Wisconsin in Political Science, was intellectually a full partner with Bob. We found it fascinating that Ellen had a special talent for being able to follow two or three different conversations intelligently at the same time. Nonetheless, she chose to be a wife, homemaker, and mother. So far as we could tell she was not even tempted to become a "career woman," and was fully supportive of Bob professionally. At the same time, Bob genuinely respected Ellen's intellectual and political knowledge and judgment; he was never patronizing toward her intellectually, and she would not have put up with it if he had been. I think it is more than a coincidence that both Andrea and Cindy [Robert and Ellen's two daughters] went on to get their doctorates and rejected the "career woman" course and, like their mother, became devoted wives, mothers, and homemakers.[10]

In years when there was a presidential election, in order to follow the results, Robert and Ellen usually got together with other couples like Elroy and Jean Peterson, Hal and Mary Davey, or Wayne and Virginia Cole. In the election of 1960 when the race between Richard Nixon and John F. Kennedy was still hanging in balance, Ellen was so worried about its possible outcome that according to Jean Peterson she left the group and went into a bedroom to lie down and compose herself.[11]

Throughout her life Ellen read widely, and while living at the Knoll at Iowa State, she used the ISU Library very often. She was especially interested in English history, so much so that until he learned differently, John C. McNee, assistant director of the library, thought that was the area of her Ph.D. study. McNee recalled,

> Mrs. Parks must have read nearly every book we had on English history. Actually, that was an area in which we were comparatively weak at the time, and Mrs. Parks helped immensely in building that section. Quite often I was able to facilitate interlibrary loans for her from other universities.

I remember, too, that we had an antiquated film reader which we trucked over to her at the Knoll so that she could read microfilm at her leisure. She must have kept that film reader for a year or two, but we could no longer use it anyway.[12]

After her daughters had left the home, Ellen spent more time adding to her collection of miniatures, many of which were replicas of homes and costumes of nineteenth-century Britain. Her miniatures of Dickensian characters, for example, had to be absolutely correct right down to every weskit and gaiter.

Mr. and Mrs. Parks Go to Washington

In the fall of 1940 the newly married couple, still graduate students at Wisconsin, had no immediate prospects of employment but agreed that Washington, D.C., was the best place for them to write their dissertations—the only hurdle yet standing between them and their degrees. The best students coming out of political science or economics in those years were going to jobs in Washington rather than to lower-paying ones in academic life. Moreover, both Robert and Ellen wanted to do theses that dealt with agriculture, and the nation's capital was a treasure trove of agricultural studies and agencies. Ellen was able to retain her social science research grant—a fellowship that paid $1800 a year. Robert still had his teaching assistantship but had to give that up when they left Madison.

So the newlyweds went to Washington with little to go on as far as money was concerned. Within a couple of months, however, Robert, having made himself known around the Department of Agriculture, was offered a job in the Bureau of Agricultural Economics.

The Bureau of Agricultural Economics, commonly called BAE, was a central planning office for the secretary of agriculture and his department. As distinguished from action agencies like the Soil Conservation Service, the Agriculture Adjustment Administration (Triple A), or the Farm Security Administration, the BAE was essentially a research agency created within the Department of Agriculture as an effort to pull together its mushrooming assortment of activities, most of which centered around the use of land.[13]

The BAE had several sections, one of which was the Land Economics Division, and this was where Parks was assigned. The division was staffed mainly with political scientists and lawyers who were expected to survey and be knowledgeable about what was going on in state legislatures affecting land use or agriculture. It was Parks's specific job to travel the New England states and talk to people in the capital cities, urging them to send their legislative bills to the BAE in Washington so that they could be analyzed and coordinated with related programs. It was his first experience with legislators and their sometimes arcane machinery.

In New Hampshire, for example, he completed a research project on rural roads and their financing. Another project sent him to Texas to do a similar study on tax assessments in the rural areas of that state. Usually such assignments outside Washington took him away from home for a month or more. It all depended upon the circumstances—how much fieldwork he had to do and how much cooperation he got from resident researchers at the particular state's college.

Through experiences at the BAE, Parks was collecting data and information he felt he needed for his dissertation. Meanwhile, Ellen, too, was working hard on hers; it was going to be a race to see who would finish first. Ellen had an advantage; she could work almost full-time on her writing because she still had her social science research grant and no bureaucratic bosses to satisfy. Taking her materials and typewriter with her, she sometimes traveled with her peripatetic husband.

Parks's Navy Career

Robert and Ellen Parks were in Atlanta, Georgia, having dinner at one of the hotels there when the news broke that the Japanese had attacked Pearl Harbor. Along with everyone else, they knew immediately that their lives would be changed by the forthcoming war. The couple went to Clemson in South Carolina the next day, and there they listened to President Roosevelt declare, "Yesterday, December 7, 1941—a date which will live in infamy—the United States of America was suddenly and deliberately attacked by naval and air forces of the Empire of Japan."

Washington, D.C., was abuzz with exigencies created by the war, and Robert Parks was kept too busy to give much attention to his dissertation. By the summer of 1943, the navy, needing a larger pool of young officers, was directly commissioning some college graduates who had demonstrated their talents and were carrying out significant responsibilities. A person so selected would go for an interview, take mental and physical examinations, and upon successful completion of all three would be commissioned outright; that's all there was to it. Parks was among this elite group and was commissioned as an ensign with orders to report for active duty on July 1, 1943.

Classified as a communications officer, he was sent to Harvard for six months of training. Parks maintains he didn't know anything about communications, but the navy's practice was to put lawyers, economists, political scientists—those who didn't have a particular specialty—into the rubric called communications.

At Harvard, Parks and three other young communications officers were assigned to a four-bed room in Matthews Hall, an older dormitory. By coincidence two of the occupants were named Bob; the other two were Als. Along with fellow ensigns, the four took courses dealing with naval regulations, traditions, and responsibilities. The green young ensigns sometimes were put in regular courses taught by Harvard professors and in which other Harvard students were enrolled. Parks described one such course:

> I remember we had an electrical engineering and radio course; we just weren't prepared for it. The professor's name was Knipp, and we jokingly called his course a Nap with Knipp. He was big on vacuum tubes and could lecture for hours on what went on inside a vacuum tube—just lost us completely. But I don't think they ever flunked anybody out of the naval group. We had our mission and were largely taught by navy persons anyway.[14]

In the middle of August 1943, Robert's roommate, Al Woodward, found an apartment in Cambridge, Massachusetts, for his wife, Jane, and their baby, Bob. The Woodwards invited Ellen and Andrea Parks to come to Cambridge to share the apartment.

Both Ellen and Robert remembered that the Woodward baby cried a lot and could easily be heard through the thin plywood walls of the apartment. Years later, after his first daughter had married, Robert Parks reminisced:

> Al was the father of Bob Woodward, whom we knew when he was just a baby. Al's wife, Jane, and Ellen shared an apartment. Our Andrea was a little baby then, and so was Bob Woodward. Now I tell Andrea that she can easily make a name for herself by saying that she shared a bedroom with Bob Woodward of Watergate fame.[15]

On January 1, 1944, Ellen moved back to Washington and resumed her job at the Bureau of the Budget where she had been writing a history of the War Manpower Mobilization. Her husband was temporarily assigned to the naval district in Norfolk and soon thereafter more permanently assigned to the vice admiral's staff there. This particular vice admiral was commander of a large naval service force—a force consisting of minesweepers, oilers, tankers, repair ships, and vessels of that sort—headquartered in the Norfolk harbor.

Ensign Parks lived on a repair ship whose only designation was R10. That designation baffled the local telephone company, which kept listing R10 as a building in the harbor area. Indeed, the ship never went anywhere and remained anchored there in the harbor. Luckily for Parks, however, personnel who lived on the stationary vessel got extra pay for being "afloat."

Parks found his naval assignment "interesting." His job entailed being custodian for messages coming into that command, and he said that he saw "an awful lot of mail" before the Normandy invasion in June 1944. Among other duties he helped train newer communications officers who were to be sent out to sea on convoy duty in the Atlantic. He developed a certain protectiveness for these fellow communications officers.

> One of the things that I sort of got a kick out of was standing up for the communications officer. Every ship that went out to sea had restricted materials—secret orders, supply stations, danger zones, escorts, information, and so on, and when one of those documents was lost or couldn't be accounted for, all hell was raised. The communications officer was nearly always the first one to take the heat. Ordinarily, his commanding officer acted immediately, without looking into the case. He just said, "The communications officer is to be recalled, and he should be reprimanded, and so on and so forth." Then he'd send this order into our headquarters. So I began to reply, "What facts about the case did you ascertain before submitting this recommendation?" Or "What did you do to help said officer in the performance of his duties?" That was one of those little fun things I got out of being an officer on the admiral's staff—playing with the big brass, and there's a lot of brass in the navy.[16]

Parks had risen to lieutenant junior grade by August of 1945, when the war ended. He stayed on for another six months and by the end of that time had been in the navy for two and a half years. Moreover, he had served in grade eighteen months, long enough to be up for promotion to full lieutenant. A career in the navy wasn't his cup of tea, however, and he was anxious to return to civilian life.

Upon getting out of uniform, he went back to his former job in the Bureau of Agricultural Economics, but he discovered there had been great changes from the time when he had been there before. In those earlier years it had been an exciting place, brimming with enthusiasm for projects considered absolutely essential to the country's welfare. With the war's end, the former excitement had waned, and the bureau was in retrenchment, having a difficult time getting adequate appropriations from Congress.

Some persons speculated that much of that difficulty resulted from a cultural survey the BAE had completed and released. Among other findings, this controversial study had claimed that in counties scattered throughout Mississippi it was not unusual for white men to sleep with black women. The accusation didn't sit well with many of the most powerful men in the House of Representatives, including those on the appropriations committee.

A different project undertaken by the BAE drew more favorable attention. This was a study directed by John Timmons—then a colleague in the BAE. Timmons' nationwide survey attempted to find out how farmers acquired title to their farms. It was an investigation that both the BAE and Congress liked; it offended nobody. Of course, in the final analysis, there were only two ways one got farm ownership: either you inherited it or you married into it! Parks was impressed with John Timmons as a researcher, not suspecting that some day the two of them would be colleagues on the same faculty at Iowa State in Ames.

A position within an important government agency was pretty "heady wine" for a young person, but it didn't keep Parks from working on his dissertation. Ellen did the same and finished hers in 1947. For the next year she was Dr. Parks while her husband remained Mr. Parks.

Professor Parks at Iowa State College

Mr. Parks continued to do a lot of traveling for the Bureau of Agricultural Economics. Among other assignments, in the summer of 1947 he came out to Minnesota, Wisconsin, and Iowa. His assignment was to find out what people in the land-grant colleges were doing with soil conservation programs. In Iowa, of course, he came to Ames and Iowa State College, where he formed an early opinion:

> My impression of the people was all right—nothing particularly good or bad about it to be honest—but my impression of the campus was awful. This was in very, very hot weather, and in Minneapolis, Madison, and here in Ames, it was 100 degrees or

more every day. The campus was brown, looked as if you set a match to it you'd have an awful fire immediately. It would have burst into flames. And I said to myself, "That's an awful looking campus," not knowing that I'd be here for most of my life.[17]

At Iowa State College in that summer of 1947, Parks met several of the major administrators, namely those in the Division of Agriculture, including Dean H. H. Kildee, Dean Robert Buchanan of the Graduate College, and Ralph K. Bliss, Director of Extension. Parks did not believe that any of them, however, had anything directly to do with his later employment.

Parks first learned of a possible job at Iowa State College through John Mashek, a professor in the Department of History, Government, and Philosophy. Mashek had come to Washington to testify in behalf of United Way, and in a discussion with Parks and several others, he mentioned that his own department head, Clarence Matterson, had casually commented that the department was considering a joint appointment with the Division of Agriculture. If they could find the right person with a background in history, government, and agriculture, Matterson thought the college would approve the appointment.

After Deans Harold Gaskill of the Division of Science, Kildee of Agriculture, and Buchanan of the Graduate School all approved the move, Parks was invited to Ames for an interview with Matterson of history, government, and philosophy and William G. Murray of agricultural economics, the two department heads to whom the appointee would be responsible. Matterson and Murray told him they were looking for somebody as a cross between their respective departments and that his experience in political science and agricultural economics seemed just right.

In those days a prospective appointee was expected to give a paper before a seminar composed of senior faculty members. Parks gave his and apparently impressed nearly everyone, winning especially high praise from the two department heads, Clarence Matterson and Bill Murray.

Parks was offered a position with the rank of associate professor beginning in the fall quarter of 1948. This was a comparatively high rank for a newcomer on the faculty because it carried tenure and entitled the person to vote in all faculty decisions, something junior members like assistant professors and instructors then could not do. The rank and concomitant salary were necessary because Parks needed incentives to leave his comfortable job with good pay at the BAE in Washington.

Upon arriving in Ames, he took a lot of ribbing about being a "split personality" because he was assigned three-fourths time in political science and one-fourth in agricultural economics. Actually, it didn't work out that way. On paper, he was supposed to do most of his teaching in political science and his research in agricultural economics, but he found himself spending more of his allotted hours and energy in the classroom.

Everyone in the Department of History, Government, and Philosophy was expected to teach at least one section in the basic course American Government 215. President Charles Friley mistakenly thought that such a course was required in all land-grant colleges. Parks and others teaching government knew better, but no one disagreed because that was the department's bread and butter. Another course that interested him very much was entitled American Political Theory. Within the next couple of years, he would introduce and teach a new course in government as well as one in agricultural administration.

In the classroom his presentations usually were tightly organized lectures, and it wasn't long before he began teaching several sections of the basic course together. After all, it was as easy to lecture to ninety students as thirty.

Television was in its infancy, but Iowa State College had led the state in securing FCC approvals for telecasting. Its home station, WOI-TV, was the envy of every university and many commercial broadcasters. The college put pressure on some of its best lecturers to present their offerings on the new medium, so Parks was encouraged to teach American Government 215 via television. He accepted but wasn't really pleased with his efforts. For one thing, he had a divided audience: some people were on campus and taking the course for academic credit; others were at home listening for pure enjoyment and information. Even the best lecturer had trouble holding the interest of persons sitting in their living or recreation rooms at home.

Producers at the station urged Parks to "spice up" his presentations. Visual aids would be the easiest way to do that. He talked over the idea with Ellen about a forthcoming program in which he intended to discuss gerrymandering. His young daughter, Andrea, was listening in and volunteered her pet salamander as a visual aid. According to her, they mounted the critter on a small piece of wallboard marked with appropriate labels and lines.[18]

There was no survey or other effort to measure audience reaction, but Parks was not pleased with his venture:

> About that salamander, they were always pushing me to use visuals, but I never liked that very much. I don't use visuals anyway. They bother me, so I just don't try to use them. Besides, it was not a good production. We had one camera—one camera which would go off in the middle of things. It was an experience but not very much fun.[19]

Despite personal dissatisfaction with his television debut, there was no doubt that Parks was gaining a reputation as one of Iowa State's best young professors, an especially hard-working one. His experience with political science both in theory and practice made him a valuable member of the graduate faculty, where he served on numerous Ph.D. committees, one of which was for Virgil Lagomarcino.

Lagomarcino had given up a public school superintendency in order to pursue further graduate study at Iowa State. Although his primary interest was in the field of education, he had chosen a minor in political science. Parks had been invited to serve on the candidate's committee and had come to like the ambitious graduate student. Lagomarcino recounted the following episode:

> I remember ... my final oral examination for the doctorate. ... He [Parks] asked me to trace the development of democratic philos-

ophy and theory from the fall of the Greek city state to the nineteenth century. ... At the end of the examination, as is the custom, the candidate is asked to leave the room while the committee discusses his fate. ... The wait seemed unending. Finally, the door opened and Parks came out, stuck out his hand, and with an expressionless face, said, "Congratulations, fellow, they outvoted me." I laughed but wasn't sure why.[20]

Professor Parks was well liked by his colleagues but said he couldn't spare the time to fraternize much or join with the daily kaffeeklatsch that met nearly every morning at ten o'clock in the Memorial Union. This informal group led by Matterson of history, government, and philosophy, Keith Huntress of English, Joe O'Mara of genetics, and Alfred Kehlenbeck of foreign languages met in a small room called the Nook.

The Nook gathering was noted for its camaraderie—a place where men from all disciplines could get together and relax, away from the problems of their respective departments. Women were not barred, but as a carryover from years of male domination on the campus, they seldom attended. Staff, faculty, and an occasional grad student—all were considered equal within the Nook. Researchers mingled with teachers; scientists sparred with humanists, artists, and once in awhile even an administrator. The group might include conservatives and liberals, but usually there were more of the latter than the former.

During a half-hour in the Nook, one could sit in on topics ranging from Aristotelian ethics to TV's latest sitcom—from foreign problems to local gossip, from general subjects to individual events, and from the sublime to the ridiculous. In the Nook it was repartee that drew participants, and the exchanges could be brilliant, frivolous, provocative, or irreverent but never dull. There was no coin in professorial language, and around the table the latter could rise to eloquence or sink into vulgarity. Praise was more scarce than criticism, the most frequent of which was aimed at authority wherever found: columnists, authors, coaches, and especially college administrators.

One participant in those Nook discussions was duly impressed and one day came back to his departmental office to find his colleague Parks at work grading papers. According to Parks the following exchange took place:

> He was very disenchanted with everything at Iowa State and said he wanted to give me some advice. "First," he said, "you made a stupid mistake in coming here. This is no place for anybody in the humanities or social sciences." Then he elaborated by saying he had studied the power structure. He added, "I'll tell you one thing more. You'll never amount to anything around here unless you're a Republican, a Presbyterian, and live in the Fourth Ward."
>
> I never met any of those requirements, and I often thought that if I ever saw him again that somehow I'd remind him that I got to be a little higher and into that top office in Beardshear Hall as president. But then I was afraid he might say, "I never said you couldn't get to be president; I just said you couldn't amount to anything!"[21]

Despite the pessimism shown by Parks's colleague on that occasion and notwithstanding Iowa State's reputation as a "cow college," Matterson, longtime head of history, government, and philosophy, had garnered some pretty high-powered, promising young professors. "Matty's" department was home base for Paul Sharp and Norman Graebner as well for Robert Parks. Sharp would become president successively of Hiram College in Ohio, University of North Carolina at Chapel Hill, and the University of Oklahoma in Norman. Graebner became a noted professor, holding the Randall Chair of History at Illinois University before accepting a similarly prestigious chair at the University of Virginia.

One of Parks's younger colleagues in the Department of History, Government, and Philosophy was Wayne Cole. Cole, a distinguished historian and friend of the Parks family, later left ISU to take a better position at the University of Maryland, and after his own retirement he offered this judgment of Robert and Ellen Parks:

Intellectually, we were impressed by Bob and Ellen's capacity to cross academic disciplines. I believe Bob may have had a joint appointment in Government and Economics for a time. If not, he was fully accepted in the economics department as one who could speak their language. Similarly, both Bob and Ellen could talk my field of history as well as I could. And both of them were ahead of the game when the civil rights movement got underway. They both were very broad gauged intellectually.[22]

Parks respected the talents of colleagues such as Sharp, Graebner, and Cole, but his greatest affection and respect went to Matterson and the elderly Earle Ross. Ross was nearing the end of his long teaching career during which he had developed a special expertise in the history of agriculture, a subject of great interest to the younger Parks. The venerable Ross was perhaps even better known for his scholarly history of Iowa State College from its founding until 1941.[23]

Parks was on the faculty at Iowa State College from 1948 until 1956. Most of his work was in the classroom teaching some phase of political science; his one-quarter time allotted to the Department of Agricultural Economics was mainly a paper arrangement, for with that time he was left to do pretty much whatever he wanted. He liked both Matterson and Murray, his department heads, and they in turn knew that his own self-discipline was stronger motivation than anything they could provide.

After eight years though, Parks became restless. There was no particular dissatisfaction with Iowa State, and he was aware that President James Hilton had taken a personal interest in his record. Wisconsin University, however, had not forgotten him and in 1956 made him an offer that forced a decision.

He and Ellen had won many friends in the Ames community. He had a comfortable position on the faculty, had bought a home, and his daughter Andrea was in the first grade. At Madison, however, he would receive a better salary and teach only graduate courses. The W. K. Kellogg Foundation had given hefty scholarships to people doing graduate work in agricultural economics at Wisconsin, and

Parks would have major responsibilities in recruitment and training of the selected scholars. It was too good an opportunity to pass up.

So Parks and his family returned to Madison for two years, from 1956 to 1958. However, President James Hilton back at Iowa State was not ready to give him up. Enrollments had swollen, and there simply was too much work for himself and Provost James Jensen—the only two administrators in the presidential office.

The working relationship between Hilton and Jensen was a good one, and as is customary in institutions having a provost, Hilton spent much of his time with the Board of Regents, alumni, and leaders within the state while Jensen was primarily concerned with on-campus matters. Both agreed that a third person was needed.

The tall, distinguished-looking James Jensen was a thoughtful administrator who liked to mull over every problem very carefully. His infrequent attempts at humor were strained and seldom successful. To underlings he appeared solemn and somewhat foreboding because his favorite pose was to sit silently behind his desk smoking a curved-stem pipe while listening to advocates of various proposals battle it out before him. Over in the Nook one day when administrators were on the pan, acerbic Joe O'Mara from the Department of Genetics quipped that Provost Jensen was "the only man known to science who could sink by his levity and rise by his gravity."

Jensen, with Hilton's urging, contacted Parks and described a new position they were considering. He invited Parks to come back to the campus for an interview. When the candidate showed up, Hilton and Jensen were somewhat vague in describing the intended duties, but they were specific in urging Parks to take the job. About all Hilton told Parks on that occasion was that academic programs being offered at Iowa State were all right for most students, but there was not enough attention being paid to the best and the worst students. If he would come aboard, Parks would be a second administration man working with Provost Jensen, particularly in academic matters.

Iowa State's offer to return brought Parks to a crucial decision: in effect he had to choose between remaining a teaching professor or becoming a full-time administrator. His fondest hope during undergraduate years as well as those spent in graduate study was that someday he might become a distinguished professor at a major university. Ellen years later recalled talks the couple had about administration and teaching.

> I remember we discussed administration as a career. I had a theory about administrators, one I still hold. I think those persons who start out wanting to go into management or to become administrators should never be one because they are just wanting power over someone else. Bob was a very good graduate teaching assistant, and later all he wanted was to become a distinguished professor.[24]

At Wisconsin, Parks was well on the road toward the goal of becoming an outstanding teacher—a goal he would have to abandon if he chose administration. Moreover, he genuinely enjoyed working directly with students.

The tenure he had earned as a professor would go with him if he moved to Iowa State, but if he relinquished teaching, his assignments and future salaries would be determined by the Iowa Board of Regents. He knew that being away from an academic discipline too long was an enormous handicap, particularly at a time when so much was happening in his field of political science. Parks, along with President James Hilton or whoever succeeded him, served at the will of the regents. Parks had great respect for Hilton, but the latter was approaching retirement age, and that event when it came posed uncertainties for his major assistants. Still, from the high ground of university administration, Parks would have opportunities for service to a broader academic community than in the classroom or directing a few graduate students. He decided to cross the Rubicon.

CHAPTER 4

Prelude Years, 1958–1965

He has half the deed done, who has made a good beginning.

Horace
Epistles, Book 1

During Robert Parks's interview with Hilton and Jensen, there had been brief discussion as to title, and Hilton had settled on dean of instruction—a description so vague that Parks himself later referred to it as "dean of everything else." He became Iowa State's first and only dean of instruction, and he frequently used an anecdote to explain the university's failure to continue the office:

> There was this baseball manager who had a rookie third baseman. The manager, a former infielder himself, said he'd show the recruit how to play the position. So the manager went out, and the first grounder that came to him was a slow bouncer, which he muffed. Soon a second one went right through his legs. He was no better on the third try, bobbling the ball twice and enabling the runner to reach first base safely. When the inning finally ended and the manager came to the bench, he said to the rookie, "Just wipe that smile off your face. See what you've done! You've loused up third base so bad no one can play it."[1]

Although Parks had moved from classroom to high-level administration, his experiences as a professor, buttressed by affection and respect for three brothers who had chosen teaching as their careers, would remain with him. In fact, throughout his administrative lifetime he was an articulate champion for both students and faculties.

That orientation guided his moves as dean of instruction. Soon after he entered his new office, he launched a double-barrelled attack: attracting more of the nation's best students and securing more appreciation for the faculty.

One of the first steps in attracting the best students was establishment of an Honors Program. As early as the fall quarter of his first year as dean of instruction, he was encouraging the Division of Home Economics to begin such a venture.

The initial Honors Program was so successful that in the following winter quarter Dean Parks strongly backed the Cardinal Guild when that student governing body asked that all divisions offer such an option. The rigidly controlled Honors Program took several forms, and students admitted into it were allowed certain exceptions to usual degree requirements. They might be placed in advanced classes, they could earn extra credit for individual projects beyond a course's regular requirements, they might be exempted from certain prerequisites, or their degree programs could be altered with advice and consent of specially selected advisers.

Although still experimental and voluntary, each of the divisions quickly put the recommendation in place. Parks kept pushing the proposal, but it was not until 1960 that the General Faculty gave its approval and the Honors Program began appearing in catalogs and other official announcements.

It wasn't enough to have an Honors Program for students after they were enrolled at Iowa State, Dean Parks argued. The university should put more effort into attracting the very best students that high schools produced. This was the motivation that resulted in a program for National Merit Scholars—a program that won endorsement and cooperation from the nation's top secondary schools. Begun in 1960, selection during the next three years was limited to twenty-two students annually, but that number rose slightly as more and more applications began appearing. By 1964, Iowa State had thirty-two Merit Scholars enrolled and had graduated twenty-one of them, more than any other Iowa or Big Eight University.

During the years of his deanship and subsequent vice presidency, Parks also stepped up efforts to secure more financial aid for students. While at Wisconsin, he had been closely involved in obtaining grants from the W. K. Kellogg Foundation, and in 1958 he helped direct a proposal from Iowa State to this same benefactor. The foundation responded with a five-year commitment of $448,550 to Iowa State for its establishment of a Center for Agricultural and Economic Adjustment. The same foundation thought highly enough of the center that in 1962 it awarded an additional $600,000. While these grants were not won by Parks alone, it is doubtful they could have been obtained without his guidance and weighty support.

Other financial grants that Vice President Parks helped secure were related even more directly to student welfare. These came from the Ford Foundation. A 1961 grant from this corporate organization brought $50,000 into Iowa State for interest-free loans to deserving students. The loans were forgiven at the rate of $1,000 per year, or 20 percent of the total amount loaned, whichever was greater, if the recipient entered the teaching profession.[2]

On Behalf of Students and Faculty

During the time he was dean of instruction, Parks argued that faculty salaries at Iowa State were "abysmally low" considering the qualifications demanded and the work accomplished. Improved salaries, therefore, were among the highest priorities, but he also wanted other recognition for faculty and staff. There were innovative steps that could be taken, and he proceeded to do so.

In his first year as dean, Parks joined with Provost James Jensen to begin a program to honor distinguished professors. Parks drafted the final proposals but was quick to give credit to his immediate superior:

I was dean of instruction, and he was provost, so it was pretty much a cooperative thing between Jensen and me, and, of course, with eventual support of President Hilton. There were initial questions about how many there should be; how open should we leave the selection; who should make the determinations; should there be a financial reward? Should it be a title which would follow a person through a whole academic career or be designated for a specific time? All of these were questions Jensen and I had to iron out.[3]

Subsequently, in 1959 one faculty member from four of the five colleges was awarded the title of Distinguished Professor—an honor that would follow each throughout his or her professional life. The first members selected were Don Kirkham from agriculture, Ernest W. Anderson from engineering, Mary S. Lyle from home economics, and Edward A. Benbrook from veterinary medicine. (The burgeoning College of Sciences and Humanities, for reasons never explained, submitted no nominee for that year.)

When President Hilton and Provost Jensen in 1958 had interviewed Parks for the position as dean of instruction they asked for his opinion of Iowa State's overall curriculum, and he had replied:

Iowa State has an excellent curriculum in what is offered, but frankly I think it's far too narrow and too limited. To be a real university—a first-class university—we will have to be stronger in the liberal arts and probably in the fine arts than we are now. Without slighting the scientific and technical areas ... we would have to bring in some new majors and minors.[4]

Hilton and Jensen agreed with this line of thought, and almost as soon as Parks's new position became official, he began moving proposals for new majors. Some of these proposals had already been submitted to President Hilton, and his new dean convinced him that the time was ripe to put a few selected ones on the agenda for the Board of Regents. Accordingly, in May of 1960, with strong backing from both Parks and Hilton and despite opposition from

Virgil Hancher, president of the University of Iowa, the regents authorized major work at Iowa State for undergraduates in the fields of English and speech, modern languages, and physical education for women. A giant step had been taken toward what Parks had described as "a first-class university."[5]

Parks's term as dean lasted only until 1961, for in that year Provost James Jensen resigned in order to take the presidency of Oregon State University. Jensen's resignation offered President Hilton an opportunity to break up the multitudinous duties that had been within the former provost's charge as well as to groom a person he was eyeing as a suitable successor. Thus Hilton abolished the offices of provost and dean of instruction and replaced them with two vice presidencies. He selected J. Boyd Page to be vice president for research, while maintaining his position as dean of the graduate college, and he upgraded Robert Parks into a vice presidency for academic affairs.

The vice presidency gave Parks a somewhat more prestigious title, but in actuality his responsibilities changed little from what he already was doing. Securing more financial aid for deserving students was an endeavor he continued to pursue as vice president. One of the reasons that Wisconsin had proved attractive to him had been the very healthy scholarships that the Kellogg Foundation was giving to graduate students there who were preparing to go into extension work. Undoubtedly, the connections Parks had made with Kellogg people and the respect he had earned from them helped smooth approaches from Iowa State for similar awards.

As vice president, Parks also was concerned with the state's need for more secondary teachers, and he thought Iowa State should do more to fill the gap. With that goal in mind, he persuaded President Hilton to appoint Virgil Lagomarcino as director of an expanded teacher education program. Shortly thereafter, Parks urged the Board of Regents to grant the university permission to prepare more elementary school teachers. His persuasions resulted in the board's approval of a broadened curriculum in the Departments of Child Development and Education in order to permit graduates to become certified as elementary teachers.

He continued pushing for more moneys to help prospective teachers, and he kept encouraging students whom he thought deserving to apply for whatever grants or awards were available in their fields. The Ford Foundation Grants were especially helpful to those students who wanted to become teachers.

Iowa State had a special curriculum for training teachers of engineering, and this program was impressive enough that the Ford Foundation added another $75,000 in forgivable loans to predoctoral students who were preparing to teach engineering. The results were so successful that by 1963 the Ford Foundation had loaned more than $185,000 to students majoring in engineering at Iowa State.[6]

Along with rising enrollments while Parks was vice president came demands for a wider range of courses and more authorized degrees. He accepted these challenges and began pressing hard for a wider curriculum at both undergraduate and graduate levels.

In his vice presidency, Parks also continued trying to gain more recognition for faculty and staff, and his efforts took several forms beyond that of designating distinguished professors. He was enthusiastic about the idea of overseas teaching experiences for members of Iowa State's faculty, and in the fall of 1960 five teachers from Baroda University in India came to Ames in order to take further graduate work as the first step in a Baroda–Iowa State–Ford Foundation project for establishing degrees in home economics at the M.S. and Ph.D. levels. A team of Iowa State professors in exchange went to India to teach graduate courses and coordinate the program.[7]

Improvement of staff and faculty welfare was always a priority item on Parks's personal agenda. Among the benefits enjoyed by the faculty was participation in a retirement program with the Teachers Insurance and Annuity Association of America (TIAA). Under the Iowa State plan, 10 percent of the teacher's gross salary each month was deposited in this pension fund. Of this 10 percent, one-third was deducted from the teacher's net pay, and the university contributed the other two-thirds.

In the fall of 1963 President Hilton, with Vice President Parks's strong advocacy, approved an increase from 10 to 15 percent on the portion of the teacher's salary above $4800. Of this 15 percent, the university continued to contribute two-thirds, and the remaining one-third was deducted from the employee's salary. Parks's warm support for such upgrading did not go unnoticed by the staff and faculty.

In the years between 1958 and 1964—years of his prelude to the presidency of Iowa State—Parks was involved in many matters not directly concerned with student or faculty welfare. One of those occurred just as he began his second year as dean.

On September 23, 1959, lead stories in national telecasts and headlines of most major newspapers featured happenings at Iowa State, for on that date, Soviet Premier Nikita Khrushchev came to the campus during a whirlwind tour of the United States. Khrushchev was at the height of his reign (1958–1964) as leader of one of the world's two superpowers, and in that position he alternated between envy toward the West and contempt for a system he could not understand. He insisted that capitalism was outdated and threatened "to bury" it figuratively. Again and again, he spoke of the day when the Soviet Union would overtake the United States in industrial might and technical know-how, yet America excited him, and he reacted to it with even more than his usual ebullience.

During his twelve-day tour of the United States, tens of millions of Americans sat entranced before television sets to watch this extraordinary man—part showman, part astute politician, part alien but strangely intriguing figure. He and his accompanying delegation made several stops in Iowa, including one at Iowa State University. Dean Robert Parks had not been a major player in the decision to invite the Soviet premier and his delegation to visit Iowa State, but as one of the university's top three officials, he was conspicuous among those on the welcoming committee.

The Russians left Moscow on September 15 for the 4800-mile nonstop flight to Washington, D.C. Their huge jet-propelled TU—114 Transport landed at Andrews Air Force Base, fifteen miles from the city, rather than at the closer National Airport because runways at Andrews were longer, and it was felt that security could be tighter than at a commercial airfield.

President Eisenhower was on hand to greet the visitors, after which they were driven to Blair House directly across Pennsylvania Avenue from the White House. Later in the day, President Eisenhower and Premier Khrushchev had a brief discussion before they climbed aboard a helicopter for a ride over the city.

From Washington, Khrushchev and his delegation went to New York City where he addressed a gathering of business leaders, and from New York he flew to California, first to Los Angeles and then aboard a special train traveling north along the beautiful coastline to San Francisco. On the train were hundreds of American journalists, and wherever the Russians stopped, there were huge crowds anxious to get a glimpse of the colorful Soviet leader.

The delegation next flew from San Francisco to Des Moines where on September 22, 1959, at the Hotel Fort Des Moines, Khrushchev spoke at a dinner hosted by the Greater Des Moines Chamber of Commerce. Everywhere he went, he was accompanied by Henry Cabot Lodge, U.S. Ambassador to the United Nations and the man President Eisenhower had chosen to be the Soviet premier's official escort.

In Iowa's capital city, Khrushchev toured the John Deere Factory and the Des Moines Packing Company. At the latter stop and to the delight of swarms of photographers who dogged the footsteps of the two men, Khrushchev and Lodge ate a hot dog. The Soviet premier, who spoke no English, through his interpreter directed a question to Lodge, "Capitalist! Have you finished your sausage?"

Lodge replied, "Yes, we capitalists get hungry, too, you know."[8]

The banter was typical of exchanges throughout much of Khrushchev's trip.

From Des Moines, the Russians were driven to Coon Rapids and the home of Roswell Garst, the person chiefly responsible for inviting Khrushchev to visit America. Garst, one of the state's wealthiest farmers, operated a large hybrid seed corn firm, owned a substantial cattle business, and farmed several thousand acres. He had twice talked with Khrushchev in Moscow, and the Soviet leader had shown great interest in American farming methods, particularly in the raising of corn—a subject on which Garst was an acknowledged expert.

At the Garst farm a crowd had gathered, waiting for the Russians to arrive, and among the onlookers was 240-pound Jack Christensen of Mason City. When Khrushchev tried to pass through the crowd, he spotted the portly Christensen and walked over in order to give the Iowan an amiable pat on his ample belly. The gesture delighted every photographer, and through his interpreter, Khrushchev remarked, "Now there's a REAL American."

Not to be outdone, Christensen pointed to the Russian's girth and replied, "Hey, we both have the same."[9]

Inside the farm home, Garst and Khrushchev talked about seed corn and related matters, after which they tramped through a nearby cornfield. Their tour was hampered by a horde of reporters and photographers. At one point, Garst, irritated by the press of people, stepped aside to pick up a handful of silage, which he angrily tossed at the journalists. Khrushchev stood smiling at his host's outburst while everyone with a camera was clicking its shutters repeatedly.

From Coon Rapids, Khrushchev and his entourage, grown huge with American journalists, motored to Iowa State. The motorcade entered the campus from the west, and the smiling, pudgy premier waved continually to spectators lining every street. As the miniparade passed slowly down Osborn Drive, four men clad in identical trenchcoats, pulled-down fedoras, and dark glasses suddenly stepped into the street. Carrying violin cases, they marched toward the car with the Russian leader.

Security men were watching from the roofs of the chemistry and home economics buildings. Four other men quickly came out of the crowd, put their arms around the trenchcoat-clad figures, and guided them firmly back among the spectators. It turned out to be nothing but a prank by fun-loving college students and was humorous only because it occurred before the decade that saw the assassinations of John F. Kennedy, Martin Luther King, and Robert Kennedy.

Khrushchev's car moved slowly through the campus, and Robert Parks was among officials standing in front of McKay Hall, waiting for him. President Hilton delivered the formal greeting to the Soviet leader and welcomed him to the university.

Then came a quick tour of the home economics building. Told that training in home economics helped prepare young people for marriage, Khrushchev was impolite enough to say, "In Russia, we don't have such schools. We learn such things from our mothers."[10]

Inside the building, Helen LeBaron, dean of the Home Economics College, stood ready to answer any questions the Russians would ask. Khrushchev went into one class of about a dozen women, and after the purpose of the class had been explained to him, he asked LeBaron, "Suppose a man marries one of these girls. How can he check to find out her knowledge and efficiency?"

Dean LeBaron replied through the interpreter, "If she's a graduate of Iowa State she receives a certificate. And all graduates from here have knowledge and efficiency."

The answer apparently didn't satisfy Khrushchev, for he grinned, "But who can believe mere words? Suppose she has a graduation certificate but doesn't know how to prepare pancakes."

When his remark was translated, Dean LeBaron, who usually was outraged by suggestions that home economics was merely cooking and sewing, avoided a possible diplomatic gaffe and did not answer. The girls, however, laughed and applauded the premier's remark. Basking in their responses, Khrushchev continued, "I think when you get married, you will settle that question without the help of the dean."

The class enjoyed the badinage, and meanwhile, several boys were thrusting arms through the open windows hoping that Khrushchev would shake their hands. He did shake several after waving away security guards who were attempting to curtail the boys' boldness.

Parks had carefully watched Khrushchev work the crowds and

noticed that he paid unusual attention to young people. Reflecting upon the way the Soviet leader conducted himself on the Iowa State campus, Parks said:

> Mr. Khrushchev proved himself a wonderful politician. He would have been elected in this country as easily as Russia, if he was really elected there. As he went down the line, he was pretty perfunctory until he got to the students, and then he made a big deal of chatting with them and shaking their hands.[11]

Nina Khrushchev accompanied her husband inside the home economics classroom, where she showed great interest in a display of cooking utensils. When it was demonstrated that one of the pans had heated evenly throughout, she said, "Now I know what to bake my pies in. Aluminum pans are best."[12]

As he emerged from the home economics building, Khrushchev found spectators jammed six to ten feet deep behind a temporary picket fence. He clasped his hands above his head in a familiar gesture that evoked hearty cheers from the mainly student crowd. Shouts of "Hi, Nikki" were heard but quieted down when President Hilton presented the Soviet premier with a book on the history of Iowa State. In making the presentation, Hilton remarked that in 1955 a Russian delegation had given him a Russian cookbook; now he wanted to reciprocate.

At that point, Diane Rasmussen, a senior in home economics, stepped up to present the premier with a popular cookbook by Lenore Sullivan of Iowa State's home economics staff.

The Russian's motorcade then left the main campus and drove to the swine nutritional farm a mile south. There Khrushchev was given a model of an Iowa meat-type hog, and he pleased the smaller crowd that had trailed him by asking, "If Soviet and American pigs can coexist, then why cannot nations coexist?"

The gift of the model pig encouraged the wisecracking Russian to add, "In my country there is an old proverb that when one does something unpleasant, you can give him a pig."

In a more serious vein, he expressed appreciation for the gift. However, he couldn't resist another quip, and for the benefit of the ever-present Henry Cabot Lodge, he gibed, "I am glad that Mr. Lodge is with me here on this farm. In all his life, he probably didn't take in as many smells as he did today."[13]

After visiting the swine nutritional farm, the Khrushchev party motored to the Des Moines Airport and flew back to Washington, D.C. The next day Khrushchev had a tête-à-tête with Vice President Richard Nixon before meeting with President Eisenhower at Camp David, a presidential retreat Eisenhower had established in the Catoctin Mountains, sixty-five miles from the White House.

Although Robert Parks did not have any active role in inviting the colorful Russian to America, he did help coordinate various side trips on campus for the Russian entourage. Several of the Soviet's top atomic officials wanted to tour the Ames atomic research laboratories. Accordingly, V. S. Yemelyanov, chief of Russia's Atomic Energy Administration, and three lesser officials met with Dr. Frank H. Spedding, director of the Institute for Atomic Research and the Ames Laboratory.

The world had learned that in the 1940s scientists at Iowa State were deeply involved in top secret research with the primary goal of producing uranium, the metal used in the atomic bomb dropped on Hiroshima—the epochal event that helped to end the war with Japan. Efforts of this small group of scientists were so successful that, in all, the Ames facility turned out about two million pounds of uranium for nuclear use.

Fourteen years after the war had ended, Spedding was able to tell the visiting Russians that the Ames Laboratory now was devoted to basic research and had not been engaged in any secret work for a year or two. He also assured the press that any information the Russian experts gained from their visit already had been published in scientific journals; their tour of Iowa State facilities only gave them a chance to see such work first-hand. Spedding had assured Hilton and Parks that permitting the Russian scientists to inspect the laboratories would in no way provide them with any information that had not been released earlier.

There would be numerous noteworthy events at Iowa State while Parks was dean of instruction and then vice president for academic affairs—the two administrative offices he held prior to his presidency. He would insist that in 1958 he had not come back to Iowa State with the presidency in mind, and it is unlikely that any solid commitments were made at that time. It is worth noting, however, that James Hilton had drawn Parks back from Wisconsin in 1958 and had engineered his vice presidency in 1961. Subsequently, Parks's appointment as the vice president made inescapable the fact that he was the number one man next to the president himself. The sixty-five-year-old Hilton was looking forward to retirement, and his selection of Parks left no doubt as to whom he wanted as his successor.

Lois Hilton, too, held great affection for Robert and Ellen Parks, and despite the differences in their respective ages, she and her husband enjoyed being in the company of their younger colleagues. Robert and Lois were outgoing and fun-loving whenever the four got together; Jim and Ellen tended to be more solemn and serious.

One time a repertory theater group came to Ames to present *Who's Afraid of Virginia Woolf.* The production represented a departure from the usual theater offerings in Iowa, and even before it was presented on a makeshift stage in the college armory, it had touched off considerable debate because of its themes and bawdy language. Hilton decided not to attend because he was in delicate budget talks with key legislators at the time and thought his presence might give critics gratuitous ammunition. His wife, however, saw nothing wrong in her going. Ellen Parks had another commitment, so Parks was delegated to escort Mrs. Hilton to the play. The two of them went together, and afterward Mrs. Hilton told her husband how much she had enjoyed the evening. He replied that "If any legislators complain about it, I'll just say that it wasn't an Iowa State show anyway—nothing but a barnstorming troupe."

By 1963, when President Hilton announced his intention to retire in the summer of 1965, the active search for a new president got underway. Parks by that year was the major spokesman for all academic matters, was well-known throughout the state, and had been meeting regularly with the Board of Regents for almost six years.

Iowa State in 1959 had changed its five divisions into five colleges, and in 1963 each voted a member of its faculty to be on a five-person ad hoc committee charged with making recommendations to the Board of Regents, who, of course, would have the final decision. The university's committee was composed of Keith Huntress from the College of Sciences and Humanities, Ercel Epright from Home Economics, Ernest Anderson from Engineering, George Browning from Agriculture, and Frank Ramsay from Veterinary Medicine. The committee unanimously voted Parks its first choice, but it's a moot question as to how much the vote was needed from the campus, where there already was an overwhelming groundswell of support for Parks.

In 1943, Iowa State College Press published *Manual for Trustees of Colleges and Universities,* written by President Emeritus Raymond Hughes, which went through three editions in its first eight years. In his work, President Hughes suggested that the desirable age range for presidential candidates should be from thirty-five to fifty-two years and that items to be considered should include marriage and children, church relations, education and degrees, publications, educational and administrative experience, financial experience, speaking ability, personality in relation to staff unity, and student goodwill. Hughes went further to suggest that consideration should first be given to members of the institution's staff. There is no evidence that members of the Iowa Board of Regents in 1964–1965 had ever read Hughes's manual, but if they had, they would have known that Robert Parks met all of the former president's criteria.

The Board of Regents had begun reviewing candidates in 1964 and announced that it hoped to reach a decision by the end of the year. Parks was fully aware of the interviewing process being conducted by the regents throughout the fall of 1964, but while informing him that interviews were taking place, several regents also saw fit to reassure him with statements such as "Now, Bob, don't you be nervous about this." Or "Don't worry about it. Everything will come out all right."

Hilton was too honor-bound to tell Parks that he himself was the prime mover in the latter's candidacy, although Parks knew that he had Hilton's backing. Hilton was bent on persuading the regents, and his endorsement of Parks was fully in line with his wife's enthusiasm for their protégé.

Parks was meeting with the Board of Regents so often on regular business that there was little need for a long or extended interview. He remembered a meeting in Des Moines in December 1964, when there was wide speculation that the board was about to make a decision. On that fateful night he ate dinner first with colleagues from the other two state universities:

> So I went there. Funny thing. Everybody knew I was being interviewed. Bill Lange, who was vice president from UNI, some others, and Howard Bowen, President of Iowa University, were eating together. I think it was at Hotel Fort Des Moines, and the waitress who was serving us was remarkably slow. Everybody around the table knew I had an appointment with the regents at seven o'clock, and they really leaned on her to hurry up the service.
>
> I had a very pleasant meeting with the regents that night. I guess you could call it an interview, but I can't even remember the questions. Some of them probably hinged around, what would you do with this protest movement? That sort of thing—just general questions and very friendly ones at that. So I guess that night after they got through with their agenda, they told me their decision. The next day they took a formal vote and announced it.[14]

Maurice Crabbe from Eagle Grove, Iowa, was the regent who formally nominated Parks, and after the nominee received the regents' unanimous vote, he told the press that the board had received over 140 recommendations for the position of president of Iowa State University.[15]

Public reactions to the announcement of Parks's selection were extremely laudatory. Among the strongest was a statement from President James Hilton: "In my opinion, the Board could not have made a better choice. He is one of the most able men with whom I have been privileged to work in my forty-two years in the field of education. Dr. Parks's appointment will be enthusiastically welcomed by staff, students, alumni, and friends of the university."[16]

So the night before it was officially announced, Robert Parks learned that he was going to be the eleventh president of Iowa State University. That same night he called Ellen back in Ames in order to tell her the good news. He might have saved himself the cost of the call, for she probably knew it even before he did. Earlier in the day, a regent had said to President Hilton, "Well, Jim, you'll be glad when you hear our choice."

That very afternoon James Hilton telephoned his own wife, who he knew was indignant that the board would even consider anyone other than Parks. Hilton relayed the impending news release, and almost as soon as he had hung up the phone, Mrs. Hilton called Ellen Parks to say:

> Ellen, this is Lois. You know that love seat in the parlor? Well, I think you ought to come over so we can talk about having it recovered.[17]

W. Robert Parks had left sizable tracks through Tennessee, Kentucky, Washington, Wisconsin, and Iowa. Now he was about to become the eleventh president of Iowa State University, where further and larger challenges awaited him.

CHAPTER 5

Outset of the Parks Presidency

Wise statesmen are those who foresee what time is thus bringing, and endeavor to shape institutions and to mold men's thought and purpose in accordance with the change that is silently surrounding them.

John, Viscount Morley
Life of Richard Cobden

On July 1, 1965, Robert Parks became the eleventh president in Iowa State's history. The institution begun as a technical school and model farm had changed considerably since October 21, 1868, when seventy-two students arrived for an eleven-week precollege program taught by President Adonijah Strong Welch, three professors, and two young women assistants. Four more faculty members were on hand March 17, 1869, when the new school on the Iowa prairie opened its doors to the sixteen women and seventy-seven men who comprised its first class. A century later, when Parks accepted the presidency, the fledging school had grown in ways almost unimaginable, and greater changes lay on the horizon.

As Robert Parks began his presidency, Iowa State had an enrollment of 12,450 students. Enrollments were a stock in trade and usually gave rise to one of his favorite quips. When asked, "How many students do you have up there in Ames?" Parks's invariable reply was, "About one out of four."

No single path leads to a university presidency. In addition to the many who come from academia are those with backgrounds in law, medicine, corporate business, the military, or various other professions. Given the diverse duties that come with leading a university, a helpful background might include courses in banking and investments, diplomacy, labor relations, door-to-door selling, public relations, juvenile delinquency, and a good measure of behavioral psychology. Above all, the person selected for such a post must have innate tact and good judgment. For more than a score of years, President W. Robert Parks demonstrated that he had a good measure of these ingredients.

Most of the faculty greeted his appointment with approval and a measure of relief that no outsider had been chosen. Parks had come from their ranks and was their overwhelming choice. Wayne Cole, professor of American history, voiced the opinion of many on ISU's staff:

> I had one very clear thought at the time of Parks' appointment to the presidency of Iowa State; it was a truth about Bob Parks. At the time I said that it seemed to me that many people reached the top by climbing over the bodies of others. Bob did not do it that way. For me it was encouraging, almost inspiring, to see a thoroughly decent person rise to the top without compromising the thoroughly decent values that he had embraced throughout his life. Bob was a decent person when he was just my office mate and one of my colleagues; he was still a thoroughly decent person when he became and served so long as a university president.[1]

A day or two after the Board of Regents announced its selection of Parks, the *Iowa State Daily,* the university's student newspaper, sent reporters to the Memorial Union to ask students what they thought about the decision. Reactions ranged from disbelief that President Hilton was going to retire, to approval of a "new man with new ideas." The preponderance of those interviewed, however, said that they hadn't heard much about the appointee. Adding an air of mystery to the selection, typical responses were printed under a bold caption reading "STUDENTS: 'WHO IS PARKS?'"

In truth, the average ISU student at that time did not know much about Parks. The older honor students were well acquainted with him as were most of the leaders in student government. Only a few of the latter group were aware that he was the person who had turned down a request they had submitted earlier that year; it was a matter of liberalizing hours for women living in the residence halls.

Colleges and universities had long regarded their role as one of in loco parentis, that is, to act in lieu of parental absence. Iowa State had quit the practice of setting hours for male students years earlier, but most of the restrictions for women residents were still in place as the 1960s opened. During Parks's vice presidency, hours for all women except freshmen were extended so that during weeknights they could stay out until midnight. Freshmen had to be in their dormitories by 10:30 P.M. Weekend hours for all women enrolled at ISU were extended to 1 A.M. for Friday and Saturday, and until midnight on Sunday.

In the months immediately following President Hilton's announcement that he would retire in the summer of 1965, student activists were at work trying to do away with all restrictions on women's hours. Andrea Parks, the incoming president's twenty-one-year-old daughter and a senior at Iowa State then, can best tell the story:

> I got very involved in city politics and student issues during my last year at Iowa State. I was elected to student government and eventually headed a committee to abolish hours for senior women. When I started college, women, freshmen women, had to be back in the dorm by 9 or 9:30 with the doors locked. ...
>
> Throughout my undergraduate years there were very strict hours for all women, so I led this group to find out what other universities were doing, and we wrote all over the country. Then we made a recommendation to abolish hourly restrictions and submitted our recommendations along with our collected evi-

dence to President Hilton. He looked at it and gave it to my dad, saying, "Well, Bob, I think you ought to be the one to make a decision on this." And Dad turned it down flat!

I graduated in the summer of 1965 and got married on the twenty-eighth of August. Dad went into office on July 1 of that year, and when the fall quarter began, he not only abolished hours for senior women, he abolished them for junior women, too. And he hadn't even been asked to do that![2]

In the eight months Parks served as president before being officially inaugurated, he agreed to a no-hours policy for senior women and for women over twenty-one. Seniors under the age of twenty-one also were eligible for the new freedom if they obtained their parents' permission. This was a major victory for student activists, and ever-afterward Andrea would tease her dad by reminding him that he didn't loosen restrictions on women's hours until after his daughter had graduated and gotten married.

If at the time of his selection Parks was not well-known to most students, that could not be said in regard to the ISU faculty. Beginning with his appointment as dean in 1958 and up through the four years of his vice presidency, he increasingly had become President Hilton's point man in academic matters, and instructors through full professors were well aware that they had an able friend in the administration's upper echelon. Also, Parks's presentations before regents and legislators as well as several notable speeches he delivered on other campuses had added to his stature as one of the Midwest's leading educators.

With his commitment to excellence, Parks was showing himself to be more than an academic bureaucrat. He enjoyed philosophizing about the character and duties of a truly educated person, and as he moved into higher administration, he gave more voice to ideas planted early in his teaching career. For example, in 1963, while vice president at Iowa State, he was invited to speak at an Honors Convocation at Wartburg College in Waverly, Iowa. Notwithstanding the seriousness of his talk that day, Parks had time for a little onstage whimsy. He whispered to the Wartburg College president, sitting in the chair next to him, "Gee, you've got a good student turnout."

The president replied, "Well, there had better be. Everybody's required to come."

So Parks asked, "That so? How do you check them?"

The president said, "Well, you know they talk about that spy in the sky? We've got a big camera up there watching and taking count."[3]

Parks entitled his speech on that occasion "Our Useable Past," and in it he listed the following characteristics of a true scholar: 1—self-discipline, 2—open-mindedness, 3—a sense of proportion, 4—humility, 5—independence, 6—courage, and finally, 7—a social conscience that aims toward discoveries that will serve human needs.[4]

In this address Parks built on ideas and quotations from some of his selected heroes. His fifth attribute, for instance—independence—clearly echoed Ralph Waldo Emerson's call for self-reliant thinking in American scholarship. Parks's credo, however, went beyond Emerson's introspective view that improvement could come best by attempting to perfect ourselves from within. Parks believed that a scholar, no matter what his field, must have a social conscience and must work toward serving human needs. In later years he contrasted his belief with what he read of Emerson:

> It seems to me that Emerson's view was that trying to perfect ourselves from within is enough. You see he was a transcendentalist and believed in union with nature—that sort of thing. Emerson engaged in introspection and seems to have felt it was enough to be a "be-er," merely a being. However, John Dewey, another philosopher, said that a scholar had to be a "doer," an active participant in human society. Dewey's philosophy centers on the world around us, and I go along more with him.[5]

Parks linked self-reliance with courage—an attribute he said was necessary for the scholar even when the pressures of other men would have him present a distorted version of truth to fit some special purpose. "The historian," he said, "must narrate past events as they actually happened rather than by giving a picture of history that pleases a special group." Further amplifying his concept of courage, Parks said that "the sociologist must present the facts about social disadvantages he discovers among minority groups" and the "nuclear scientist must tell the truth about radiation and fallout." He closed the address by declaring that the scholar must have a social conscience; he could not be isolated from the issues of the day.[6]

The speech was Robert Parks at his best, for it revealed some of his deepest convictions: his commitment to independent thought and his willingness to risk public censure by involvement in society's greatest controversies. When questioned about ideas he presented that day at Wartburg, Parks answered:

> Now as to the substance of that talk, I'd say that in many ways the speech was a retread. The term "useable past" I had used often in my teaching and really had taken from Edmund Burke, a famous British conservative statesman. I think that particular term may be the most meaningful one in real conservatism.
>
> ... Burke later became a Whig, but the term "useable past" was an especially good term because it's not so stuffy. It immediately gives purpose to what you are doing, and it's far better than saying, "Hey, I want to tell about history or what took place." It's a meaningful term for the scholar's goals.[7]

The bedrock of Parks's educational philosophy is found in his sixth and seventh criteria for the scholar, namely, *courage* and *involvement* in social issues. Parks was not the first, of course, to call for scholarly involvement in society's problems. As a political scientist, he was well aware that the tenet hearkened back to the very cradle of democracy, when in the fifth century B.C., the eloquent Athenian statesman Pericles declared, "In a democracy we are the only people who think him who does not meddle in public affairs not only indolent, but good for nothing." Likewise the credo appears in writings and speeches of many founders of our American democracy. In the middle of the nineteenth century, speakers began shifting the call for involvement in public matters onto persons with formal education.

Among those who urged scholars to respond to social needs was George William Curtis, American author and reformer for more than half of the nineteenth century. Curtis viewed education as one of the greatest of all powers in human affairs, and in an eloquent college commencement address entitled "The Public Duty of Educated Men," he explained:

> By the words public duty I do not necessarily mean official duty, although it may include that. I mean simply that constant and active practical participation in details of politics without which, upon the part of the most intelligent citizens, the conduct of public affairs falls under the control of selfish and ignorant, or crafty and venal men.[8]

There is no direct evidence that Parks had read this particular speech by Curtis although he was not unfamiliar with Curtis's name and contributions to educational philosophy.

In 1965, when Parks took the reins at Iowa State, the university already was a huge enterprise, and the image of any large enterprise—be it university or industrial corporation—is in first part reflected by the persona of its chief administrator.

It was traditional for the institution's president to address faculty and staff at the beginning of every fall quarter, and although most of these persons had lined up solidly behind Parks's appointment, they did not know just what would be his initial actions. The Great Hall of the Memorial Union, therefore, was filled at ten o'clock in the morning of September 7, 1965, when the fall convocation was held and Parks addressed the ISU faculty and staff for the first time as their president.

He began by saying that he had sat among them while listening to two former presidents and that their position was more comfortable than where he now found himself. And he previewed his talk by announcing his intention to paint in broad strokes that morning his philosophy of the kind of university he wanted Iowa State to become in the latter years of the twentieth century.

Parks declared that he was not marking out new or different paths, but there were three central goals he wanted to help Iowa State achieve—excellence, diversity, and service.

He said the first of these goals—excellence—was a "process of becoming" rather than a state of being; there had to be continual striving and effort to move toward it. Excellence in a community of learning was not synonymous with size. He noted Iowa State's student enrollment was more than fourteen thousand and predicted that it would grow even more rapidly, but size, he insisted, was an unreliable standard for measuring the worth of an educational institution. Excellence was like the turf at Buckingham Palace, where the head gardener explained the secret of the beautiful velvet lawn: "You sow the seed, and then you water it daily for five hundred years."

Although Parks declared he was charting no new paths, he gave clear signals of the different directions the university would follow during his tenure. The clearest concerned his second goal, namely, to make Iowa State a "truly broad-based university." He recognized that ISU had attained its leadership position among land-grant universities, but its most distinguishing characteristic had come from expertise in science and technology. "The day has long since passed," he proclaimed, "when a university of true excellence and distinction can be narrowly specialized."

The third goal for Iowa State as he saw it was one of service—a "knowledge center" to help people no matter whether they lived in cities or towns or on farms. The challenge must be to provide the individual citizen with greater educational and training opportunities.[9]

Parks did not quote Shakespeare in this convocation address, but he must have been familiar with the bard's writing: "There is a tide in the affairs of men, which, taken at the flood, leads on to fortune."[10]

In this address President Parks paraphrased Shakespeare by stating: "There comes a time in the development of many institutions when conditions are present which will permit them to make large moves forward, if they will but take advantage of them." Iowa State, it seemed to him, had reached that stage in its institutional growth.

One of the first changes President Parks made was not a large, consequential one, and it occurred on the social scene in the opening weeks of that fall quarter of 1965. It had been President Charles Friley's custom to hold an annual reception for the faculty, and his successor, James Hilton, had continued the practice. It usually turned out to be an expensive evening for young instructors whose salaries were in the neighborhood of $3300 to $3500 for nine months. Moreover, the gatherings on the whole were rather dreary, formal affairs that all young or incoming members were expected to attend. So every fall, wives would rummage through their wardrobes to find a former best dress, often a bridesmaid dress, to make over and hope it would be suitable. Their husbands would rent a tuxedo or borrow one from a father or uncle.

The improvisations frequently were ill fitting and uncomfortable. The wife had outgrown the dress that had dazzled her beaux at the high school prom or the husband found the borrowed coat a size too large and the pants a size too small. It wasn't unusual for a man to wear a sweat shirt or sweater under his white dress shirt in order to pad his frame and make the coat fit a little better or to stuff toilet paper around his toes because his friend's black shoes were too big.

At the appointed time on the Saturday night chosen for the gala, the couple, usually joined by one or two others, would go to the Memorial Union, where they would meet their respective department head. This worthy would then escort his motley crew through the door into the Great Hall, where a long line consisting of deans, directors, and other administrators already had formed around the perimeter of the room. The department head would introduce his party to a designated greeter who in turn would present the visiting couple to a waiting dean or dignitary. The process was repeated at each of numerous stations, where perfunctory remarks were exchanged and forgotten as readily as uttered.

At the very end of the line stood the president and his lady. After the guests had passed this final outpost, they could make their way over to a long table and be served coffee or tea and a small piece of cake. Then as soon as convenient, the couple would slip away for a more informal party in a private home where they could return to their normal lives.

By 1948, when he had first joined the Iowa State faculty, Parks had been in Washington long enough to be thoroughly at home at formal affairs, but then he came to Ames and ran Iowa State's gauntlet. Along with other attendees, he was offended by the affair's artificiality. When asked about his impressions of Friley's and Hilton's formal receptions, Parks gave this response:

> I resented them really. Here was a cow college, and none of us had a lot of money, and we didn't get very good salaries. Then we were forced to sort of put on the dog. And believe me, we were pressured to be there—to meet people with whom you didn't particularly have much in common, and you had to rent tuxedos if you didn't have one of your own. And you were made to feel out of place if you didn't have one. Yes, I resented all that—not deeply, but I didn't think it was a very good idea. That carried over into my own administration, and I wasn't wildly enthusiastic about them then either although conditions had changed.[11]

The fall receptions did continue, but they were greatly changed. Robert and Ellen Parks wanted to make the evenings less formal and more enjoyable. Invitations were duly sent to the faculty, but the new presidential couple stressed that attendance was entirely voluntary. Invitations also made it clear that dress would be optional. When guests arrived, they did not find a long receiving line but people already dancing to light music from a small ensemble. A wider variety of refreshments was available and included hors d'oeuvres, small pastries, coffee, tea, and two kinds of nonalcoholic punch. (Iowa then did not permit even licensed establishments to serve liquor by the drink.) The change did not affect Iowa State's well-being, but it did suggest that a different approach would be taken by the institution's top official. Other changes began to occur that would have more significance.

Some of the changes were in the personal lives of Robert and Ellen Parks. Their circle of intimates grew smaller, and even relationships with old friends were altered. Harry Truman, the nation's thirty-third president, described the White House as "the great white jail" because in it he felt isolated from social and political contacts he formerly had enjoyed. Robert Parks in the presidency of Iowa State had a parallel problem—a problem perhaps worsened because he worked almost daily with former associates. Truman in the Oval Office had the advantages of having moved away from his home base in Missouri and furthermore had no need to daily encounter former colleagues from the U.S. Senate. At Iowa State, Parks lived in the comparatively small town of Ames and on the campus where he had won many friends.

Parks wore his new rank gracefully and toiled in the same vineyard as professors, but his work now was entirely different. He was among the faculty but no longer one of them. He might meet teachers face-to-face in the parking lot, on the steps of Beardshear Hall, where central administration was housed, or in a building where he was attending a conference called by a dean or chair of an essential university committee, but the old camaraderie was gone. He continued to be surrounded by friends and well-wishers, but essentially his position as head of one of the state's largest institutions put him in a unique category. He could not help but notice that restraint and respect from former peers tinged nearly every conversation. Moreover, he had to be more circumspect in whatever he said because a careless remark might be quoted, remembered, and sometimes given unwarranted interpretations. He could no longer slip quietly into the stands with old friends like Matty Matterson or Elroy Peterson to watch an Ames High football game; someone was sure to point out, "That's Dr. Parks, president of Iowa State."

He and Ellen had accepted a tremendous responsibility, and they could not escape the public attention that came with their changed status. The entire family was affected. Ellen hated to leave the friendly neighborhood in west Ames, but the president of the university was expected to live at the Knoll. Andrea, their older daughter, had married and was a graduate student along with her husband at Indiana University, but Cindy, eleven years old and still in elementary school, moved into the Knoll with them.

The Knoll has been the home of Iowa State presidents since its construction for that purpose in 1900. Nestled among large trees and sitting a considerable distance from the street to its east, the home is only partially visible to persons walking to the Memorial Union or elsewhere on central campus. Construction of the residence was begun in August of 1900 at an initial cost of $10,067.75. President William Beardshear and his family moved into the new house the next year. The home had not yet been given an official name, and in 1912 when South Hall, the building where music was taught, was destroyed by fire, the president's home was taken over and the rooms turned into classrooms and practice areas.

The switch was feasible because the college was between presidents and the home, therefore, was not occupied. Raymond Pearson arrived in September of 1912 to begin his term as the school's seventh president and promptly moved into the Knoll to make it his residence. Actually, Pearson's immediate predecessor, Albert B. Storms, had named the eight-bedroom house the "Knole" after one of England's baronial estates, but Pearson believed that was a misspelling and changed it to the "Knoll."[12]

Shortly before Parks entered office, the Iowa Board of Regents had authorized the university to take preliminary steps toward construction of a new, off-campus presidential residence, but Parks, with his strong sense of history, felt the home should be preserved because of its importance to Iowa State tradition. Upon his recommendation, therefore, the plan was dropped and approval was given instead to redecorating and remodeling the Knoll.

Renovations were begun a year before the Parks family moved in. The remodeling included additions of a family room and a large entry hall. A breakfast nook was created with a pass-through to a kitchen more modernized. The work also involved interior and exterior painting, installation of casement windows in the "morning room," refinishing the woodwork, wallpapering throughout, and construction of a circular drive around a brick-walled planter. The renovations, which were completed before the Parks's occupancy, likewise included redoing the study on the first floor and the sleeping porch as well as an adjoining small room on the second floor.

Upstairs were three comfortable bedrooms, one of which the parents furnished to the tastes of the teenaged Cindy; otherwise, these bedrooms were untouched.

Life for the Parks family in the Knoll was meant to be comfortable, but living there took away much of the privacy they might otherwise have had. Old neighbors like the families of Matty Matterson and Wayne Cole did not find it so easy to drop over after supper for dessert or iced watermelon during the humid Iowa nights of July and August.

One activity Robert and Ellen Parks were determined to continue was a monthly book club. This informal group consisted of Robert and Ellen, Elroy Peterson, M.D., and his wife, Jean, Ellis and Jo Hicks, Martin and Helen Ulmer, Bernard "Vin" and Ann Vinograde, and Hal and Mary Davey.* The group met after each member had read the book chosen for that month. The book might be fiction or nonfiction, drama, or short story. One reader was expected to give a brief summary of his or her interpretation of the work, after which other members joined in a free-flowing discussion. Jean Peterson said that in its fifty-year existence the tightly knit club read classics as well as trash. Her husband added that in their monthly meetings "rank had no privileges." Bob Parks might be a university president, but when that group met in the home of one of its members, he was only one of eight equal readers.[13]

The first family on a college campus lives in a glass house where their daily activities are readily watched, and whether they wish it or not, a university president and every member of his or her family become role models. How would Robert and Ellen Parks cope with the realities of his new position?

The position carried with it great power and tremendous responsibility. In accepting the presidency Parks would owe responsibilities to students, faculty, alumni, and the public, and experience had taught him that it was not unusual for interests of the four

---

*This "club," which was more than fifty years old in 1999, currently includes the Parkses, the Petersons, David and Judie Hoffman, David and Julie Wilson, George and Sandra McJimsey, and Gilda Hansen.

groups to be in direct conflict. Now every day he would make decisions that could affect the lives of hundreds of faculty members as well as generations of students. Moreover, as university president he would be expected to interpret and administer broad policies adopted by the Board of Regents. He would also have to remember that as the university's highest administrator he was a political figure whose decisions, statements, and actions could arouse ire or endorsement from the all-important American taxpayer and voter.

University presidents carry out these responsibilities through widely varying methods of administration. At one end of the spectrum is a person who bestrides his campus like a colossus and on the opposite point might be a shadowy figure seen only at public ceremonies or highly staged events.

President Parks made it clear from the onset that he would be at neither of these extremes. He could expect some former colleagues to become critics or sycophants—sometimes both—but the fellowship he had enjoyed with former coworkers was no longer feasible or possible. How would his best friends react when he had to rule against their wishes?

And there were the students. He meant to look out always for their welfare, but there were certain to be times when he could not accede to the requests of a particular student group. He hoped students would think of him as a friendly guardian of their interests.

Moreover, there was the Ames community and citizens throughout the state to be considered. Every Iowan had a stake in Iowa State University—the huge educational institution he had agreed to head.

What was it the Bible said about a man serving two masters? Parks now had more than two masters. The groundswell of faculty support that had helped propel him into office had been encouraging, and he fervently hoped that he could live up to such high expectations. He had the normal instincts of wanting to be liked, yet when conflicts arose and difficult choices had to be made, how would his supporters react? There were sure to be some complaints. He could only try his best to be fair to all contending parties. It would take tact, honesty, and willing helpers.

Despite its recent designation as a university, Parks had accepted leadership for a school whose national reputation had been earned through its technical and scientific accomplishments; he accepted that fact and was determined there would be no slacking in those fields. As dean in 1958 he had joined the ever-growing group of persons pressing for a wider curriculum, and now as president he was in a position where his voice would be heard above all others. He could accomplish nothing by himself, but faculty groups and committees, clamoring for changes, could count on his support for some of the recommendations President Hilton had decided to hold and pass on to his successor.

The first step in making Iowa State a broad-based university was enlargement of the curriculum, which in turn was linked to securing approval for additional majors and degrees. Parks moved in this direction at once. In 1964 shortly after he had been designated as the university's next president, the Board of Regents at his urging approved a Ph.D. program for the Department of Child Development. The institution had offered a master of science degree in that field since 1928. At the same meeting, the board also authorized a Ph.D. program in the Department of Psychology and a master of science degree in government. The Department of Psychology had offered a master of science degree since 1938.[14]

In its March 1965 meeting, the board accepted Parks's recommendation that the restrictive term "vocational" be dropped from the formerly named "master of vocational education" in favor of simply "master of education degree." At the same meeting, the regents authorized graduate programs at Iowa State leading to the master of science and the doctor of philosophy in computer science.[15]

Parks also acted quickly on reorganization of several departments. A department is the fundamental teaching unit within a university's structure, and Iowa State had a few very large ones that housed disparate academic disciplines. Economics and sociology, for example, was a huge department as was one which combined history, government, and philosophy. Another merged English, speech, drama, and telecommunicative arts, each of which had a sizable faculty and offered a range of courses. Such conglomerates were products of periods when enrollments were slight or of the Great Depression era, when budgets were slashed unmercifully.

Parks said to friends that the ultimate goal of every university president ought to be creation of the best possible "learning community for students and teachers." He believed Iowa State had outgrown the notion of combined departments. The lack of unified purpose within such academic behemoths tended to dilute the quality of their teaching and other contributions toward the "learning community" he envisioned.

In part because of his experiences as a teacher in the multifaceted Department of History, Government, and Philosophy, and in part due to his preference for tight organization, he felt the time had come to make the departments more discipline oriented:

> To be a first-class university, we had to do everything we could to attract and keep the best possible faculty, and I felt it was in the interest of their prestige, their self-respect, standings within their professional associations—in the interests of nearly everything—it was good to separate these groups into their own identities. When our people went to conventions, they were asked, "What in the world are you doing attached to that department? It isn't much professional recognition and sounds like an old-fashioned teachers' college or a very small operation." So breaking up those giant departments was another thing I did attack early in my presidency.[16]

The Board of Regents approved his recommendation for division of the Department of Economics and Sociology into two separate units to take effect July 1, 1966, the new ones being the Department of Economics and the Department of Sociology and Anthropology. He did not think the university had a strong enough curriculum in anthropology to warrant further separation.

It took a little longer to break up two other academic conglomerates, and it was not until the spring of 1969 that Parks and his committees saw fit to present the regents with relevant recommendations. Board action again was favorable, and on July 1, 1969, the former Department of History, Government, and Philosophy became three departments: history, political science, and philosophy. In similar action and on the same date, the former Department of English and Speech was separated into the Department of English and the Department of Speech.[17]

Throughout the first two years of his presidency, Parks kept bombarding the regents with requests for new degrees and widening the university's curriculum. The majority of regents agreed with his aims for a broader-based university, so most of his proposals were accepted.

Between 1965, when Parks assumed the presidency, and the summer of 1967, when he took a short, two-week vacation, there was a flurry of requests for new degrees and curricular additions. Some of the recommendations had been pending since the last years of Hilton's presidency, and others had been returned to committees by Parks because of his insistence upon more careful preparation of evidence showing need as well as assurance that the proposals would measure up to the university's standards. He wanted to make certain no deviations from excellence occurred during his watch.

In 1966 the regents approved four advanced degree programs: doctor of philosophy in forestry, master of forestry, master of science in history of science and technology, and master of science in industrial relations, all effective June 1, 1966. In that year, too, a change was made in the reading knowledge examination of foreign languages for graduate students. Instead of being administered individually by the Department of Modern Languages as was done previously and somewhat haphazardly, examinations prepared by the Educational Testing Service of Princeton, New Jersey, were administered by the Graduate College and the Testing Bureau of Iowa State's Student Counseling Service. Not long afterward the regents gave tacit approval to broadening the scope for new courses within the Department of Modern Languages when they agreed to change the department's name to the more descriptive title—the Department of Foreign Languages.

Next the board approved four new degree programs that enabled the university to award the bachelor of science degree in computer science, music, and philosophy, and the master of science degree in English, beginning in the fall of 1967.

In addition to curricular matters, Parks had to move quickly to choose personnel for key positions. His elevation to the presidency coupled with Jensen's departure a few years earlier and Hilton's retirement had left big gaps in the top administration. No one knew better than he the importance of having a right-hand man to deal with academic matters. The new president's most pressing appointment, therefore, was to find someone to fill the post he had just vacated, namely, vice president for academic affairs.

The person Parks selected, in what he quipped was the most rapid national search ever conducted, was George Christensen. Christensen had been dean of the veterinary medicine college for the prior two years, and long after they both had left office, Parks gave these reasons for the selection:

> I had made up my mind. As I looked around, the person I thought had real potential was George Christensen. The fact that he was a biological scientist would go well with my interest in the liberal arts and my background in the social sciences. Those factors helped make my choice. George had done very well: he'd been chairman of the Faculty Council when he was a professor here; then he went to Purdue, and he came back here as dean of veterinary medicine. He just had so many of the personal qualities that I felt would be good in the office. Remember I had just come out of it, so I had some notion of what he would be doing. Also, I thought he had the professional qualifications and type of personality that would mesh well with our administration.[18]

Christensen quickly accepted Parks's offer and from 1965 until 1986 served as the president's number one man in academic areas. Christensen's major and most visible function was as the university's chief personnel officer, a position that entailed responsibility for all faculty or staff appointments, salaries, and tenure matters in addition to overseeing curricular changes, new majors or degrees, the library, assignments of offices and classrooms, and schedules, along with an assortment of other duties. When called upon, he was expected to present personnel requests to the Board of Regents or to members of the legislature. His duties would expand each year he was in office.

Another critical appointment Parks made early—one that would grow more important as years passed—was his decision to appoint Carl Hamilton, head of the Department of Technical Journalism and an Iowa State College graduate of 1936, as director of university relations. In addition to undeniable talents with words, Hamilton had the kind of experience Parks knew would be needed in dealing with legislators and the public. Hamilton had grown up on an Iowa farm during the lean years of the Great Depression; he had been editor and publisher of a newspaper, the *Iowa Falls Citizen,* and during the war he had served in Washington, D.C., in the office of the secretary of agriculture. Those who knew him said Hamilton was an impressive person and one who got things done.

Parks had inherited a vexing problem involving the university's radio and television stations, and he wanted to turn that trouble over to a reliable subordinate. The stations were very profitable commercially, but although educationally owned, they had to meet the strict broadcasting standards set up by the Federal Communications Commission. In part because of these standards, in part because of growing pains within the stations themselves (WOI-AM, WOI-FM, and WOI-TV), and in part due to ambitious personalities, considerable friction had developed between the stations' personnel and university personnel who taught courses in radio and television. Parks wanted to create an authority who could ride shotgun on both factions:

> In appointing Carl Hamilton as director of university relations, I had in mind a broader sweep than had been held by his predecessor ... I wanted to bring the television station and the radio stations effectively under one person's control. Somebody was

needed between me and those operating the stations. So that combined with the Film Production Unit and others, I thought could all be brought together under one major administrator, and Carl had the experience and a personality strong enough to do it.[19]

Within a year, Hamilton's position would be upgraded into a vice presidency for information and development with added responsibilities for relations with the Iowa State Foundation, the Alumni Association, and the Memorial Union.

Parks likewise was confronted with problems in extension, a keystone in Iowa State's mission. He had come into the presidency convinced that the university's extension program ought to be reorganized. Personal experiences in Washington, Wisconsin, and Iowa had taught him that such programs could be uncoordinated and duplicative. Furthermore, there could be expensive rivalry between colleges within the same university over staff and short courses. Iowa State was no exception in this regard, and he summarized reasons for his early action:

> I had the feeling all along that our extension program was just too fragmented—that something could be gained by bringing engineering extension together with agricultural extension, which of course was a biggie—and short courses, and so forth, under a dean separated out from individual colleges. So I set up a dean for extension and chose Marv Anderson. At the same time, I changed the concept of county by county extension agents and created area or regional offices which would be appropriate for all our extension efforts within the state. That also permitted some consolidation of functions from individual counties into a more regional type. So that was one thing I thought could be done quickly.[20]

Parks was right in describing extension, especially agricultural, as a "biggie." He expanded his new dean of extension's responsibilities to include the Cooperative Extension Service in Agriculture and Home Economics, Engineering Extension Service, the Center for

Industrial Research and Service, and the Short Course Office. The latter enterprise itself was no small undertaking, for in 1965–1966 total short course attendance was 22,941—a gain of 2349 over the previous year. There were eighty-one different short courses and conferences in agriculture with an attendance of 4587 persons; thirteen courses in home economics attended by 2032, and eight in veterinary medicine with an attendance of 259. Thus Parks was taking visible steps toward his goal of "service" to the state.

Other appointments Parks made early in his presidency were Wayne Moore as vice president for business and finance effective July 1, 1966; Wilbur (Bill) Layton in 1967 as vice president for student affairs, with supervision over the Office of Admissions and Records, the Department of Residence, the Dean of Students Office, and the Student Health Services.

There were more shake-ups in the organizational pattern within the university. Arthur Gowan's longtime position as director of admissions was upgraded to dean of admissions and records, effective at the beginning of October 1965. Ralph L. Kitchell, D.V.M. 1943, replaced Christensen as dean of the veterinary college; James W. Schwartz, a 1941 graduate, succeeded Hamilton as head of the Department of Technical Journalism; Robert S. Hansen was appointed chairman of the Department of Chemistry and chief of the chemistry division in the Institute for Atomic Research. Parks with Christensen's steady concurrence was assembling a first-string administrative team.

Parks had some personal characteristics that coworkers would recognize and appreciate; one of those traits involved effort. He believed that any worthwhile endeavor called for hard work. That was a dictum he followed ever since his days at Berea College and one he carried into his presidential office on the second floor of Beardshear Hall at Iowa State.

Usually his workday began early. If it called for decisions or talks that could be done from campus, he liked to walk from the Knoll to Beardshear Hall, where he would climb the stairs to his office. If he expected to go out of town or visit places in different parts of the far-flung campus, he would drive his own car to the faculty parking lot. It was not unusual for teachers with 7:30 or 8:00 A.M. classes to walk across campus in company with the president who was beginning his day at the same hour. Parks's capable secretary, Joyce Van Pilsum, would have a typed agenda ready by the time he arrived. Emergencies or pressing matters often changed plans, but without the script the pace in his office would have been even more hectic.

There were many times, of course, when a trip to a distant city kept him from getting home until after midnight. For him old habits died hard, however, and he thought he ought to be in his office as soon as other workers. Moreover, a quick perusal of the campus newspaper or a few glances at briefing notes or memoranda gave him a head start on the day's agenda.

To outsiders he might give the appearance of quiet authority and dignity, but friends who knew him saw another side of his personality. Far from being a stodgy executive, he appreciated lighter moments and incongruous situations. He preferred subtle humor and with intimates might enjoy repartee or even a reductio ad absurdum or non sequitur. Although defacing public property irritated him, one bit of graffiti, which he quickly ordered removed from a wall in the mens' restroom at Beardshear, amused him. Someone, presumably a student, had scratched, "I'd rather have a bottle in front of me than a frontal lobotomy."

Although he had his favorite anecdotes, most of the time for humor he liked puns and plays on words. If a legislator or nonacademician sidled up to suggest an action that he did not favor, he might say with a grin, "That might work in practice, but it'll never work in theory!"

Concerning an ISU professor known to be especially long-winded during faculty meetings, Parks admitted to an associate, "Yes, unfortunately he always passes up a chance to keep his mouth shut." And for a colleague whose credentials were consistently overblown, he remarked, "Down deep he's really pretty superficial."

Once while regents were exchanging views over the "publish or perish" pattern common with promotion and tenure policies at the three universities, someone asked if administrators were held to the same standard. Parks replied, "No, we're not. We've already perished!"[21]

Speeches play almost as important a part in the life of a university president as sermons do in the life of a pastor of a church, and to some extent a university president and a minister of the gospel are faced with similar challenges. Each must address traditional problems yet fire inspiration for attacking them as well as for developing new approaches for immediate crises.

Parks's ability to stand before an audience and speak extemporaneously on broad aspects of human society, often with subtle humor and impressive references to history, added immeasurably to his stature. Actually, he was a better extempore speaker than when reading from a manuscript. Without a script before him, he could give free play to his agile mind; his personality showed better, and his voice grew more animated.

While speaking impromptu, Parks would also attempt more humor—some of which went over simply because the ideas were so ridiculous. Examples of this group included questions like: "Do you know that 90 percent of all bananas produced in Iowa are grown at ISU atop the plant sciences building?" Or "Are you aware that there are fifty-seven miles of sidewalks on ISU's campus, all of which drain toward the center in order to hold the maximum of water?"

There were formal occasions like graduation ceremonies when all persons sitting on the stage were garbed in academic robes and swathed in solemn dignity, but even at such times Parks would exchange quips in sotto voce. Moreover, behind the pomp and ceremony there could be happenings of which spectators were unaware. At least one dean, who attended only when he could find no valid excuse for a substitute, was so stage frightened that he relied on prescribed medicine to prepare himself to read a short announcement, and one preacher, who often was there to give the benediction, fortified himself beforehand with vodka.

It was President Parks's practice to personally hand each graduate his or her diploma at the instant a reader announced that individual's name, and if Parks knew the graduate was a son or daughter of a faculty member, he was apt to whisper, "Your dad wasn't sure about this, but we are." To a daughter, it might be, "Congratulations, honey. Your parents did well." To a known varsity athlete, he might say, "Best gain you ever made" or "Congratulations! You've made the team."

There were public addresses, of course, that demanded careful utterance—addresses important enough to be remembered and to take their place in history. In those situations, a manuscript was imperative. During the fall of 1965, pressures from daily duties as the university's new president robbed Parks of time to prepare what he knew was going to be the most important speech of his life, namely, his inaugural address. The event was scheduled for March 22, 1966—a convenient date that also represented the 108th anniversary of the founding of Iowa State.

An inaugural address is not the only speech a university president makes, but it is one of his most important. The address marks a special occasion that, more than any other during his administration, has an almost sacramental element. When well-done, it mixes symbol and substance. Pomp, procession, and academic garb add solemnity to the occasion, and listeners and readers look to the message for indications of what to expect from their new chief executive.

After Christmas 1965, in the evenings or whenever his schedule permitted, Parks began working on his inaugural speech. He approached it somewhat like a freshman preparing for his first examination. Unlike many high-level executives, he didn't use other people for speech writing. Although he occasionally asked a staff member to help prepare short comments for a news release or dedication event, longer speeches were personal productions in which he took too much pride to turn them over to others. As a student of language, he tried especially hard to avoid hackneyed phrases—verbal cholesterol—which clogged the message.

The inaugural represented an occasion on which he would have an opportunity to take a comprehensive view of the place and purpose of education in human society. He wanted it to be a thoughtful address, but because he would be making a philosophical statement and expressing his own ideas, it wasn't a matter of doing a lot of research. He would use a few quotations and plenty of respected sources, but he wouldn't have to scurry around to find them; rather he meant to draw upon his readings and previous teaching experiences.

He penned the speech through four drafts himself and talked over the major points with his most reliable critic:

> I think I can say that the only person that was helpful in preparing this address was Ellen, of course. She had the same training I did and was a very bright girl in addition to being my wife. She was always helpful in everything I did and the best critic I ever had. She had some especially good ideas about organization.[22]

A far better typist than her husband, Ellen went over each of these four drafts, and it was only the week before the inaugural occasion that Parks was satisfied enough to read the final version aloud to himself, marking pauses and phrases he wanted to emphasize. He worried about the talk's length and hoped it would be no more than half an hour. Actually, as delivered, the address took two minutes less than that because under the excitement of the moment he spoke somewhat faster than usual.

Indeed, what criticism the speech drew came from those who thought it a trifle too long, but it wasn't a collection of random ideas Parks had cobbled together for the occasion. He did not aim the address toward casual listeners or those who wanted light touches or entertainment; nor did he expect the address to stir members of his audience to some kind of immediate action. He meant for the speech to be an intellectual challenge, and he crafted it in the hope that it would stimulate men and women to think about the impact inventions and technology were having on their lives and to realize that among the enjoyable fruits of modern science were certain poisoned apples.

The message contained Parks's concepts of a modern university, and because those concepts guided Iowa State for the next two decades, an outline of the speech reveals the breadth of his thinking.

The Role of Iowa State University in the Scientific Age:
A New Humanism

INTRODUCTION

I. Throughout history, people have attempted to identify purposes of life.
   A. Attempts have been fitted with dominant interests of the period.
      1. Ancient Celts found explanations in superstitions and magic.
      2. In past three centuries interpretations have been dominated by science.
   B. Education must play a deciding role in our scientific age.
      1. Education has technological, economic, social, and political consequences.
      2. Schism exists between thoughts about science and thoughts about culture.

BODY

I. Science has become the "magic" of the modern world.
   A. Benefits of science include abundance, convenience, and leisure.
      1. Science seems a purposeless "magic" without values.
   B. We fail to grapple with science's impacts on our lives.
      1. Examples: "vulgar impact of the bomb"; habits, ethics, and patterns of conduct.
   C. ISU has three goals: excellence, diversity, and service.
II. Fourth goal must be to bring science into society's decision-making processes.
   A. Universities tend to produce professional skills.
      1. Resulting in narrowness of specialized knowledge.
      2. Hence, a failure to integrate science into our culture.
   B. Goal should be to bring all disciplines within sciences and humanities into a new educational unity.
      1. "New Humanism" has appeared before.
   C. Science can be a liberalizing force in developing human goals and values.

1. Poverty and slums were ignored in Augustan Age of Literature.
   2. Today science must be concerned with humanistic education.
   3. So-called liberal education has permitted science to set up its own system of values.
   4. Science must be at the core of modern liberal education.
III. Liberal education must be broad based.
   A. Liberal education must not shut itself off from modern science.
      1. Liberally educated person must understand language of science.
         a. Examples: properties of the DNA molecule, role it plays in heredity, phenomena of the university, light, space, and time, etc.
   B. Basic understanding of science and technology is necessary for intelligent decisions affecting life and society.
   C. Corollary is that education of the scientist must be within the context of human and humane purposes of life.
      1. Some scientists have disdained arts and humanities.
      2. Similarly, some humanities people view science as unesthetic and pedestrian.
         a. High scholarship is found in both science and the arts.
   D. Isolation within a special field leads only to partial knowledge.
IV. Concern at ISU should be to bring scholars from special areas of knowledge together into a common intellectual community.
   A. Community should reflect the most basic principle of humanism.
      1. Principle is man-centered, oriented around the human and the humane.
   B. True scholars must relate their specialties to a larger truth.

CONCLUSION

I. Iowa State must widen and diversify.
   A. ISU should put concern for larger truths at the core of its educational philosophy.

B. ISU education oriented around human and humane needs will not deter specialized competencies in respective fields of sciences and humanities.
   C. Let us begin by asking: "Can we afford not to achieve unity" of our disciplines?
   D. Goals are ideals not immediately attained.
II. Iowa State University can be an institution of high excellence.
   A. ISU will bring its disciplines in science, technology, and the humanities together in a common concern for the human and the humane.[23]

The usual practice for most speakers who read their messages is to have the manuscript typed in double or even triple spaces, but Parks preferred single-spacing and paragraphs. That form, he said, let him see where he was going, and he then could cut out a paragraph if the program was running longer than expected.

When asked how he thought the speech went over, Parks answered:

> Well, I think it went over well enough. Of course, you get a lot of compliments. It was a ceremonial occasion with everybody happy, so a lot of people said they liked it.
>
> ... It went over well, too, because there were people present who had that kind of mind. Now it would have been more popular—much more quoted—if I just dealt in facts—as if I had said I wanted to build sixteen buildings in the next five years. I want to put on a capital campaign of 42 million dollars or want to hire seventeen new professors. That's the sort of thing that would get quoted, but one has to hope that the impact of this talk is something that mattered.[24]

New Humanism to Parks meant blending science education with a certain amount of arts and humanities as well as vice versa. His theme was the cultural gap—growing ever wider—between inventions and scientific discoveries and society's ability to handle their impacts on human lives. The address was idealistic yet rational and highly relevant to the responsibilities he had accepted.

Only a few, if any, of the recognized physical and biological scientists at Iowa State were uneasy about his pronouncements. Actually, he found that some of the strongest support for goals he had in mind came from the scientific community. Social scientists and humanists seemed more reluctant to think outside of their fields than did the "hard" scientists, and on several occasions he said that he encountered more trouble with friends in the humanities and social sciences than with the associates from the other side.

During the late 1960s when their older daughter, Andrea, was doing her own graduate work in the history of science at Indiana University, Robert and Ellen Parks talked at length with her about the cleft between scientific advances and society's inability to channel them toward human welfare. Growing in part from such discussions, Andrea chose to do her dissertation on this concept by examining the development of the contraceptive pill and its relationship to the world's ballooning population. The birth control pill raised huge questions about population control for places in the world that clearly were overpopulated, and the daughter's study gave evidence of just what her father had talked about in his New Humanism address, namely, a cultural lag between integrating scientific discoveries and new technology with society's evaluations.

In retrospect, Parks's inaugural address was the launching pad for new and exciting, even revolutionary, ideas about Iowa State's mission, and few listeners could predict the ultimate orbits his persuasions would take. Indeed, directing the university toward a truly broad-based mission would bring changes in the lives of every student and faculty member in ways yet to be seen.

Family of Benjamin Newton Parks and Minnie Angeline Parks in 1925. Standing: Lorraine, Horace, Joe, Mary Badgett, Claude, Floyd Farrar (in-law). Sitting: Robert, Benjamin Newton, Parks Farrar (grandson), Minnie, and Taylor. *Photographs courtesy of the Parks family.*

Robert Parks at age four with his sister Lorraine, nine.

Ellen Sorge, age 20.

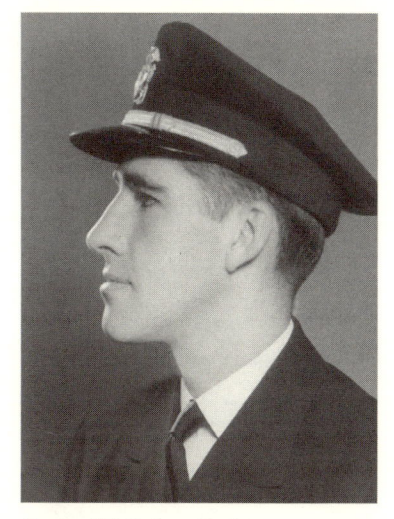

Ensign W. Robert Parks in July 1943.

Robert and Ellen Parks on their wedding day, July 1, 1940.

Robert Parks being greeted by well-wishers on the steps of Beardshear Hall (December 1964) upon his return to Ames from the meeting of the Board of Regents where it had been announced that he would be Iowa State's next president.

James Hilton, Iowa State president, upon retirement handing over the office key to his successor, Robert Parks, 1965.

The Parkses' twenty-fifth wedding anniversary—and a celebration of the announcement that Robert Parks would become president of Iowa State University.

The Robert Parks family in 1965. Daughter Andrea is standing; Cynthia is seated.

The Knoll in 1980. *Courtesy, Iowa State University Photo Archives.*

The presidents of Iowa's three state universities in 1975: (*left to right*) J. W. Mauker (University of Northern Iowa), Willard "Sandy" Boyd (University of Iowa), and Robert Parks.

Major administrators during most of the Parks presidency: (*left to right*) Carl Hamilton, Wayne Moore, Dan Zaffarano, Joyce Van Pilsum, President Parks, and George Christensen.

President Parks addressing Cyclone fans at the Peach Bowl in Atlanta, Georgia, December 31, 1977. To the right of Parks is Don Gustofson, Executive Director of the ISU Alumni Association, and to Parks's left is Arnie Gaarde, Assistant Director of Alumni Affairs.

President Parks in 1970 talking with students in his Beardshear Hall office. *Courtesy Parks Library, Special Collections.*

President Parks in 1975 with his grandson Robert Van Houweling at the entrance to the Knoll with Cy, Iowa State's mascot.

Iowa Governor Robert Ray and Robert Parks sharing refreshments and conversation at a reception in 1980.

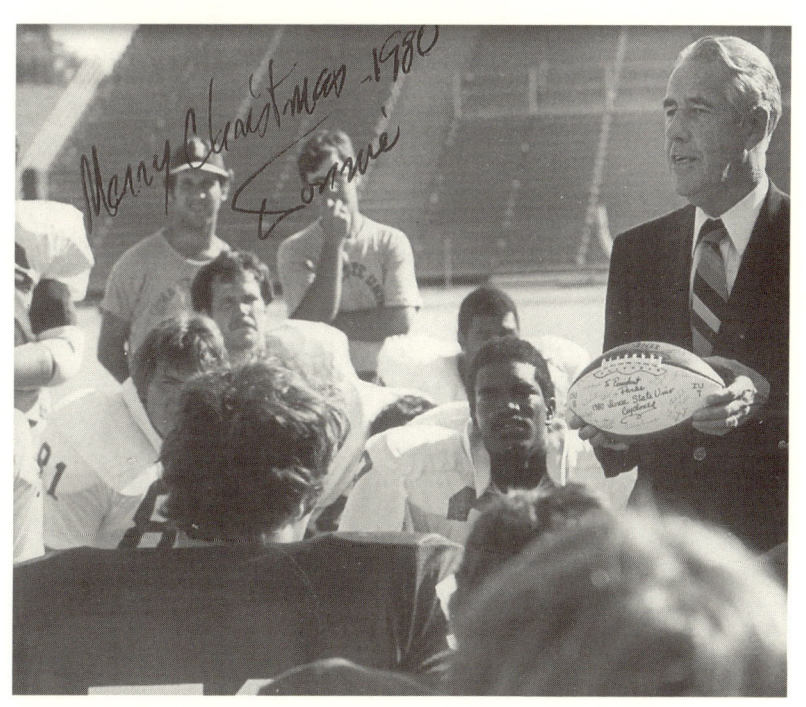

President Parks accepting the game ball presented by football coach Donnie Duncan after the victory over Iowa in 1980.

Robert and Ellen, hosts of a reception in 1985.

Ellen Parks (1919–1999), a true bibliophile, reading in the room she loved best.

Robert Parks, after retirement and in his seventies, launches a twenty-five-yard field goal to kick off the United Way Campaign of which he was chairman.

The Parkses standing in front of the ISU building named in their honor, the William Robert Parks and Ellen Sorge Parks Library.

CHAPTER 6

The Vietnam Issue

The debate [over Vietnam] will go on so long as we are a democracy. ... The debate will go on, and it will have its price.

President Lyndon B. Johnson
May 2, 1967

    The Japanese attack on Pearl Harbor in December of 1941 united American citizens more than any other event in the nation's history. Unshakable patriotism had swept the country as a generation that had come into adulthood during the Great Depression accepted the challenge to fight fascism and tyranny abroad no matter what the cost. Flushed by adventures and victory, Americans at the war's end tended to be a confident, boisterous lot. They had triumphed over evil and were ready to live in a simple either-or world where everything was black or white, rich or poor, moral or immoral, but our country right or wrong.

    The trend of the fifth decade of the twentieth century, therefore, was passivity on college campuses. Students appeared to be content with American society and mainly concerned with finishing their school careers in order to enjoy its attractions. Many young men saw themselves as future executives, and hence more of them enrolled in business and commerce courses than in the sciences and liberal arts combined. What was important was preparation for a professional career—something that would be safe and steady. A college man, meanwhile, was expected to search for the right girl who would make a fine wife and mother.

By 1960 an ever-increasing number of women were going to college, but usually they found themselves channeled into traditional female fields: teaching, nursing, or home economics. "Coeds," as male professors termed them, tended to be more silent than men; they were expected not to break the rules or remain single, which meant becoming an old maid.

Although the Korean War, which broke out in the summer of 1950, was never a popular one, there was little public outcry—no great antiwar movements, mass demonstrations, or stirring slogans, and the very thought that fifty thousand collegians might march on the Pentagon in protest would have been preposterous.

Western democracies had destroyed a Nazi dictatorship, and America was the bulwark of freedom against Communist totalitarianism. The Truman Doctrine, the Marshall Plan, and NATO were in place and fitted in nicely with the administration of likeable President Eisenhower. Capitalism, student rights, antiestablishment movements, race relations, and Vietnam—explosive elements that would produce the "Movement of the Sixties"—had not yet coalesced.

Most of the nation's attention in 1960 was drawn to the presidential campaign waged by two aggressive young aspirants—Richard Nixon and John F. Kennedy. The election, one of the closest in history, found Kennedy winning by a razor-thin edge. Out of 68,836,000 popular votes cast, he received 34,227,000, or 49.7 percent; his opponent Nixon garnered 34,109,000, or 49.6 percent. (The remaining 502,000 votes were divided among thirteen minor candidates.)

As the 1960s opened, a great many other happenings besides the presidential election were taking place in the United States: passage of progressive legislation, some of which had been pending since the 1930s, major changes in race relations, a developing readiness to question established institutions, a growing level of violence often culminating in urban riots with street battles between police and protestors, assassinations of acknowledged leaders, and within a few years deepening dismay over what President Lyndon Johnson would term "that goddamned war."

At the beginning of the 1960s, American involvement in South Vietnam was not yet called a "war," but informed citizens were aware that an unpopular regime there was being held together by American money and advisers. More and more Americans were being sent into the embattled region, purportedly to support South Vietnamese troops and guerilla activity but in effect setting up an American shadow government. A logistical buildup accompanied the American personnel, and officials in Washington, including Secretary of Defense Robert McNamara, talked confidently about how "we were winning the war."

In the midterm elections of 1962, President Kennedy was accused of being "less than candid" about American involvement in Vietnam. The Republican National Committee charged that "we were moving toward another Korea."

In an eloquent inaugural address, Kennedy promised that the United States would "pay any price and bear any burden" to hold the line against Communist expansion. The promise proved easier to phrase than fulfil. The American-sponsored invasion of the Bay of Pigs in early spring of 1961 had turned into a fiasco. After Chinese Communists later in that year crushed a revolt in Tibet and were engineering a penetration deep into Laos, Kennedy began a series of clandestine measures aimed toward halting further Red advances in both Laos and neighboring Vietnam.

President Kennedy agreed to a compromise on the confused civil war taking place in Laos, but he would not yield on South Vietnam. Instead, he authorized sending four hundred U.S. Special Forces troops into the troubled area for the purpose of expanding harassment and sabotage tactics being conducted against North Vietnam. Before long this small trickle became a torrent.

At first little opposition was mounted by either press or citizens against American intervention in Vietnam; most people agreed with the need to prevent a non-Communist country from being taken over by Communists if it was possible to do so with moderate costs. Another reason for small initial concern over Vietnam was that in the first year or two of the Kennedy presidency, Vietnam was only one of several countries in turmoil. The Soviets had built the Berlin Wall, and Vietnam seemed less newsworthy than occupied Berlin, satellite governments in Europe, or crises brought on by civil war in underdeveloped countries of Africa.

The charisma of the nation's thirty-fifth president captured more admiration from college students than did the grandfatherly attributes of Eisenhower. Kennedy's public demeanor was gracious; his rhetoric uplifting. Students believed in the New Frontier, signed up for the Peace Corps, and subscribed to the idealism the youthful president expressed so well. Inevitably, Kennedy's words echoed across college campuses, and as a result students became interested in the issues that confronted him during his short, critical time in office.

Political radicalism in the mid-1950s for the most part had attracted only a few thousand adherents who belonged to sects such as the Communist Party, the Socialist Workers Party, or the social democratic League of Industrial Democracy. Such disparate units were far from the cutting edge of social change.

At the beginning of the 1960s, young activist groups, encouraged by successes of civil rights campaigners and anti–nuclear-test protesters, began connecting with one another, and because the majority of these activists were college students, it was inevitable that college campuses would become social and political arenas.

Everywhere, in loco parentis—the concept that a college or university not only controlled academic programs but acted in place of parents in matters of student behavior and conduct—was buried under the avalanche of student rallies and demonstrations.

Student concerns varied from personal lifestyle to domestic and international issues, although few individuals embraced the whole range. Often arguments were over civil rights, and in that area there were some notable winners. Civil rights, although a popular issue among college students, did not carry the initial force of the Vietnam question.

From the oval office, President Kennedy declared that South Vietnam was the corner of the Free World in Southeast Asia, the keystone to the arch, the finger in the dike. In February 1962, more than four thousand college students trekked to Washington, D.C., to urge the Kennedy administration to change its policies toward the Soviet Union from confrontational to more conciliatory. Among student groups organizing that particular demonstration were the Student Peace Union (SPU), students for SANE (Committee for a Sane Nuclear Policy), Student Nonviolent Coordinating Committee (SNCC), Students for a Democratic Society (SDS), and the Young Peoples Socialist League (YPSL).

A year later, a splinter group calling itself the War Resisters League orchestrated its first demonstration against U.S. involvement in Vietnam.

Added to concerns over Vietnam was the matter of race relations; college campuses especially were sensitive to this problem. In early 1962, fifty-nine students from widely separated colleges had gathered in a trade union at Port Huron, Michigan, and formed Students for a Democratic Society. Out of this meeting came a resolution decrying the "feelings of helplessness and indifference" that many people saw in the political, economic, and social milieu of the country. It was necessary, claimed the group's initiators, to organize in order to change society, and the changes had to be led by "people of this generation, bred in at least modern comfort, housed now in universities." The original motivation for the meeting in Port Huron had been violation of civil rights in the South, but as college administrators were soon to find out, the society would align itself with other divisive issues, especially Vietnam.

In August of 1964, just weeks before most students returned to classes, President Lyndon Johnson declared that North Vietnam had attacked U.S. ships in the Gulf of Tonkin. Responding to his request, Congress passed the Gulf of Tonkin Resolution—a vague resolution that was interpreted as broad Constitutional authority giving the president power to wage war in Indochina. "The resolution," said George Reedy, the president's press secretary, "is like Grandmother's shirt; it covers everything."[1]

The nation rallied to Johnson's actions, and most college students fell in line with the huge majority of voters, who endorsed his moves; Lyndon Johnson's approval rating soared to more than 70 percent. In the presidential election that fall of 1964, he faced Republican Senator Barry Goldwater and was elected with the highest margin of victory in American history until that time.

Throughout 1965 the unity that had swept Johnson into office a year earlier began coming apart, and political debate erupted on campuses across the nation. As more and more U.S. men and money were poured into Vietnam, the protests mounted. In 1967 two hundred thousand people in New York City marched against the war. Religious spokesmen, political leaders from both major parties, and respected educators began speaking out more forcefully against the widening conflict. Nowhere were protests more volatile than on college campuses.

Although Vietnam was the single event that brought protesting groups together, the student unrest that widened dramatically in 1965 had several dimensions, including concerns over racial matters, civil rights, corporate business, and college administrations. The military draft that accompanied the escalating war had very real meaning to most students. Students for a Democratic Society quickly seized upon Vietnam, but there was not a great deal of interest on the part of most students in the larger agenda of SDS. Minority students in particular were not overly enthusiastic about SDS because many black students felt that the organization was led by white liberals. Within their separate groups, blacks began saying, "We can lead our own movements."

The University of California campus in Berkeley had come to be regarded as the spawning ground of student rebellions, and indeed the "Free Speech" movement that arose there in 1964 was an early incident, but the belief that student unrest in the 1960s is traceable to a single campus is misleading. In fact, the emergence of student power was a national phenomenon that occurred throughout the decade and on numerous campuses. These were the arenas where passions soared highest with both civil rights and Vietnam heating rhetoric to its boiling point.

In Iowa, college unrest had been noted even before Robert Parks became ISU's president. During a cursory interview with the regents in the spring of 1965, he had been asked how he would handle campus disturbances. His answer, relatively brief, was that he would keep an open channel of communication with protesting students.

That approach seemed satisfactory, for up until then any unrest at Iowa colleges had been relatively minor and usually had stemmed from athletic events or local grievances. Most students simply were too busy with studies and more orthodox academic activities, but a few students, particularly if they are well organized, can build a nucleus around which problems accumulate. Disruptions on Iowa campuses had not reached their peaks when Parks took office, but greater disturbances were in the offing. His promise to keep open the channels of communication would be given severe tests, especially throughout the first seven years of his presidency.

Across the nation campus rallies grew like dandelions after a spring rain; there were demonstrations against the war in Vietnam, the draft, the materialism of modern America, and violations of civil rights. Sometimes the rallies were led by students who described themselves as members of a political philosophy known as the New Left.

Outside of Iowa, protests were often directed at administrations that students considered as out of touch with their needs. That did not seem to be true in Iowa, and particularly at Iowa State, where according to surveys of student opinions the administration came off with very high marks. For example, a scientific survey of opinion taken in 1967 by Professor Charles Wiggins and Don Hadwiger of the Department of Government questioned 1500 students representing a cross section of the ISU student body and found that slightly more than 76 percent gave the Parks administration a favorable rating. Only 23 percent expressed the belief that the top administration at ISU was not sympathetic to student desires.[2]

Earlier in that year, many Iowans were surprised when Iowa State students elected Don Smith president of their student government. Described by the *Des Moines Register* as the "left-wing, bearded, sockless president of the student body," Smith was an avowed adherent of the emergent New Left group that liked to gather around tables in the Commons of the Memorial Union in order to deplore economic inequality and talk revolution. He and his adherents vowed to abolish all student conduct rules and drag ISU "kicking and screaming into the twentieth century"—a phrase borrowed from lectures of a few liberal professors.

The majority of ISU students, however, seemed to take a dim view of the effectiveness of their student leaders. Only 15 percent of the enrolled students bothered to vote in that year's election, and slightly more than 71 percent of the students surveyed disagreed with the statement that student government was "an effective instrument for solving student problems at ISU."[3]

The election of Don Smith welded Iowa State with Stanford as the only two major universities in the country having an active member of SDS as president of the student body. Notwithstanding the confidence most ISU students had expressed toward ISU's top administration, Smith immediately mounted a charge against university authority. A coterie of his supporters in the student senate passed what was called a Student's Bill of Rights. The bill was sent to President Parks, and Smith asked for a private meeting so that he could explain it further. Parks, who had not yet met the student leader, agreed to the request and recalled the occasion:

> Don really liked to shock people. His predecessors had all been more traditional—short hair, usually combed, shaved, and conservatively dressed. Don had very long hair, and he dressed very casually. Joyce [Joyce Van Pilsum, Parks's private secretary] was so shocked at his appearance she could hardly believe it.
>
> I remember the first time Don came in to see me. He was very polite and said he had come in to tell me what they were going to do. His actions after that followed the protest script almost as he had talked it out; he predicted the protests pretty well. And this is what he said, "Now, President Parks, where academic matters are concerned, you're in charge. But anything else a student does, you're not in charge. We're in charge of our own lives."[4]

The bill of rights that Smith put before Parks contained five major provisions: (1) no student shall be expelled or suspended by the university except for academic failure, (2) the administration does not have the right to tell any student where he may live, with whom he may live, or under what rules he may live, (3) all resident rules shall be determined by the occupants of the residence and not by the administration, (4) a student's grades are not to be released to any person or group outside the campus without the specific permission of the student involved, and (5) any action of the government of the student body involving the allocation of student fees shall not be subject to veto by any group outside the government of the student body.

Parks listened courteously to Smith's presentation and told him that he would like to get the views of others in the administration before making any decisions. Within days Parks contacted Mary Lou Lefka, who was vice president of the student body and in that role presided over meetings of the student senate, and asked if he could attend the next student senate meeting in order to explain his response to this bill of rights.

While many students did not approve of Smith's personal lifestyle, numerous ones had endorsed some of his ideas concerning increased student responsibility. So the situation was tense the following Tuesday night when more than 350 students crowded into the Gallery of the Memorial Union, anxious to hear what the university president was going to do.

It was common practice for the vice president of student government to offer an invocation at the opening of the meeting, and Mary Lou Lefka, farther left in her views than her colleague Don Smith, gave an opening prayer that ended with, "And God bless the Viet Cong."

After a short introduction, President Parks began his extemporaneous remarks. He said that in general he favored a high degree of student participation in decisions that affect students, but he was quick to add that the proposed bill of rights was "too absolute, too sweeping to win my endorsement." His language was unequivocal as he explained his reasons for rejecting four of the five provisions in the bill. For example, he said the proposal stating that "the administration does not have the right to tell any student where he may live, with whom he may live, or under what rules he may live" would take away from the university the authority to make regulations that were needed in behalf of all students.

Likewise, the request for absolute student control over allocation of student fees was another item he rejected forthright. Student fees, he explained, were really public funds—as public as any funds coming out of any other portion of tuition—and he reminded the students that although there was an administration committee that could overrule and make the final decision on allocation of student fees, the committee under his administration had very seldom used that authority.

One aspect of the bill of rights was accepted by Parks. That was the one concerning release of a student's grades. It was a time when the law required young men to register for the draft, and more and more students were being called up as demands for military personnel kept spiraling. Passions over the draft were running high, and the issue sparked protests at campuses everywhere. Draft boards insisted they had to ascertain if a young man really was enrolled and making academic progress or just trying to avoid the draft. In their zeal, draft boards frequently badgered university admissions offices for enrollment data. Everyone was getting pretty short tempered about the practice. At Iowa State, admissions officials had become increasingly reluctant to give out information, and in the U.S. Congress there was movement toward what eventually became the Privacy Act of 1974, prohibiting release of personal data to unauthorized individuals.

Parks had sought no advice from Iowa's attorney general or other counsel as to the legality of withholding grades from draft boards, but he felt he was on pretty firm ground in doing so. He told the student senate that night that he believed in the moral propriety of this fourth provision of the bill of rights and that he would take necessary measures to see that grades would not be released to unauthorized persons. The only exceptions, he said, would be that "parents of unmarried students under 21 can get their children's grades, and that agencies which grant scholarships can get the grades of scholarship applicants."[5]

Parks's talk with the student senate that night went over well. His remarks showed that he understood some of their concerns and that he respected the manner in which they had submitted the bill of rights. Yet he was firm in stating why he had rejected most of its provisions. Except for a few inveterate nonconformists, listeners accepted his explanations, and nearly all students admired his forthrightness in coming to address them in person rather than replying by memo, press release, or reliance upon a subordinate.

The confrontation was his first serious one with student unrest. The affair hadn't been particularly pleasant—somewhat like learning to swim by falling off the end of a pier—but it was an experience that helped prepare him for larger student uprisings to come.

Soon after Parks's response to the Student's Bill of Rights, the aura around Don Smith began fading. Other student leaders became disenchanted with his slogans and personal habits and were distressed particularly over his boast of smoking marijuana in open defiance of campus rules and state laws. A movement to impeach him arose in the senate, and elsewhere on campus he was hanged in effigy. When he realized he wasn't getting the kind of support he wanted, Smith got on his motorcycle and drove west toward the setting sun. However, after a year of two in California, he became dissatisfied there, too (someone stole his bike for one thing), so he came back to ISU and finished his undergraduate degree in engineering. Later he went on to graduate study for an advanced degree in history at the University of Iowa.

Years afterward in reflecting upon the Don Smith episode, Parks said:

When he came back to ISU and finished up his degree in engineering, I had the pleasure of handing him his diploma. Then Don went on to the University of Iowa and worked in something closer to his interests in social affairs, perhaps in the humanities or history. ... You know, people will say this, "I'm glad he finally straightened out." But Don Smith really wasn't so bad when he wasn't straightened out. ... Although his role wasn't immediate, it was there; it came with the liberalization of dormitory rules, coed dormitories, and that sort of thing. The whole affair opened up more freedom for students.

So if you look back at it, he advocated some good things. They were shockers at the time, but they were not mean things; they were not nasty things. So I'm glad he straightened out, if that term is going to be used, but I never thought he was so bad at the time.[6]

There was no antitoxin to protect the state of Iowa from the virulent fever of campus disruptions. Many Iowans had long considered the University of Iowa as the bastion of liberalism among midwestern schools, and indeed, some of the earliest disruptions occurred there. In the fall of 1967, shortly after a new school year had begun, students at the Iowa City school mounted a threatening rally against U.S. Marine recruiting. Protestors blocked the entrance to the school's Memorial Union, and police had to be called in to clear an entrance to the building. More than one hundred students were arrested as local police—fifty to a hundred strong—waded through the shoving, kicking, and screaming crowd.

Near the end of the 1960s, U.S. actions in Vietnam began to push aside other issues contributing to campus upheavals. At the close of 1968 President Lyndon Johnson ordered a halt to the bombing of North Vietnam. In March of that year he had announced that he would not run for reelection, and that summer, after a tumultuous convention in Chicago, Democrats chose Hubert Humphrey as their standard-bearer. However, in the fall election Richard Nixon garnered 301 of the available 538 electoral votes, thereby defeating his rival and carrying thirty-two states.

Nixon understood as well as Johnson that Vietnam was tearing America apart, and he seemed determined to reconcile the government's inherently contradictory commitments to military withdrawal and establishment of an independent South Vietnam government. Yet in March of 1970 South Vietnamese military forces, with encouragement and matériel from the United States, invaded Cambodia. Officially, the U.S. government denied that it was involved in Saigon's decision to invade its neighbor, but it was generally understood that the attack could not have taken place without encouragement and military aid from America.

On Thursday evening, April 30, President Nixon announced that he had ordered U.S. forces to join South Vietnamese troops in the Cambodian invasion, and across America student reaction was immediate and angry. The day after Nixon made his announcement, ISU students staged a mammoth rally. Hundreds of them massed before Curtiss Hall on central campus, where President Parks spoke extemporaneously. Restrained in his criticism, he nevertheless questioned the wisdom of enlarging the conflict in Southeast Asia, complimented the students for addressing the issue, and praised them for doing so without resorting to violence or ignoring the rights of those whose views might differ. Subsequently, a group of four hundred people donned black armbands and marched peacefully from the city's band shell through downtown Ames to protest America's widening involvement in the Indochina war.

Elsewhere, reactions to the Cambodian invasion were more violent. The very evening President Nixon announced that U.S. troops were participating in the invasion, 2500 students at Princeton University assembled and voted to go on strike. Over the weekend, hastily organized demonstrations flared on campuses all across the country. From east to west and from north to south, college students boycotted classes, made banners, and marched with boisterous shouts condemning American involvement in Southeast Asia.

On May 2, a rally at Yale University appealed for a national student strike demanding an immediate U.S. withdrawal from Vietnam; the idea was endorsed by student newspapers in seven of the Ivy League schools. In Cincinnati a thousand students marched to a sit-in within the downtown business area. At Stanford University, students battled police in the worst rioting in that school's history.

Typical of the protests was the size of the student gatherings: 5000 at Harvard, 2000 at Boston University, 1000 at Tufts, 1800 at Northeastern University, 2000 at Brandeis, 2500 at MIT. Nearly every college or university in Massachusetts voted to strike: at Clark University 1100 students—two-thirds of the student body signed on and were quickly joined by Simmons, Holy Cross, Assumption,

Worcester State, Springfield, and the University of Massachusetts in Amherst.

Farther west, at Case Western Reserve University in Cleveland, students voted a strike intended to shut down all campuses in Ohio, and in the state of Washington more than two thousand students surged through downtown Seattle, stopping traffic in a march protesting escalation of the war. At Oregon State in Corvallis, students hurled fire bombs at local police who had been called in to prevent threatened violence.

The great majority of protests in the immediate wake of the Cambodian invasion were peaceful, but some were not. The most serious and consequential confrontation occurred on May 4, 1970, at Kent State University in Kent, Ohio, a town of eighteen thousand near Akron. On Friday, the day after President Nixon's announcement, a rally at Kent State drew more than two thousand students who watched and cheered as a copy of the Constitution was buried. A veteran with a Silver Star and a Bronze Star burned his discharge papers. The next night the ROTC building on campus was burned down.

On Monday another rally formed on the Commons. A speaker climbed onto the base of the Liberty Bell monument and urged students to strike against the university. An army jeep with three National Guardsmen and one state trooper in it pulled up. Using a bullhorn, the trooper said, "Please leave the area. Please leave the area. This is an illegal gathering. Leave, before someone is hurt."

As students began heaving rocks, a company of uniformed National Guardsmen appeared, and soon gas canisters were thrown toward the assembled students. More than one student picked up a canister and threw it back. Several more truckloads of guardsmen arrived, and the guardsmen got out, formed a single line, fixed their bayonets, put on tear gas masks, and started marching up the hill toward the milling crowd.[7]

Accounts of the actual firings at Kent State differ, but the sad results were undeniable. The guardsmen shot into the crowd, killing four people, wounding thirteen, and raising the crisis on American campuses to a new level of seriousness. Within days, approximately

1.5 million students left classes, shutting down about a fifth of the nation's campuses for periods ranging from one day to the rest of the school year.

In the aftermath of the Kent State incident, protests and demonstrations at Iowa's three regents' schools moved into higher gear. At the University of Iowa, egg-throwing students disrupted an ROTC awards program. The campus armory was burned, and although no definite cause was ever discovered, it was widely believed that radical protestors were responsible. National Guard units were assembled in an Iowa City park but were held off campus largely through the efforts of Willard "Sandy" Boyd, president of the university, and Board of Regents president Stanley Redeker.

Boyd, President of the University of Iowa from September 1969 until September 1981, was viewed by most students at Iowa City as a fair and dignified administrator, yet he came under severe attack from outsiders, some of whom said he needed to deal forcefully with protestors and others who claimed his administration was too repressive. Repeatedly, he explained that in a pluralistic society a state university had to be tolerant of differing views. Boyd met with protestors and did his best to listen to their complaints. He also asked some of the school's most respected professors to go into the dormitories, chat with students, and in general try to head off any violence before it could occur. Among faculty members responding to his request for help was the world-famous physicist and astronomer Professor James Van Allen, discoverer of the Van Allen radiation belts. Van Allen's presence in the dormitories led one regent to quip that it might be the only time that underclassmen at Iowa University got to see a full professor in the flesh.[8]

Redeker was on the Iowa Board of Regents from 1961 until 1973, and in the spring of 1970 he was frequently on the scene at each of the three universities under the board's authority. A quarter-century later he gave an account of his role at Iowa University during the most critical days of 1970:

> I flew down there [to Iowa City] whenever I was asked by university officials to do so. They had a farmhouse out in the coun-

try where we stayed. It sounds all very clandestine, but nevertheless I was there with Sandy Boyd and some of his key administrators. Actually, the public-at-large and the students didn't know that such a command post existed. I was there, you might say, to fend off other board members, some of whom wanted to take a very active role in controlling the disorders. I made every effort to keep the other eight board members up-to-date on what was going on, and Governor Robert Ray came back and forth to join us from time to time. Quite frankly, we all, including Governor Ray, were trying our best to keep the National Guard off the campus. We thought it would be bad to move troops onto the campus unless absolutely necessary.[9]

Both Parks and Boyd praised Stanley Redeker and his colleagues on the Board of Regents as well as Governor Robert Ray for understanding what was happening on their respective campuses. Boyd said that during the most critical times at the University of Iowa both Governor Ray and President Redeker grasped the gravity of the situation and were extremely helpful. Boyd stressed that neither Ray nor Redeker ever interfered in any way, and both made it a point never to come to the University of Iowa unless invited by the university president.[10]

Notwithstanding the best efforts of President Boyd and his staff to allay tensions, student unrest at the University of Iowa continued to mount, and officials there deemed the threat of further violence so great that classes were canceled for the remainder of the semester.

Student upheaval at the University of Northern Iowa in Cedar Falls was more explosive than most Iowans had expected because it was the smallest of the three universities, but students there, too, formed angry demonstrations and sit-ins. Moreover, UNI had on its faculty several members who were less restrained in speech and agitation than faculty members at sister institutions. Four years before Kent State, an English instructor at the Cedar Falls school was meeting regularly with student protestors, urging them to refuse to register for the draft, to burn their draft cards, and to prepare for violence.

J. W. Maucker, president of the University of Northern Iowa, defended his young faculty member from legislators and others who wanted the man fired for encouraging students to violate existing laws. Maucker, however, was openly sympathetic with the causes espoused by the most vocal student groups, and whenever he attempted to explain his position, he made statements so ambiguous that many students were encouraged to believe he would take no strong actions against them. Accordingly, in the tumultuous May of 1970, protests on the Cedar Falls campus grew increasingly ugly. Property was destroyed, and one group took over the administration building, ousting Maucker and his chief associates.

The Kent State incident likewise set off angry explosions at Iowa State, where the traditional Veishea celebration was scheduled for that same week. The name *Veishea* was created from the initial letter of each of the five divisions of the college existing on May 11, 1922, when the first Veishea celebration was held—veterinary medicine, engineering, industrial science, home economics, and agriculture. After the tragedy at the Ohio school became known, some students and faculty at ISU urged cancellation of all plans for that year's Veishea celebration; other leaders argued that preparations were too far along and that if properly managed the three-day gala could still be held.

Veishea had long been touted as the largest student-run festival in the nation, and preparations for it began at least a year in advance. Even before Kent State and in contrast with the 1969 celebration, when protestors were considered a problem to be dealt with, student leaders for the 1970 Veishea had endeavored insofar as possible to bring campus dissidents into the planning stages for the event.

The shootings at Kent State occurred on Monday, May 4, 1970, and Veishea was scheduled to open officially on Wednesday, May 6, two days later. The ISU Veishea Central Committee—the group mainly responsible for planning the whole Veishea affair—met almost continuously in efforts to develop appropriate responses to the inflamed emotions on campus. All agreed that the parade on Saturday morning would be the most vulnerable time.

Neil Harl, Distinguished Professor of Agriculture, was faculty advisor for Veishea that year, and he related that the Central Committee decided on a four-pronged strategy: (1) a live microphone would be installed on central campus and would be open twenty-four hours a day for students wanting to express their views, (2) television commentator David Susskind, who was scheduled to appear for an address in Stephens Auditorium, would participate in a question and answer session to give students a chance to talk about their concerns, (3) there would be *no weapons* carried by participants in the Veishea parade, including military units of the ROTC or visiting drill teams, and (4) the parade would be expanded to include a unit of unlimited size that was to be called the "March of Concern," wherein individuals with protests could participate and then reunite on central campus for further discussions.[11]

Meanwhile, in the administrative offices on the second floor of Beardshear Hall, there was great concern as to whether the parade should even be attempted in light of the dangerous situation. Reports were rife that busloads of outside "agitators" would be coming in on Saturday to disrupt the floats and marchers.

President Parks asked Professor Harl to join him and other top administrators for a discussion of the worsening situation and to decide whether the parade ought to be canceled. When Harl arrived at the president's office early in the afternoon of Tuesday, May 5, he found it was like a "war room." Vice President Wayne Moore had been dispatched to Des Moines to talk with Iowa's attorney general about seeking an injunction against disruptive dissidents, but the other three vice presidents—Hamilton, Christensen, and Layton—were in attendance. Harl gave the following account of the meeting:

> I was advised as soon as I entered the room that there had been a break-in at the Armory and that the place was out of control. This came from Carl Hamilton. Carl was sort of flitting here and there and was obviously very perturbed. Bill Layton, Vice president for Student Affairs, was rather quiet as was George Christensen. Carl was the energy source of the group—in and out of the room—taking calls and informing everyone of the latest reports.

Parks was the center of attention and the voice of calm. After the vice presidents had said their pieces, he turned to me and asked, "Well, what do you think, Harl?"

I said I had come to tell him what the Central Committee had in mind, but Hamilton interrupted to ask, "What's that?"

I replied that there were four points that could become the centerpiece for a solution. Our recommendations might not be a total solution, but we thought they would help.

Hamilton broke in again before I had a chance to explain and said, "That won't work. It will never work."

He made his judgment without even listening to what we were proposing! Then he asked rather angrily, "Do you know the highway patrol is massed right now at the edge of town? Do you realize the Armory was broken into? Why should we listen to you?"

At that point, Parks broke in to say, "Just a moment. I want to hear what Harl has to say."

There was absolutely no question that Parks was in control of the meeting and would be making the ultimate decision. So then without further interruption I laid out our four points.

Hamilton repeated, "It won't work. There's no use in trying it. It just won't work."

But Parks said, "Well, we need to think about it. We need to talk about it."[12]

Christensen recalled the critical discussion somewhat differently and said that it was a very wide-ranging exchange:

> I don't remember that anybody was that specific or that firm on what to do. Options from A to Z were discussed, and bringing in the National Guard may have been one of them. As I say, I don't recall anything that specific, but it could have been because we discussed everything possible as to what would be the best way of dealing with the crisis. But we were all talking options, not from the standpoint of saying this is the way it's got to be. It was not a hawk-dove situation.[13]

In meetings of this sort, it was Parks's habit to listen more than talk. Before making a critical decision, he wanted to hear what colleagues had to say, for he understood that once he gave an opinion, subordinates were not likely to speak freely. Few would express views differing from his. That was a fact that came with the presidency. He tried to encourage open and comprehensive discussions, but that practice was not always followed.

Carl Hamilton, one of Parks's closest and most reliable aides, had an excellent perception of public sentiment and attitudes. For that reason as well as others, Parks usually followed his advice. In this instance, however, he may have gone against the counsel of this vice president, for as Harl further reported:

> That exchange ended the meeting as far as I was concerned, and the next morning I met President Parks on the stairs of C. Y. Stephens Auditorium, where the opening ceremonies were to be held. He thanked me and said, "It isn't perfect, but it's the best set of solutions we've had, and we're going to go with them."[14]

Vice President Wayne Moore came back crestfallen from Des Moines and reported that his attempt to seek guidance for a possible legal injunction against disruptive protestors had come to naught. He first had talked with Betty Nolan, an attorney who usually handled most legal problems for the regents. She said that they needed to take the matter up immediately with Richard Turner, the attorney general. The latter was not impressed, however, and according to Moore said, "What's wrong with you pantywaists up there? Can't you handle something as small as this? If you think there's a chance student protestors might try to capture the armory, why not just send over the football team to guard it?" Weeks later when Moore related this incident during a board meeting, Board of Regents president Stanley Redeker, never shy of friendly needling of Iowa Staters in regard to the school's dismal football record, asked, "Did he mean *that* football team?"[15]

Otherwise, the Veishea Central Committee's plans were implemented, and the traditional parade went off with scarcely a ripple.

The ban on weapons did produce some controversy, for an all-female drill unit from Des Moines was accustomed to using wooden replicas of rifles in its marching routine. The director of the drill team insisted that the mock weapons were an integral part of the girls' formations and also involved protecting the American flag. The Central Committee, however, was not persuaded and rebutted that only one American flag was permitted in the parade anyway. Unfortunately, later news stories depicted the Veishea Central Committee as having banned display of the American flag because of tensions over the conflict in Southeast Asia, but such was not the case. The limitation to one American flag had been in effect for several years because bystanders were accustomed to standing for it once, the first time it passed.

The precautionary measures urged by the Veishea Central Committee proved highly successful. In his talk with about 750 students gathered in C. Y. Stephens Auditorium, television personality David Susskind declared the war was "unconscionable, unthinkable, and immoral." The open microphone on central campus was heavily utilized, and the March of Concern drew an estimated five thousand marchers. Until the Veishea parade that Saturday morning, many Iowans had thought of campus protestors mainly as longhaired, unkempt dissidents, but the thousands of spectators lining the streets saw instead marchers who were predominantly middle class young men and women.

When the parade ended, many persons returned to central campus, where they were addressed by a list of speakers headed by President Parks. His impromptu words were brief and impressive:

> I am glad that this peaceful rally is being held. I can understand your deep concern about what happened at Kent State University and about recent developments in Southeast Asia.
>
> I am concerned, too. We are all concerned because the problem of how to attain peace in this world is the most important problem facing us all. If the university is not concerned with deep human values related to the attainment of peace, then what should it be concerned with?

> I will continue to exert every effort to insure that ISU will remain an open campus where differing views can be freely expressed, challenged, and debated.
>
> I ask you for your help in keeping our university an open campus. I ask you to help me resist pressures which would make this university a closed and oppressive campus. I ask you and every Iowan to be peaceful in your protests, in demonstrations, rallies, and in other expressions of concern. Violence and disruption would not only drive away potential supporters of your cause but would also make it extraordinarily difficult to retain an open campus for the expression of different points of view.
>
> I am glad that you are holding this peaceful rally. Meetings such as this are in harmony with the methods and purposes of a great university.[16]

At the conclusion of this short talk, Parks received a standing ovation from the assembled listeners. Harl, who was among the crowd, thought it was Parks's finest moment and offered this judgment:

> It was just exactly what needed to be said. The crowd, estimated at 4000 persons, included those who wanted strong action of some sort. It was an extremely volatile situation. To me, Parks's remarks were clearly the high point of his presidency. I don't believe there is any other event in his career that can approach his effectiveness on that occasion.[17]

There was more behind Parks's plea for help in resisting "pressures which would make this university a closed and oppressive campus" than his listeners realized. In February two years earlier the Board of Regents, disturbed by what was taking place on the three university campuses, had adopted a stiff resolution relating to student conduct, particularly in regard to disruptive acts. The regents wanted to be sure that universities under their supervision were taking measures to handle campus disruptions, so they passed what was called the Regents Rules of Conduct.

Parks viewed these rules as taking some of the discretion formerly allowed university authorities out of their hands. He didn't recall that any one regent was more hawkish than others but offered this opinion:

> If I wanted to name a person who was particularly hawkish, it would be the lieutenant governor at the time. That was Roger Jepsen, who later became a U.S. Senator ... but we were very fortunate in having as our governor Bob Ray, who was calm in a crisis and whose judgment prevailed. Ray, Stuart Smith as mayor of Ames, and Arnie Siedelmann, chief of police in Ames—all three of them were moderate in their view of things.
>
> The whole chain of authority was very supportive. Governor Ray could have made a name for himself by sending in state police and the National Guard. Stuart Smith could have done the same thing and have ordered more action by Siedelmann. ... I'll always remember Arnie Siedelmann; he never lost his cool. If he had to arrest some kids, and he had to do that at times, he wouldn't do it right there in the Memorial Union where it would cause a big flurry. He'd wait and find a better time and place. In general, Siedelmann wasn't keen on law enforcement just to show authority.[18]

As Parks recognized, Chief of Police Arnie Siedelmann was no small player throughout the Vietnam protests in Ames. Siedelmann was more low-keyed in handling the confrontations than some officers on his staff at the time thought desirable. Siedelmann's successor, Dennis Ballantine, was a patrolman in 1970, and years later when Ballantine himself had become Ames police chief, he gave this assessment:

> Arnie was very laid back. He had the cool head when some of us younger people thought we ought to go in and beat some heads. On Arnie's orders we spent a lot of time negotiating, talking, and backing away from situations so that they wouldn't escalate. From the perspective of my age and position now, I know that he was absolutely correct, but at the time there were a lot of us

young police officers who were really upset that we were allowing these demonstrators to do what they were doing without us taking any action.[19]

Although violence had been avoided during the 1970 Veishea parade, tensions at Iowa State were stretched to the utmost. Each day brought reports of what actions other colleges and universities were taking in response to protests sweeping the nation. At hundreds of schools, strikes and rallies resulted in dismissals or curtailments of classes. Within a week some 227 colleges and universities were closed in the face of the broadening demonstrations against U.S. actions in Vietnam and the shooting of the four Kent State students.

In Madison at Wisconsin University, Parks's alma mater, President Fred Harrington, who was under intense pressure from protesting students, had gone to Washington to confer with President Nixon about the crisis. Harrington returned from the nation's capital and announced that he would relinquish his presidency, thereby joining the ranks of administrators at other schools who due to the widening anger over Vietnam were forced out of office. History would show that during the tumultuous decade between 1965 and 1975 the average presidential tenure in the nation's major universities was slightly less than five years.

As more and more reports began coming in that other schools were canceling classes for the rest of the semester, agitation for similar action at ISU mounted. The government of the student body sent a recommendation to the Faculty Council that a program of "optional classes" should be established for the remainder of the spring term in order that students might be able to pursue nonviolent protests if they felt so inclined. The Faculty Council debated the issue but decided not to endorse it, and when that decision became known, one young history instructor announced that he intended to give all students in his classes an A as his personal protest against the war in Southeast Asia.

The Faculty Council at ISU, in response to the student government recommendation, said that while there was some "educational merit" in the concern that motivated a desire to participate in avenues chosen for protests, in effect the students' recommendation asked the administration to "intrude upon the most significant relationship to be found anywhere in the university, namely, the relationship between the student as an individual and the instructor as an individual." The council took the position that it was entirely proper for members of the university community as individuals to be active in political matters, but for the university to take a formal political position would be to deny its purpose as an "open" institution and to threaten its very existence.

Parks agreed with those arguments and added adaptations of his own, saying that a student whose concern compelled him or her to devote full energies to the political situation ought to seek counsel and advice from instructors. Moreover, instructors so contacted should make all reasonable efforts to accommodate the needs of such students. Parks recommended that agreements between students and instructors be made in writing so that they would be clear and completely understood. He went further to commend the parties in reaching such accommodations and complimented the students for expressing themselves in a mature manner. In effect, Parks was adamant in vowing that an "open campus" grew from a fundamental relationship between students and instructors—a relationship that was not to be infringed upon. ISU classes, therefore, would be continued until the end of the quarter.[20] On this question, the Parks statement, issued at 5 P.M. during the hectic day of May 11, 1970, represented an iron fist in a velvet glove.

At ISU over the weekend of Veishea, there were a few random, minor acts of vandalism. Slogans and threats were painted on sidewalks and buildings, and miscreants put epoxy glue in door locks at the Hub, Beardshear, Marston, and the engineering building. Food coloring was dumped in the fountain outside the Memorial Union, and in scattered places across the campus, windows were broken, but Parks heeded the restraining counsel of Vice President Wayne Moore, who said, "Let's not get too excited over a couple of broken windows."[21]

Everyone was elated that the Veishea parade had gone off so smoothly, but the dangers of campus violence were not yet over.

The university had planned to hold its annual Governor's Day on Tuesday in the week following Veishea, and all the military training units—marines, navy, air force, and army ROTC cadets—had drilled for a parade to be held on central campus. It was standard practice on this occasion for cadets from all branches of the ROTC to be awarded medals and honors they had earned during their careers at ISU. Then after the awards ceremony the cadets would march in front of assembled reviewing officials, including the governor.

A reviewing stand had been erected, and all plans were in place, but some officials remembered events of Governor's Day a year earlier. On that occasion, even before Kent State had fired higher passions, the ROTC parade had been interrupted by the mocking protestors who would say something like, "Oh, I've got to go to the library," and then step between ranks of the marching cadets. Despite Vice President Bill Layton warning the dissidents not to interfere, some of them had fallen down in front of the marchers and wouldn't get up. It was hard on the young ROTC cadets, but they handled it well and stepped around the blockers. One disheveled student in history strode angrily to within three feet of President Parks, who was sitting in the reviewing stand, called him a warmonger and berated him repeatedly for permitting the parade to be held. The student's tirade was laced with the worst obscenities he knew, but Parks sat impassively and let the invective run its course.[22]

In the spring of 1970, however, tensions were so strained and tempers so near the boiling point that ROTC commanders, fearful of confrontation between protestors and marching cadets, recommended that the awards ceremony and usual parade be canceled.

Parks respected the professionals within the ROTC units and appreciated the ways in which they had cooperated to dampen threats of campus disruptions. He agreed, therefore, with the officers' recommendation and released the following statement:

> I reluctantly concur in the decision of the Officer Education Departments to cancel the Governor's Day Ceremony at Iowa State

University. The tense and difficult situation which already has caused similar occasions to be cancelled throughout the state and throughout the nation and which has even caused many colleges and universities to prematurely close their campuses and terminate the school year indicates to us that we should not take the chance of possible physical injury to participants in the ceremony or to innocent bystanders.

Although I agree with the decision, I find it particularly regrettable inasmuch as ISU has experienced no violence or threat in the form of bodily harm. Our student body has shown remarkable restraint, maturity, and good sense. A military review, however, might well become the focal point which protesting groups would consider offensive at colleges and universities throughout the state. Under such circumstances, a level of violence might develop which would pose a threat to personal security beyond the university's power to prevent or control.[23]

The cancellation of the military parade on Governor's Day was the last major demonstration at Iowa State against the war in Vietnam. Everyone was pleased that things got no more out of hand than they did, and the school year ended as scheduled. Why did Iowa State suffer less from violent disruptions during the Vietnam protests than other universities? There might be several explanations, including the fact that ISU had an experienced and effective administrative team in place at the time nationwide disruptions were at their fullest. Vice Presidents George Christensen, Wayne Moore, Carl Hamilton, and Bill Layton had worked together long enough to develop an objective approach to most problems as well as respect for one another's abilities. It was a team the university president could rely upon.

Parks was inclined to give great credit to his associates and said,

> An awful lot of people at ISU were very helpful to me because they were just doing their jobs and doing them well. For instance, Wayne Moore, Vice President for Finance, was pretty cool and

> useful in so many ways. We put him sort of in charge of security, and he always had the highway patrol alerted in other towns.
> ... Shorty Schilletter [J. C. Schilletter, Director of Residence] was another stalwart. He ran a good operation over in the residence halls where students set up their councils and were able to talk things over. Shorty and his assistants had a lot to do with keeping things peaceful and quiet in the residences.[24]

Notwithstanding the effectiveness of ISU's administrative team, no one can overlook the importance of Parks himself throughout this critical period. Although an occasional critic might state otherwise, there was never any doubt as to who was in charge. Some complainants claimed that President Parks was not forceful enough in quelling disturbances and dispelling protestors. Others argued that he relied too much upon his vice presidents, particularly Carl Hamilton. Undeniably, Hamilton, the talented and energetic vice president for public relations, was a dominant figure on campus and throughout the state. Some observers went so far as to rate him as the most influential person at ISU, even above President Parks, but such judgments may have been flawed because they came from fellow journalists or from persons unfamiliar with the administrative style of Robert Parks.

President Sandy Boyd of the University of Iowa gave the best statement of relationships between Parks and his administrative associates:

> They [Parks's vice presidents] totaled out their responsibilities, but they did so clearly within Bob Parks's purview. I mean nobody went out on their own. Whatever they were doing, they were doing with his blessing; there was never a maverick operation. Certainly Hamilton was dependable and very able, but he was never power driven. If anyone were to suggest that he exceeded his authority, Carl would have been deeply embarrassed because he was so loyal to Bob.[25]

The great advantage held by Parks was that most students and their parents at home had come to regard him not as an austere academician but as a friendly leader to whom they could turn—a leader dedicated to the best purposes of education. Such judgment seemed warranted, for on numerous occasions and in many ways, he had shown that he was genuinely interested in student welfare. In the opinion of Board of Regents President Stanley Redeker, "Bob Parks was particularly well tuned to the moods of students. They respected him, but I think they looked at him more as a distinguished peer or colleague rather than a remote, authoritative figure."[26]

Undoubtedly, there were a few students at ISU who would have condoned violence; many others were vocal and sympathetic to the so-called radical cause, but persons in this group were not dangerous or obnoxious. They were the students who grasped leadership and were able to turn frustrations and anger into productive channels.

In response to questions about Veishea 1970, Arthur Sandeen, Dean of Students at ISU from 1969 to 1973, evaluated the role president Parks played in the dramatic episode.

> I believe the major reason Iowa State University did not experience the kinds of serious difficulty as many other institutions did during the period was Dr. Parks. Because of the high respect he had earned over the years throughout the state of Iowa, he was able to assure state leaders, faculty, students, and the police that Iowa State could best handle its problems without outside interference. At times he was subjected to some criticism for his views, but in the long run he was right and Iowa State benefited greatly from his leadership. Through all of these troubled years, no external police forces, including the National Guard was ever called to the Iowa State campus. Moreover, Dr. Parks was willing to speak publicly on issues of great concern to the society and to Iowa State students at the time. He did this in a calm fashion, whether through the newspaper, through his office as President, or directly to throngs of students.[27]

Many years later, Parks was asked if he thought the student body at ISU had played a big part in lessening the turmoil on campus, and he replied:

No doubt about it. I think the students at Iowa State were more rural in their orientation, and their traditional interests lay in agriculture, engineering, science and technology. The liberal arts before I came were subjugated, and the liberal arts were where you got most of your protests—in the schools which were a little strong in liberal arts, like Iowa and several others. Our students were more conservative to start with; they didn't go for all this stuff that took place on other campuses.[28]

In the week following the Kent State tragedy, President Nixon met with students who protested the Cambodian "incursion," and although this action didn't end the wave of college tumult then sweeping the country, the meeting as well as the close of the academic year at most schools seemed to slow down the number of further disorders.

Later in that fall of 1970, the Pentagon began withdrawing troops from Southeast Asia. In October the Third Brigade of the Ninth Infantry Division came home, and the next month two more divisions (the Fourth and the Twenty-fifth) were ordered out of the area.

Throughout 1971 citizen support for the Vietnam War dropped rapidly as television and print journalists began reporting grim details of what was happening there. In addition to dividing American citizenry, Vietnam was exacting a heavy toll on the battlefields. Graphic pictures of war's cruelty and suffering were seen nightly on television newscasts in millions of American homes, and not all of the pictures brought credit to America. In March, Lieutenant William L. Calley, Jr., a U.S. infantry officer, was brought back to Fort Benning, Georgia, where he was court martialed and found guilty of premeditated murder of Vietnamese civilians at My Lai three years earlier.

In November of 1971, President Nixon announced that hereafter U.S. ground forces in Vietnam would be in a defensive role; however, offensive activities by South Vietnamese escalated, and before the year was out the U.S. Air Force resumed bombing attacks.

As 1972 began, Nixon disclosed that Secretary of State Henry

Kissinger had been secretly negotiating with the North Vietnamese since 1969. Notwithstanding the administration's carefully crafted press releases, peace talks seemed to be going nowhere, and twelve months later Kissinger admitted that negotiations were deadlocked. It was not until early in 1973 that a cease-fire agreement was signed in Paris by Kissinger and Le Duc Tho from North Vietnam. Even after this signed truce, South Vietnamese troops continued fighting in attempts to recapture villages and territories seized by the Communists.

When Nixon entered the Oval Office in 1969, there were more than one-half million Americans stationed in Southeast Asia. He had inherited the most unpopular war in his country's history, yet it was the end of March 1973 before 595 American war prisoners were released by the authorities in Hanoi and the last U.S. troops were airlifted out of South Vietnam. The United States had poured billions of dollars into the Indochina war, and the cost in human lives was incalculable. There were no reliable estimates of deaths of civilians or the number of enemy soldiers killed, but the ten-year war brought death to 46,163 Americans, while an estimated 223,748 soldiers from South Vietnam had been killed in action.

In the fall of 1972, President Nixon was reelected by a landslide over George McGovern. Nixon resigned the office two years later, but it was Watergate not Vietnam that doomed his presidency.

Watergate, at first only a swank office and apartment building in Washington, D.C., became a symbol for one of the sorriest episodes in the history of the presidency. The affair involved burglarizing of the Democratic National Committee headquarters during the 1972 presidential campaign, trials and imprisonment of those apprehended, firing or resignation of top aides to the president, wiretapping of White House conversations, and sensational televised hearings before a Senate investigating committee.

The dispute involved all three branches of government—executive, legislative, and judicial—and was a bonanza for television and press. The acrimonious relationship between Nixon and the press went back many years, but because of Watergate it fell to its nadir soon after he began his second term. Throughout the spring and summer of 1974, his credibility plummeted, and by August of that year it was beyond rescue. Even his staunchest supporters realized that leaving him in office would have crippled the presidency until 1977 and would have rent the country more than it had been torn since the onset of the Civil War, so on August 9, 1974, Richard Nixon gave up the position he had fought so long and hard to win—the only chief executive in American history to resign from office.

In the aftermath of Watergate and with the bombing and war in Vietnam ended, two of the factors in the divisiveness that had engulfed college campuses were removed. Young and disenchanted students had challenged the old order. Wounds from their enthusiastic and occasionally violent challenges had been deep but not incurable. Another wound, however, remained and was even more threatening.

America's attitude toward and treatment of racial minorities had set off demonstrations at numerous colleges since the early 1960s. Perhaps the furor aroused by Vietnam produced more direct confrontations on campuses than did arguments over civil rights, but the latter carried potential for greater violence and danger to the nation itself.

CHAPTER 7

Race Relations at Iowa State University

PREJUDICE: a vagrant opinion without visible means of support.

Ambrose Bierce
The Devil's Dictionary

    Added to the antiwar movement that tore American society apart throughout the late 1960s and early 1970s was a second and even more volatile issue, namely, civil rights. Protests over Vietnam often occurred at the same time and in the same place as demonstrations over the plight of blacks. The two issues, intertwined like serpents of the caduceus, were major threats to a community's well-being, but at Iowa State University and in the city of Ames, it was the civil rights issue that led to violence and injury.
    In 1958, when Robert Parks returned to Iowa State from his stint as a professor at Wisconsin University, the full divisiveness in race relations had not yet come about, although a few warning signals of its seriousness had appeared in scattered regions. Of course, even before World War II and throughout that period, there were innumerable instances when blacks faced Jim Crowism, but two specific happenings during the postwar era caught the media's attention and became national news.
    On December 1, 1955, a white bus driver in Montgomery, Alabama,

demanded that Rosa Parks, a black woman, give up her seat to a white woman. Rosa Parks, no relation to the subject of this book but a lady he sometimes referred to as "the most famous person with this name," refused to do so and was promptly arrested for violating a city ordinance that called for segregated seating. The incident led first to formation of a local coalition between black groups and churches in Montgomery. The local coalition, known as the Montgomery Improvement Association, grew into a more regional organization that by 1957 had become the Southern Christian Leadership Conference, led by Martin Luther King, the civil rights movement's most eloquent speaker. King called for nonviolent but direct action, including boycotts and sit-ins. Such tactics were successful enough to attract substantial financial aid from northern blacks and liberal whites.

Another incident that helped focus national attention on racial discrimination occurred in February of 1960, when four black students from North Carolina A&T College sat down at a lunch counter in a Woolworth store in Greensboro. The waitress refused to serve them, saying that it was the store's policy not to serve "negroes." Her refusal spread across the A&T campus that night, and the next morning in a carefully planned sit-in, thirty male and female black students walked into the Woolworth store and seated themselves at the counter. There was no violence, just polite occupation, and before that year ended, more than seventy thousand black and white students participated in similar sit-ins to protest the Greensboro incident.

In 1961 college students calling themselves "freedom riders" further tested segregation laws throughout the Deep South. The Student Nonviolent Coordinating Committee (SNCC) began conducting voter registration in the same region.

In the next half-dozen years, a series of public murders added fuel to the firestorm over civil rights. The assassination of President John F. Kennedy in 1963 did more than just remove the nation's elected leader; his murder shattered much of the idealism he had helped spread. In 1965 the killing of Malcolm X shocked young blacks, for to many of them the black Muslim leader was a hero and martyr—a champion of African heritage, a preacher of black pride.

Three years after Malcolm X was killed came murders of two other prominent public figures. In April of 1968, Dr. Martin Luther King went to Memphis, Tennessee, to support a strike of garbage workers in that city. There, standing on a balcony outside his motel room, he was shot to death by an unseen marksman. King's murder brought new urban outbreaks of violence all over the country. Two months later, Senator Robert Kennedy, elected from the state of New York, was cut down by an assassin's bullet in the Ambassador Hotel in Los Angeles. It seemed as if American society was becoming conditioned to violence, both individual and general.

Meanwhile, angry confrontations between protesting groups and authorities were breaking out everywhere. College campuses were especially sensitive to problems of race relations and civil rights. Numbers in the ranks of Students for a Democratic Society (SDS) swelled, and the organization that had begun as a moderate, idealistic movement turned to radicalism and violence.[1]

In the fall of 1962 at the time the original fifty-nine members of SDS were going back to their college classrooms, James Meredith, a former Air Force sergeant, sought entrance as the first black to enroll at the University of Mississippi. His attempt was blocked by a police force ordered to the scene by the governor of the state, Ross Barnett, who had won election as an ardent segregationist. Meredith obtained a federal court order, and President Kennedy federalized the Mississippi National Guard and sent other troops to nearby Memphis. The governor yielded, but rioting on the campus of "Ol' Miss" broke out when Meredith, protected by U.S. marshals, tried to enter the college. Two persons were killed by snipers, and newspeople were beaten or fired upon. After a day of disorder and while clouds of tear gas still hung in the air, Meredith finally was registered.

The civil rights issue continued to boil all over the South, and in June of 1964, while most of the country was paying attention to presidential politics, more than a thousand white college students headed south in an organized effort to enroll more blacks as voters. Three of the migrating civil rights workers disappeared near Philadelphia, Mississippi, where they had gone to investigate the burning of a church. On June 23 their burned car was discovered in a swamp, and six weeks later, on the night the United States made its reprisal strikes for the Tonkin gulf incident, the FBI found the three bodies, two of them northern whites and the third a southern black, buried in an earthen and concrete bridge.

The disastrous period was not without some notable advances for blacks. In 1963 Dr. King led a huge civil rights march on Washington, D.C., and in the following year was awarded the Nobel Peace Prize. In 1967, Thurgood Marshall became the first black Supreme Court justice, and twelve months later Shirley Chisholm from New York achieved the distinction of being the first black woman elected to Congress.

Under pressure from President Lyndon Johnson, Congress in 1964 had passed a civil rights act. The act desegregated all public facilities and most companies, authorized the federal government to withhold funds from any program practicing discrimination, and established the Equal Employment Opportunity Commission. Despite the significance of this monumental legislation, discriminatory practices continued. It was easier to pass laws than to change attitudes.

In 1967, in the black ghettos of the country came the greatest urban riots in American history. Six days of racial violence in Newark, New Jersey, left twenty-three dead, and a week-long riot by blacks in Detroit resulted in forty-three deaths. The following year four black student demonstrators were killed by police in Orangeburg, South Carolina. In 1969 Fred Hampton and Mark Clark, active members of the Black Panthers organization, were shot by Chicago police.

The next year, the President's National Advisory Committee on Civil Disorders, dubbed the Kerner Commission after its chairman, Otto Kerner, Governor of Illinois at the time, released a summary of its 1400-page report on the summer riots of 1967. Among the commission's major findings were (1) The United States "is moving toward two societies, one black, one white—separate and unequal." (2) White racism is the chief cause of black violence and riots. (3) The upheavals were not organized or part of any conspiracy but came from an accumulation of social ills, including unemployment, inadequate housing, discriminatory police practices, and various complex social processes. The advisory committee also reported that in the period under study there had been eight major uprisings, thirty-three "serious but not major" outbreaks, and 123 "minor" disorders. Eighty-three persons died from gunfire, mostly in Newark and Detroit.[2]

Thus the national scene was anything but peaceful during the first decade of Robert Parks's twenty-one-year presidency at Iowa State University. Neither the ISU campus nor the surrounding community of Ames could escape involvement in the ugly, dangerous upheavals taking place in the United States.

John Milton, incomparable poet of the seventeenth century, tells us, "Childhood shows the man, as morning shows the day."[3]

If Milton's statement is true, we can better understand Robert Parks's approach to problems of race relations by taking another look into his boyhood. What attitudes did Parks form while a boy growing up in segregated Tennessee that help explain decisions he made as a man, particularly as a man responsible for heading a major university during a time of racial strife and protests?

Indisputably, the history of Parks's native region as well as attitudes of his parents helped shape his outlook on race relations. It will be remembered that middle Tennessee, where Robert Parks spent his boyhood, was quite different in terrain and social attitudes than the eastern or western portions of that Volunteer State. East Tennessee—the mountain area—was prounion at the outset of the Civil War and has remained largely Republican ever since. In the cotton country of west Tennessee, sentiments regarding slavery were pretty well unified in antebellum years. In middle Tennessee people cared less about slavery and had supported the South only after the state had seceded from the Union. It is worth noting, too, that Tennessee was the very first of the seceded states to come back into the Union.

Parks maintained that even though his grandfather had fought on the Confederate side, no member of his family was a professional Southerner, and none went "around whistling Dixie or waving the Stars and Bars on Independence Day." He was lucky enough to have been brought up in a friendly environment with close family ties. In discussing his youth, he recalled:

> I remember we used to sit around the fireplace in a semicircle for family discussions; it was right in the living room. That was about the only fire we had in the house. It was a very tolerant family.
>
> Take this race relations business, for example. There was, of course, a very strict set of social customs, but my parents always demanded that we children have much consideration for the colored people. And—oh, the terminology is important here. In those days you wouldn't dare call them African-Americans; they wouldn't understand it, and we wouldn't have understood it. Lots of people called them "nigger." That word was never used in our house; my mother would have washed my mouth out with soap! We called them "colored people."[4]

When asked if the word "negro" was common, Parks answered,

> Well, you could use that, but "colored people" implied more of a community relationship. To us it meant a closeness that "negro" didn't. Strangely enough, "darkies" then seemed all right for some people, but "colored" was by far the most acceptable term in our family.[5]

Young Parks's relationship with one particular family of color—George and Annie Mae Fox—was very close. George—partly hired hand and partly tenant farmer—lived with his wife Annie Mae in a little cabin back of the main house on Benjamin Parks's hardscrabble acreage, where he did all kinds of work in the fields as well as odd jobs for Robert's mother. When Benjamin was away, George was the only man watching over the homestead, but Minnie Parks always felt perfectly secure with George around—just as if he were her grown son. Robert in his adult years said, "I think he was as near a son as one from a different race could be in those days."

George came from a large family, and one of his sisters had an illegitimate son who became Robert Parks's closest companion. According to Parks:

> George had beaucoup brothers and sisters, and one of his several sisters had an illegitimate child whom she named Robert Fox—after me, incidentally—and was three years younger than I was. The very best friend I ever had. He was black, and we were very close to each other. ...
>
> Spud was his nickname, and I think our friendship demonstrates a couple of things about race relationships in Tennessee way back in that time—in the 1920s. It demonstrates first of all that little kids didn't mind the race difference. It didn't concern them much—maybe not at all—not at all until they got older and had it drilled into them.
>
> Another thing was drilled into black kids from the very beginning: "Be careful how you work with whites. Be sure to let them think they're in charge."
>
> Spud did that; he always let me think I was in charge, but really he was. He chose the games and offered all the ideas. He could think up games with a tin can, a rock, a piece of string, whatever materials we had at hand. Spud was such a sharp kid.
>
> What I'm trying to say is that Spud was probably smarter; at least he was the leader. We became separated after I left home for Berea College, and I heard that he didn't turn out so well, but in the terrible system back in those days that was to be expected. ... Spud's life showed what environment can do to a person.[6]

Berea College in Kentucky had been established in the 1850s for the joint education of blacks and whites, and that college provided Robert Parks with a second liberal environment. In 1934, when he enrolled at Berea, he lived in Howard Hall, a dormitory built in large part with funds from the Freedman's Bureau. Consequently, during the time Parks was an undergraduate at Berea, there was an easy and good companionship between blacks and whites.

Later and farther north at the University of Wisconsin, he found comparatively little racial tension. His future wife, however, remembered that as a young girl she often had read tirades of the Ku Klux Klan against blacks, Catholics, and Jews. Ellen forever would be upset and angered by words or acts of discrimination.

Throughout the years of World War II, Washington, D.C., was a segregated city, and the navy—the branch in which Parks served as an officer at Norfolk, Virginia—was conspicuous for its policies on racial separations. During that period, Robert and Ellen Parks had little contact with blacks or other minorities, and there is no record that the family fought against the system or was unduly disturbed by it; the young couple had a new daughter and were intent on launching their professional careers. Consequently, they didn't have much time for social matters or discussions of local issues.

Robert Parks, however, never forgot injustices he felt had been dealt his boyhood buddy Spud Fox and other blacks. When Parks came to Ames first as a professor of political science and economics, Iowa State had a reasonably good record on race relations. The school had helped start George Washington Carver on his illustrious career. Carver had first been an art student at Simpson College in Indianola, Iowa, but in 1891 an instructor encouraged him to transfer to Ames so that he could study the more practical sciences of agriculture.

Carver was the first black student at Iowa State and earned his bachelor's degree in 1894, after which he was given responsibility for managing the Agriculture Experiment Station's greenhouse. He also became the school's first black faculty member. In 1896, Carver finished his master's degree and left Iowa State for Tuskegee Institute, where he accomplished his massive research that led to development of hundreds of uses for products like sweet potatoes, soybeans, peanuts, cotton, and Alabama clay.

Notwithstanding the record of Carver, there weren't many minority students enrolled at Iowa State College in 1958, when Parks took up his administrative post as dean of instruction. Iowa State always had been open to blacks, but the institution itself had not been particularly hospitable. There did not seem to be much overt racism, although careful observers could note that the numerous graduate students from India or countries in the Middle East usually wore turbans in part to distinguish themselves from American blacks.

Soon after he left Wisconsin to return to ISU, Robert Parks undertook efforts to improve the status of the school's minority students. In 1963, two years before he was named president, he established a committee on human relations and charged it with advising the university administration on "problems arising from injustices based on race, creed, or color prejudice." To head the new committee, he selected William G. Murray, a senior professor of economics.

During his retirement years, Parks revealed a factor in his decision to name Murray, an acknowledged Republican who in a close campaign once lost a bid to become governor of Iowa, to lead this seminal committee:

> I remember very clearly that we needed somebody like Bill Murray to head it. He had been the Republican candidate for governor, and you didn't want a wild-eyed liberal leading it. You wanted somebody who was substantial and on the conservative side, actually, because what we were going to be doing was not necessarily a conservative thing. ... I met with the committee on several occasions and saw all their work, of course, but I was never a part of their deliberations.[7]

Murray reported that black male athletes told his committee they were reluctant to come to ISU because so few black women were in Ames. Murray's committee set out to remedy that situation and under his leadership did excellent work. Slowly the number of black students at ISU began rising.

The Human Relations Committee at ISU and a counterpart committee at the University of Iowa were primarily responsible for getting the Board of Regents to adopt, six months after Parks had been selected to succeed James Hilton, a policy statement on human rights stating: "Neither the Board of Regents nor any official who is responsible to the Board of Regents, shall, therefore, in policy or practice, discriminate on the basis of race, color, religion, national origin, or ancestry." The statement didn't seem like much at the time, but it marked intentions and future actions.

Notwithstanding the best efforts of regents and Iowa State administrators, dissatisfied black students and their sympathizers grew more active. A primary goal of many black students was to bring more of their own race to the school—a goal that Parks shared. He told colleagues, "We should do the best we can to recruit minority students, but there's a limit here. We're in competition with other states, but we just don't have many blacks in Iowa."

At the time, nearly all blacks at ISU were in some way connected with the athletic department—as varsity players, physical education majors, or junior members of the athletic staff—or they were employed as custodians by the physical plant. In fact, at a convocation talk with the staff, Parks, showing a tinge of grouchiness, growled, "This minority business doesn't apply just to athletics or the physical plant."

In 1954 Thurgood Marshall, then head of the NAACP Legal Defense Fund, had helped persuade the Supreme Court to declare in its landmark *Brown v. Board of Education* school-desegregation decision that separate facilities are inherently unequal and even damaging to black children. Despite this pivotal ruling and its implementation, the number of black students enrolled in institutions of higher learning remained discouragingly low.

Determined to change that situation, President Parks in the fall quarter of 1968 created a pilot program for bringing more black students to ISU. He realized that most of the targeted students would be unable to meet the school's normal admission standards and that his envisioned program would be running counter to policies set in place by committees within the separate colleges and the overall university. In his judgment, however, the goal was important enough to face the opposition that came from such sources as the highly respected dean of admissions and records, Arthur Gowan. The amiable, efficient Gowan was not a racist by any standard, but his voice was among the chorus of protests that arose from chairs of several academic standards committees who were against any lowering of the university's enrollment requirements.[8]

Parks did not back down, however, and authorized the first step in his plan, which involved sending Dean of Students Arthur Sandeen along with other deans to Chicago to select seventeen of the inner city's disadvantaged students. These students, primarily black and not chosen because of their athletic skills, formed a nucleus intended to encourage other blacks to come to Iowa State. This initial recruitment program, not particularly popular at the time it was started, drew attention and approval from the Board of Regents, and the board soon adopted measures that encouraged all three state universities to enroll more minority students as well as to hire more minority staff members.

At about the same time and long before the term "diversity" became a political shibboleth, Parks made another move toward opening more opportunities for blacks. He asked the National Association of State Universities and Land-Grant Colleges (NASULGC), a prestigious organization that five years later would choose him as its head, which black institutions in the South would be most congenial for ISU to associate with in faculty exchange programs. Officers in the NASULGC headquarters in Washington, D.C., encouraged him to contact Prairie View University near Hempstead, Texas. Parks did that and subsequently invited Al Thomas, President of Prairie View, and a few of his colleagues to visit Ames in order to discuss ways in which ISU might be of help.

Thomas made it clear that what his school needed most was advice and guidance on the engineering program it wanted to start in the coming July. The needs of Prairie View fitted in nicely with the Faculty Improvement Leave program Parks had helped launch a few years earlier, so he threw his weight behind selection of several top ISU engineering professors to go down to the Texas institution. President Thomas of Prairie View was generous in his praise of Parks and the Iowa State professors for helping get his school's engineering program accredited.

In that same year Parks decided that ISU needed a person who was familiar with the backgrounds and concerns of minority students, so he created a position called "director of minority affairs." When announcement of the new position went out, William Bell, professor of physical education, head coach, and athletic director at North Carolina A&T College at Greensboro, responded by telephoning President Parks and saying, "Well, Dr. Parks, I think I can help you." Parks was quick to hire Bell, who had been a big-time football player during his college years at Ohio State. In Parks's opinion, Bell "was a gentlemanly black fellow." With Bell on board, black students at ISU began to feel that they had a spokesman in the administration at Beardshear Hall.

President Parks's personal standing among black students on campus was high because most of them did not forget his actions in behalf of minorities. He had met with them numerous times and had encouraged them to use lecterns and ballot boxes for redress of grievances; those, he insisted, were the avenues for real and lasting advancement of civil rights. Moreover, he had initiated efforts to recruit black students, had encouraged inclusion of black studies into certain curricula, and had hired Bill Bell as a special assistant.

Thus noticeable actions to improve the lot of black students at ISU had been undertaken within the first five years Parks was in office. After a meeting with him, black students usually reported to their colleagues that the ISU president was a person who listened to their concerns and genuinely wanted to promote better channels of communication.

Parks had taken one very significant action that won unqualified approval from the black community. It was a step visible to all and would have lasting value—namely, creation of the Black Cultural Center.

With strong goading from Parks, ISU administrators were doing their best to speed integration of black students with other residents in dormitories and Greek houses, yet it was understandable that blacks wanted to get together sometimes in separate racial gatherings. In 1969 the few black students on campus had begun banding together in a loosely knit group called the Black Student Organization, but they had no place where they could assemble, collect relevant histories, or voice common concerns. They took their complaint first to Bill Bell, who explained it to Parks. Parks appreciated their situation and said that what was needed was a place where blacks could meet with one another and not feel they were outsiders.

Professor Neil Harl, Veishea faculty advisor, was known to be sympathetic to the problems black students faced at ISU, and with Bell's help Harl contacted Luther Glanton, a prominent black judge in Des Moines. Bell and Harl next located a vacant house in Ames on Welch Avenue—just a block away from the campus proper. When the three took their proposal to Parks, he was very enthusiastic about buying the property and turning it into a Black Cultural Center. He suggested people to contact who he knew would be supportive of the project.

Parks informed the Board of Regents about intentions for the center, but in his words, "They were pretty stuffy about it and said, 'All right, but be sure you don't use any state funds.'"

With that warning in mind, he sent assistants scurrying for nonpublic funds. The search netted donations from several university organizations, private subscriptions, and a substantial loan from the Alumni Achievement Fund. Having acquired sufficient financing, the Black Cultural Center was able to begin operating on January 1, 1969. Seven months later on August 18, 1969, the center was legally incorporated with the three names William Bell, Neil Harl, and Luther Glanton on court documents as the legal incorporators.*

Meanwhile, campus turmoil was on the agenda whenever and wherever university presidents met, and the conventional wisdom among them was "Try not to let the two causes, viz. Vietnam and black protests, come together." However, as the volume and intensity of Vietnam protests continued to rise throughout the nation, so did demonstrations and rallies over racial grievances. Parks and his counterparts could no more halt protests arising over the one cause

---

*The Black Cultural Center, 517 Welch Avenue, was formally dedicated on September 27, 1970, the same day as the dedication of Carver Hall, named in honor of George Washington Carver.

than they could from the other; the causes were separate, but at Iowa State passions raised by the two issues spilled over at the same time.

A normal April brings bountiful rain to Iowa, but that month in 1970 also brought showers of protests. As the month began, a large delegation of Vietnam protestors from ISU marched from the campus to downtown Ames and sat in front of the bus station, where the newest draftees were scheduled to depart. It was not an unruly gathering, and at the station numerous spectators as well as local police watched a forty-year-old professor with great bravado burn his outdated draft card. Demonstrations and actions by blacks in days immediately ahead, however, were more ominous and violent.

Less than 1 percent of the Ames community in 1970 was black, and practically all of that percentage was connected with the university. Two weeks before the Veishea confrontation that was of so much concern, an incident growing out of black dissatisfaction resulted in more actual injury and property destruction than anything done by Vietnam protestors. What began as just another barroom brawl became a cause célèbre.

The whole incident with its ugly aftermath started during the second week of April when three ISU students were arrested in a downtown Ames tavern. Two of the three, Larry Munger and Chuck Jean, were white, and the third, Roosevelt Roby was black. Details of the actual fracas became so muddled that it was impossible to tell which parties were at greater fault, but it was incontestable that Jean was hit with a beer mug wielded by Roby and suffered a head wound that required forty stitches. Munger and Jean were charged with fighting, and Roby with assault and battery.

The following day, Munger and Jean appeared before Municipal Court Judge John L. McKinney and pleaded guilty. Police went to Roby's residence at 2514 Lincoln Way, just across from the huge Friley Hall complex on central campus, with the intention of arresting him. The two officers had handcuffed Roby and were leading him to the squad car when a number of blacks arrived and separated them from their captive. Among the blacks surrounding the arresting officers was Charles Knox, a former felon and head of the Black Panther organization in Des Moines. Roby started running toward Friley Hall, protected by Knox and other blacks on the scene. The officers did not pursue Roby then and later explained that to do so might have led to unnecessary injuries.

The officers were reluctant to enter the residence hall where Roby had sought sanctuary, but they contacted the Office of Student Affairs. Discussions between municipal and university authorities next took place, but police were not granted permission to enter the residence hall without a search warrant. Director of Minority Affairs William Bell, however, offered to go over to Friley to try to talk Roby into surrendering. When Bell arrived at Friley Hall and attempted to go into the room where Roby was thought to be hiding, black persons would not allow him to enter. In consequence, Bell never was able to say whether or not Roby was actually there.

The brouhaha mounted when a second warrant for Roby's arrest was issued, this one charging him with "resisting execution of due process." Within the Iowa Code assault and battery, fighting, and disturbing the peace are all misdemeanors carrying a maximum penalty of a $100 fine and/or thirty days in jail, while resisting execution of due process is an indictable misdemeanor with a maximum penalty of a $1000 fine and/or one year in jail. The upgraded warrant against Roby meant that he now was charged with a more serious offense than either of the coculprits, Munger and Jean.

Charles Knox also was charged with resisting execution of due process because he allegedly had aided and abetted in the escape of a fugitive facing arrest. A trial date was set, with the trial to be heard in the municipal court presided over by Judge John McKinney.

The story was just beginning, for tempers kept rising. In the third week of April, a group of angry black students gathered in the Commons of the Memorial Union for a noisy, disturbing demonstration. One black student was reported as having carried a rifle; university administrators took no discernible action in regard to this incident.

The next day, Friday, April 24, an estimated crowd of fifty blacks massed in front of City Hall in Ames to protest what they termed unfair police treatment. Relations between local authorities and those at the university were being tested, and some Ames citizens blamed the Office of Student Affairs for "shoving all their problems downtown."

Robert Crom, Director of Alumni Affairs, disclosed that his office was receiving an increasing number of letters from former graduates who were upset because ISU administrators were not taking stronger actions against campus disrupters, and much of the blame fell either by name or implication on ISU's chief administrator, Robert Parks.

The pressure on him mounted daily. Not only was he facing the danger of Vietnam protests getting out of hand; now he had to deal with the added threats of racial violence. His critics, including some students and other Iowa citizens beyond Ames, complained that local blacks were using Roby's arrest and trial as an excuse to get into violent tactics like those taking place on more militant campuses. Nor could Parks escape criticism from some members of the state legislature.

State senator Francis Messerly (R–Cedar Falls), chairman of the powerful Senate Appropriations Committee and vice chairman of the Legislative Budget and Financial Control Committee, came to the campus and conferred with Parks about the alleged behavior of blacks in the Memorial Union. The influential senator told a reporter: "Every disruptive act harms the image of the university. I have over and over again stressed that the universities must present a better image or the taxpayers will not support the schools." The legislator went on to say that he had received "piles and piles of letters" from citizens demanding stronger leadership from ISU administrators.[9]

By coincidence, a few days before Messerly's talks with Parks, Judge John McKinney had begun hearing testimony in the assault and battery case against Roby. During the next weekend, while the court was in recess, complaints by black students against alleged unfair treatment by Ames police gained momentum.

The hearing resumed on Monday, April 27, 1970, and that evening Judge McKinney went into the garage of his home at 2613 Pierce Avenue in the northernmost section of Ames. As he stepped into the garage, he discovered that a bomb of sorts had been placed just inside the door. The device consisted of a one-gallon lacquer can bearing the brand name "Cook's Paint" and a dry cell battery on top of the metal can. Attached to the battery was an alarm clock from which straps led to a chemical lower in the can. The clock was ticking, so McKinney realized he might have little time. He rushed back into the house where to his wife he spelled out the threat, "Mary, there's a *B-O-M-B* in the garage. Get the kids out, and take them across the street!" Then from the neighbor's house, McKinney called police.

The police arrived quickly and a fire truck soon thereafter. Officers put the device in a large garbage can that they then filled with sand before taking it to a nearby field. There they shot holes in the canister, but nothing happened, so they took the device out of the garbage can to examine it more closely. They found a couple of kitchen-type matches attached to the clock. As the clock hands moved downward, these matches would have struck pieces of flint held in place next to the chemical in the can. Later after laboratory analysis, the FBI announced that the primitive contraption would have worked but technically it was an "incendiary device," not a bomb.[10]

No evidence as to who constructed the device and placed it in McKinney's garage was ever discovered, and motivation for the act likewise remained speculative. The Ames community was shaken. No one knew what, if anything, might come next. If a judge's home were to be attacked, wasn't anyone in a position of authority vulnerable? The concern reached even the Knoll, where the Parkses lived. Times when her husband had to be out of town and she was alone in the home with her teenaged daughter, Cindy, were worrisome for Ellen Parks. Once she called on two of her closest friends—Elroy Peterson and his wife, Jean. Dr. Peterson described the occasion:

> During that time when there was so much upheaval, Bob [Parks] had to go away for a meeting, and Ellen asked Jean and me to come over to be with her that evening because she was afraid. And before we left her that night, she asked me to go down into

the basement to make sure there wasn't anybody lurking there. She didn't want to call campus security because she didn't want them to know she was such a chicken.[11]

The Petersons said that Parks himself never expressed to them fears for his own safety or for that of his family, but in view of what was occurring in the community, they were sure that as parents both Parks and his wife were concerned over dangers for their young daughter. Jean Peterson added, "Ellen was worried about Cindy and the house, of course, but she was particularly worried about Bob—thinking he was too trusting and that somebody might attack him."[12]

Beyond the Knoll, Judge McKinney and other citizens were convinced that blacks were responsible and that the bomb was linked to Roby's trial. Judge McKinney added that in his opinion Roby's deed and trial had nothing at all to do with legitimate complaints over infringements of civil rights. Most blacks seemed to take a different view, and one member of the Black Student Organization at ISU declared that the entire bomb incident "was a hoax—nothing but a political stunt" designed to swing public opinion against Roby.[13]

Meanwhile, President Parks was driving to Des Moines daily for important budget negotiations with the Board of Regents and legislative leaders. Meetings with staff and students aimed toward lowering the rhetoric over either Vietnam or civil rights had to be squeezed in at unpopular hours or late at night. Although he was opposed to enlargement of the war in Southeast Asia and he agreed with many grievances of blacks, he abhorred violence of any sort. With the volatile 1970 Veishea celebration only a week away, unruly demonstrations by black protesters could not have come at a more inopportune time. The deluge of phone calls and letters mounted from people charging him with inaction against disruptions caused by protestors.

Critics clamored for him to do something—almost anything—no matter what. Yet hasty action or the wrong decision could bring disaster to the institution he cherished. A lesser man might have buckled under the strain, but Parks set emotions aside and put all of his powers of analysis to work on confronting the twin dangers of local riots over Vietnam and over black demands.

Having attributed the bomb in his garage to somebody associated with Roby or the Black Student Organization, Judge McKinney promptly recused himself from presiding over Roby's assault case—a case in which Roby was found guilty of simple assault.

On May 20, the case against Roby and Knox for "resisting execution of due process" began. The Des Moines attorney who had represented Roby in the assault case asked McKinney to preside over the trial on the more serious charge, but McKinney refused. Consequently, a substitute judge presided over this trial, which lasted two days before the jury returned a verdict of not guilty for both Roby and Knox.

The next day, which was Friday, May 22, Judge McKinney was in his office on the second floor of City Hall in downtown Ames. The office overlooked an alley, and the judge was donning his robes in preparation for traffic court scheduled to begin at nine o'clock when he and the court bailiff heard a terrific noise. McKinney recalled the incident:

> All of a sudden we heard this explosion. My first reaction was that a truck or something had blown up in the alley because there always were a lot of trucks with propane tanks there in the alley. Then some of the women started screaming, and dust began filtering all around the place, so I knew it must be somewhere in the building. ... At first, I didn't associate this at all with any kind of bomb; I just thought it must be some sort of internal explosion—something just went wrong and blew up. It never occurred to me that somebody might have set off a bomb.[14]

It was a bomb all right, and a powerful one at that. The most amazing fact about the explosion was that no one was killed. Thirteen people were injured, most of them from flying glass, and one state trooper was permanently blinded in one eye. A citizen who had been picked up on an intoxication charge the night before was in the holding area below ground level, and he was struck in the throat by a sliver of steel from the window bars of his cell. Fortunately for him, the sliver stayed in his throat long enough to help stanch the bleeding while he was being rushed to the hospital. Physical damage to the building was extensive, and all communication facilities were knocked out, so the Iowa Patrol brought in a semitruck equipped as a mobile communications center and parked it in front of the shattered building for the next several days.

Within the span of thirty-six hours, there were similar bombings in Omaha and Des Moines, but the one in the Ames City Hall caused the most injuries. The common belief was that the three assaults were coordinated and aimed at police as an establishment rather than at individuals. Nevertheless, there seemed to be a discernible pattern of attacks toward persons in authority. For example, after the bombing in downtown Des Moines, a second bomb was thrown at the home of Luther Glanton, the city's only black judge. Expecting that such follow-ups might occur in Ames, police put Judge McKinney's house under twenty-four-hour surveillance. The judge also secured permits for him and his wife to carry loaded pistols, and for several days after local police ended official surveillance, citizen volunteers took over and watched McKinney's home throughout the nights.

Two weeks after Veishea and the bombing, a relative calm began settling over the ISU campus and nearby city. Final examinations went off on schedule, and the university ended its spring quarter without further disruptions. Parks and his team of administrators had kept violence away from the campus itself but had been unable to protect the entire community. From his presidential pulpit, he continued to plead for public discussion and debate rather than violence. His reputation among black students enrolled at the university was intact; they still respected and trusted him.

At Iowa State during the fall quarter of 1970, black protests were not as intense as in the previous spring. Parks continued taking measures to retain the confidence of black groups on campus and encouraged other administrators to be sympathetic to their needs and concerns. However, there remained a small, hard core of black militants whose demands were beyond the will or indeed the power of Parks to grant. Spokespersons for this group always wanted a private conference with the president and usually refused to talk with any other administrator.

The president made every effort to accommodate the students' requests, but sometimes such meetings simply could not be worked into his crowded schedule. If he were out of town, for instance, black leaders insisted they were being given the runaround. Threats of campus upheaval by disgruntled black students remained worrisome for several more years.

President Parks said that in many ways the black protests were more dangerous than those over Vietnam; Vice President George Christensen took a slightly different view:

> I don't know that I'd call the black protests more dangerous, but they certainly were more pertinent to the university and to its responsibilities toward society. The university couldn't take any stand against stopping the war in Vietnam, but in regard to the black students, they were coming to us with very legitimate concerns that affected the functions of the university. ... First of all, they didn't feel comfortable that the university had done enough to get a critical mass of black students on this campus, so they felt very isolated. Secondly, they didn't feel there was enough black representation on the faculty, someone they could relate to.[15]

Numerous meetings with black protestors were held at various levels of administration. The meetings seemed productive, but black discontent continued, and sometimes protestors got very angry. For example, once a group of about twenty burst into the president's office, demanding to talk with President Parks. He was not available, so his secretary, Joyce Van Pilsum, summoned Christensen, who gave his version of the encounter:

> The group appeared in Dr. Parks's office, en masse, without any warning. He was out of town, and they felt they needed to get Christensen in. Joyce Van Pilsum came and told me they all were in the big conference room waiting for me.
>
> I said, "Fine," and just as I was going into the room, she whispered, "Dr. Christensen, they've got guns." Her warning alerted me, but I have to say that I never saw any signs of weapons. Whether or not they really had them, I do not know. It was a meeting which grew out of a sense of frustration. The black students presented a list of demands which they had worked out. I don't recall the exact number, but it was twenty plus.
>
> They shoved this list in front of me and wanted to know right away, "How are you going to react to this or what will you do about that?" Some demands we could talk about; others were entirely unacceptable. ... There was a lot of yelling, and they might say something like, "You're not leaving here." Well, I saw no reason to leave anyway and was ready to talk about every issue and as long as they wanted, so our meeting went on for about eight hours.[16]

The reality of physical danger to persons in authority at Iowa State was further dramatized during the third week in May 1974. Black students had continued to be unhappy in part because of alleged unfair treatment by Ames police, and one day another boisterous group invaded Beardshear Hall, advancing into the president's offices. No one had called for an appointment, but the more than two dozen unannounced protestors, led by Fred McConico and Albert Linton, coleaders of the Black Student Organization at the time, demanded to see Parks. Fred McConico was an ISU student and was joined on this occasion by his brother Tony, a nonstudent who had come from Chicago to visit him.

The group did not believe Joyce Van Pilsum when she told them the president was out of town. Van Pilsum then called Bill Layton, Vice President for Student Affairs, whose office was only a few doors away. Layton hurried over to see what he could do, and he described the incident that followed:

The students were noisy and insisting that they see Parks. Two of the young women, nineteen or twenty years old and very fit physically, tried to force their way into Joyce's office. She made the mistake of pushing one of them away. Both of the young black girls reacted physically, and I thought they might severely injure Joyce. ... So, hero me, I stood in the door of Joyce's office to stop them from getting to her. Tony, or someone, shouted, "He hit Brenda."

Tony had a galvanized one-inch iron pipe about two feet long. He hit me alongside the head with the pipe. It dazed me, but I didn't fall down. As soon as he hit me, the office became very quiet. I went back to my office and met briefly with Fred and Albert. They apologized for the attack, and we agreed to meet with the group in the president's conference room. ...

I then went to the Student Health Service and Jay Gardner, director of the health service, closed my wound with six stitches. I called Gloria [Mrs. Layton], who brought me a clean shirt, and then I went to the meeting. ... The students evidently were satisfied, for I don't recall any further incidents.[17]

The meeting in the conference room subsequent to the attack on Layton was orderly enough. Black leaders again apologized for the injury to Layton and pointed out that the attacker was not an ISU student. Someone had called Ames Police Chief Arnie Siedelmann, who attended the subsequent meeting even though he was in mourning for his seventeen-year-old son who had died the day before. Siedelmann asked Layton if he wanted to press charges against Tony McConico, but Layton refused to do so, saying, "I don't think anything positive would come from my bringing charges."[18]

Parks and others at Iowa State did not see fit to publicize the physical attack on one of the university's vice presidents, and as a result most people were unaware it had happened. In reality, the incident may have caused responsible leaders among the black students on campus to consider future actions more carefully. In any event, this was the last major act of violence carried out by black protestors during the presidency of Robert Parks.

In the beginning of the 1970s—a decade that saw many campuses torn apart by black disruptions—few major institutions were making significant efforts to recruit African-American students. For the next fifteen years, however, Iowa State, with unrelenting pressure from Robert Parks, became a leader in bringing black students into higher education. At ISU, for instance, enrollment figures for 1971 show only 247 American black students (1.3 percent of the total enrollment). In 1985, the year in which Parks announced his retirement, enrollment had climbed over three times as high to 1121 (4.2 percent of ISU's total enrollment).[19]

Years later as the century neared its end, this increase in the number of African-Americans at Iowa State might seem small to some observers, but if viewed from the perspective of that time, the record is truly remarkable. It was not always easy to persuade black students to come to the school, for it was common knowledge that the black population within the state was less than 8 percent. Although other faculty members helped immeasurably, the rise in the number of black students enrolled at Iowa State in the 1970s came about largely through the determination of its president.

The movement to bring more blacks into the country's colleges and universities spread slowly and gained momentum in part because of lobbying groups and pressures upon institutions hoping for state or federal financial assistance. With Robert Parks, though, improving educational opportunities for blacks was not a matter of political expediency; it was the right thing to do based on conscience and convictions.

CHAPTER 8

Parks and ISU Extension

Extension is the most distinguishing feature of land-grant universities—the one branch that has made land-grant universities different from all others.

W. Robert Parks

Anyone attending a football or basketball game at Iowa State University will probably hear the band play the school's fight song, and similarly anyone who attends a meeting where the mission of the university is under review should expect at least one speaker to intone the phrase "teaching, research, and service." These words have been beacons guiding Iowa State since its founding.

The Iowa State University Extension Service, often called Cooperative Extension, owes it existence to these triple lanterns—teaching, research, and service. Certainly, the institution could not have maintained its course or attained its reputation without them. The earliest extension efforts at ISU revolved around a limited concept of agriculture; today's offerings are broader but still traceable to the three guiding lights.

The history of extension education in America is a long one, going back even before the formation of the republic. Probably the first U.S. organization to disseminate information about agriculture was the American Philosophical Society, founded in 1743. Among its originators and foremost leaders was Benjamin Franklin.

Soon after the nation had been created, state legislatures began establishing boards of agriculture with the primary purpose of sharing knowledge about crops and farming practices. The first endeavors were quite informal and very limited, however, and through the first half of the nineteenth century, few colleges, if any, offered academic courses related to agriculture.

As more and more science trod onto the national stage, agitation for agricultural and other "practical" education spread. States began establishing their separate universities, and as explained in an earlier chapter, Vermont Congressman Justin Smith Morrill in 1857 introduced a land-grant college bill. Another five years passed before the bill reached the desk of President Abraham Lincoln, who signed it on July 2, 1862.

The Morrill Act of 1862 put into effect a radical idea of a nationwide system of higher education whereby knowledge could be taken to people living beyond the confines of a college campus. The act provided for measured plots of thirty thousand acres to each state. The number of plots was equal to the number of senators and representatives that the state had under the apportionment of 1860. These lands were to be sold, and 10 percent of the proceeds used, if necessary, to purchase a college site, which could include an experimental farm. The balance was to be permanently invested at 5 percent interest. By enabling land-grant institutions to establish direct contacts with every county in the United States, the act brought education closer to the people and gave rise to the slogan that a land-grant college is by its nature a "people's college."

Another Morrill act was passed in 1890. A key provision in this second legislation was a requirement that land-grant institutions, which had multiplied in numbers and size since passage of the first act, be opened to both white and black students or that "separate, but equal" facilities be established.

Meanwhile, teachers at land-grant colleges, particularly teachers of agricultural subjects or home economics, were being called upon to disseminate their expertise to farm families scattered across rural America. By the turn of the century, many citizens throughout the country had access to resource persons at one or more of these land-grant schools.

One of the most aggressive pioneers in early efforts to take knowledge to farm families was Kenyon L. Butterfield, president of Massachusetts Agricultural College. Kenyon also became chairman of a committee within the Association of American Agricultural Colleges, and this committee started sponsoring farmers' institutes, lectures, publications, exhibits, stock and poultry judging contests, tours, and related activities. The offerings were forerunners of modern extension work.

By 1914 Butterfield and his coworkers had garnered enough political support to have agricultural extension teaching established as a responsibility of land-grant colleges, and in that year the responsibility was enacted into law with passage of the Smith-Lever Act—an act that formally created the Cooperative Extension Service.

Another pioneer in linking extension education to land-grant institutions was Seaman A. Knapp of Iowa. Knapp, a man with unlimited energy and talents to match, was a native of northern New York. He obtained a classical education at Union College, where he was an honor student and elected to Phi Beta Kappa. Shortly after the Civil War he moved to Iowa, where the change of scene and outdoor work on a farm improved his precarious health.

Knapp gained a statewide reputation for his improvement in the quality of livestock, particularly Poland China hogs. He had a brief career in the ministry, served for five years as superintendent of the Iowa School for the Blind, organized and became president of the Iowa Improved Stock Breeders' Association, was editor of the *Western Stock Journal and Farmer,* and wrote numerous articles for *Progressive Farmer*—a publication put out by what then was called the Iowa Agricultural College in Ames.

Knapp was appointed "professor of practical and experimental agriculture" at the Iowa Agricultural College by President Adonijah Strong Welch. At the time of his appointment, it was reported that Knapp had been offered the presidency both of the Kansas Agricultural College and of Purdue University.[1]

Knapp's approach to extension education sprang from a conviction that merely observing model farms wouldn't motivate farmers to change their own practices. He argued instead that diversified agriculture and other desirable changes would come only through demonstrations conducted by farmers themselves on their own farms and under ordinary farm conditions.

In 1903 he proved his point through a widely publicized demonstration with seventy acres on a farm near Terrell, Texas. The field was planted half in corn and half in cotton. Knapp's objective in the test was to demonstrate the effects of using different seed varieties, fertilizers, methods of planting, and cultivation. A local committee raised a $1000 indemnity fund just in case the demonstration failed, but instead of failing, the experiment made $700 more for its owner than could have been expected using conventional methods.[2]

During the years innovators like Butterfield and Knapp were promoting their causes, numerous states were taking steps toward making the practical knowledge gained at government-supported colleges available to persons who for various reasons were not residents at any school. The outreaching education was so successful that demands for more of the same kept growing. Soon proponents in several states were calling for better coordination and more regular offerings. The result was creation of the county extension agent, a post made possible through cooperation among the chief funding sources, namely, the U.S. Department of Agriculture, land-grant colleges, and local or county organizations.

The first full-time county extension agent, or director, had been appointed in Texas in 1906. Other states followed with similar appointments, and in 1912 Clinton and Scott counties were the first ones in Iowa to appoint individuals for the jobs.

Among activities initiated, promoted, and often conducted by county extension agents were exhibits at all sorts of farm meetings: preparation and distribution of charts showing results of giving various feeds to livestock and poultry, judging contests, and special trains paid to carry observers to exemplary farms, dairies, or cornfields. There were also lectures, picnics, and other events wherever farmers and their families gathered.

One of the most popular means of getting new knowledge to information-hungry farmers was the so-called short course; it might be held on a college campus or conducted within a chosen community. A short course of anywhere from three days to two weeks could center on such agricultural matters as judging a class of beef or dairy cattle; hogs, horses, or sheep; or seed corn. If the course was to be taught in a community away from the college, it was necessary to find a room with heat, good light, and seating for a hundred or more people. If the course involved something like selecting seed corn, the room had to be large enough to seat as many as two hundred people, each with a tray of corn to study.

Or a course might present an aspect of home economics, usually referred to then as domestic science. The course could offer instruction in such everyday work as weaving, spinning, knitting, sewing, cooking, or other household arts. For the home economics courses, rooms with cooking stoves, cupboards, tables, and demonstration material usually were required.

Other ways of making information available to citizens living beyond a land-grant college campus included farm institutes (similar to short courses but less structured), demonstrations either in a home or on a farm, lectures, pamphlets, and personal visits from specialists on the staff of the agricultural college. Among subjects included in the wide-ranging programs were better handling of soils, selection of better animals for breeding purposes, control of animal diseases, creamery management, landscape architecture, farm buildings, orchard management, and marketing practices for farm products.

The range of topics was almost unlimited. In addition to overt instructional programs, extension personnel initiated and supervised boys' and girls' 4-H clubs—clubs that in turn divided into more specific groups such as beef club work, pig club work, garden and canning clubs, and a host of activities related to rural living.

Demonstrations were always in demand. Animal husbandry specialists, for example, were among those who gave great assistance to both farm men and women. Farm butchering demonstrations were particularly popular throughout the 1920s and well into the 1930s. In a one-year period, 1920–1921, farm butchering specialists gave sixty-three demonstrations in seventeen counties of Iowa. In some instances, the specialists themselves did the butchering, and in others they supervised local farmers who did the work.

Farm women often attended such demonstrations, asking questions and frequently telling the men how to cut the carcass. In effect, the better ways of killing, curing, and canning of meats provided farm families with high-grade meat at a cheaper cost than if purchased from retailers.

According to Ralph K. Bliss, a longtime director of extension at Iowa State, farm women were particularly interested in demonstrations of butchering, and one woman wrote: "I was delighted to find that our home-killed hogs, done according to ... instructions, furnished us with pork chops, where we had never before had anything but backbone."[3]

James Hilton, Iowa State's tenth president and Robert Parks's immediate predecessor, remembered one butchering demonstration, however, that went awry. Shortly after graduating from Iowa State in 1923, Hilton accepted a position as county extension agent in Clinton County, Iowa, and one day he visited a farm where he intended to demonstrate the best way to butcher a hog. His version of the story, which he delighted in telling, went as follows:

> Often in home butchering the blood from a carcass was not drained out quickly and properly. I got eight to ten men around me, and together we hoisted this three hundred–pound hog onto the butchering table. While one man held the hog's head, I made a deep slice with my butchering knife across the hog's throat so that the blood could drain down through a trough on the side of the table and into a funnel connected to a bucket below.
>
> Well, a little blood ran out all right, but then the holder released his hold on the animal's head. To my surprise and chagrin, that big old hog merely shook his head a couple of times, slid off the table, and walked away.[4]

Fortunately Hilton's other achievements were far more successful as were instructions and demonstrations given out by his fellow agents in the state.

An important component of Iowa State University's extension program is the Iowa Agriculture and Home Economics Experiment Station. The rationale for this indispensable branch was embodied in the original Morrill Act of 1857, which specifically permitted that a portion of a land-grant college's capital fund (not more than 10 percent, however) could be used for purchase of a site or of an experimental farm. This provision spurred the Iowa Agricultural College at Ames, with its emphasis upon research dealing with animal husbandry, dairy industry, and farm crops, to seek further funding from the state. Accordingly, in May of 1888 the Iowa General Assembly passed an act to establish the Iowa Experiment Station at the Agricultural College. The first experiments of this newest venture involved tests with crops, soils, horticulture, and dairying—the same general matters that were of concern to the pioneering extension efforts.

As with any major enterprise, the rise of extension did not come without controversy. The most enduring one concerned the relationship college extension departments had with existing farm organizations. The first farm organization of any consequence in America was a social establishment begun in 1867. The new association named itself the National Grange of the Patrons of Husbandry, and soon local chapters were called simply the Grange. The Grange developed as a means of bringing farm men and women together where knowledge about scientific agriculture and markets could be exchanged—knowledge hitherto unavailable in most rural communities. The original purposes of the organization were social, cultural, and educational, but when the national economy worsened in 1873, the organization that had begun mainly to combat the isolation and drabness of rural life quickly turned into an agency of agrarian protest. By 1875 the Grange could count over eight hundred thousand members and twenty thousand lodges. The Grange's greatest strengths were found in the corn- and wheat-producing states of the Middle West, including Iowa.

The Grange movement flourished for nearly twenty years but was weakened by a return of prosperity. By 1880 its membership had shrunk to one hundred thousand, and laws it had espoused, particularly those relating to railroad rates and practices, had not been enacted or were proving ineffective. Embattled farmers, therefore, left the Grange fold and resumed their old, individualistic ways. It would take another depression to impel them into organizations more politically militant.

Organizing farmers into political blocs has proved difficult, in part because farmers are more isolated than urban dwellers and produce crops with varying market problems. Also, the independent nature of many rural families encourages them to individualistic ways. For these and other reasons, farmers' organizations in the main have been less cohesive than labor and craft unions.

Following the demise of the Grange movement, numerous farm alliances sprang up across the country. One named the Agricultural Wheel appeared in Arkansas, the Texas State Alliance was formed in the Southwest, the Farmers' Union developed in Louisiana, and the National Farmers' Alliance formed in the Northwest.

The first platforms of these splintered alliances did not advocate political action, but that began changing in 1890, particularly in the Middle West. In this vast region—a region extending westward from Ohio across Indiana and Illinois as well as embracing Iowa, Kansas, Minnesota, and Nebraska—farmers were very hard pressed. The Great Plains, essentially a wheat and corn region but one that also produced over half the nation's oats, hay, barley, and rye, was parched by drought and swept by hot, dry winds that robbed the soil of the little moisture it had held. Such natural disasters added to the farmers' plight, and they turned toward political action. A People's Party was formally launched in Kansas in June 1890, and immediately there were candidates running for office under this banner.

Very soon the People's Party became known as Populists. As the party swelled, every conceivable gathering place—schoolhouse, church, rural town hall, open square, and meadow—was thronged with crowds who had come to listen, sing, shout, and cheer leaders who had sprung up almost miraculously. Many of the Populist leaders were colorful characters, and many of them became known for their incisive attacks and fiery rhetoric.

One of Populism's proponents was Ignatius Donnelly, who attempted to found Nininger City in Minnesota. With his restless mind, Donnelly played to the hilt his role as the "Sage of Nininger." He also wrote several books, one of which claimed location for the lost isle of Atlantis, another arguing that Francis Bacon wrote Shakespeare's plays, and a novel describing a Populist utopia.

Although begun in the embittered Midwest, Populism soon spread throughout the country and attracted spokespersons that included men with nicknames like "Pitchfork" Ben Tillman of South Carolina, "Bloody Bridles" Davis H. Waite of Colorado, and "Sockless" Jerry Simpson of Kansas. Hardly any of the Populist Party leaders were farmers; the great majority were of the rural middle class—editors, lawyers, or professional politicians and agitators. Tillman earned his nickname through the violence of his vocabulary as did Waite, a Colorado governor who announced he would rather see blood flowing to the horses' bridles than popular liberties destroyed. Simpson from Kansas ridiculed a rival candidate for wearing silk socks and thereafter won the title "Sockless Jerry, the Socrates of the prairies."

The men were joined by a flock of female orators, the most famous of whom was Mary B. Lease of Kansas. Although hostile critics said a woman should not be a stump speaker, Mrs. Lease talked frequently and vividly, delivering more than 160 speeches in 1890, firing many of them with her famous utterance: "What you farmers need to do is raise less corn and more Hell!"

Iowa's outstanding Populist was James B. Weaver, a former general from the Civil War who had helped form the Farmers' Alliance. In 1892, Weaver ran as the Populist Party's presidential candidate. He was defeated but polled over one million popular votes and garnered twenty-two electoral ones. He then became an important leader of the free-silver movement and backed William Jennings Bryan in the 1896 presidential race.

It was Bryan, the boy orator of the Platte as he was often called, who with strong support from Populists ran on the Democratic ticket for the U.S. presidency first in 1896 and again in 1900 and 1908. Defeated in his three tries for the presidency, Bryan remained a Democratic leader and eloquent Chatauqua speaker. Although the nation consistently rejected Bryan for the presidency, it eventually adopted many of the reforms he urged—the income tax, popular election of senators, women's suffrage, public knowledge of newspaper ownership, and prohibition.

Populism, land-grant colleges, and extension programs. No formal documents ever directly linked the three, but all were interrelated. Agrarian discontent as expressed in Populism gave impetus to formation of the Farm Bureau Federation, which inevitably was linked with extension programs offered through land-grant colleges. Extension programs in turn frequently were arranged by county extension agents.

Extension programs from Iowa State became official when the Iowa General Assembly passed what was known as the Extension Act of 1906. The act came about largely through the successful work of Perry G. Holden. Holden, a seed corn expert from the University of Illinois, had joined the agronomy faculty at Iowa State College in 1902. At several short courses sponsored by the college, he gave talks on corn production. Sponsoring officials at first feared that the subject would be so boring that farmers would walk out of the meeting. Instead, farmers in attendance reacted warmly to Holden's enthusiastic presentations and asked for more of the same. Holden responded that the short course program cut into time he was supposed to spend on regular classes and jokingly said that the only way he could make additional presentations was to schedule them from 2 A.M. to 8 A.M. His listeners conferred with other farmers and came back suggesting that if the class could be held at 5 A.M. they would attend. When President William Beardshear heard that he had a professor on his staff who could "coax farmers out to a 5 A.M. class," he raised Holden's salary and made him vice dean of agriculture.

President Beardshear further arranged for Holden to travel throughout the state sharing his expertise on corn production. The first short course held away from the Iowa State campus was given at Red Oak in January of 1905 and drew 250 local farmers, each of whom paid $2.50 a ticket. The gathering was such a success that within the next winter Holden and his staff received thirty-seven thousand inquiries about such courses.[5]

Holden's work attracted supporters from beyond the college, including the Iowa Grain Dealers Association, Henry Wallace, editor of *Wallaces' Farmer*, and the *Des Moines Register*, the state's most prominent newspaper. Holden was urged to draft a bill calling for creation of a state extension service. He did that, and with only slight revisions the bill passed the Iowa General Assembly and became the Extension Act of 1906. Small wonder, therefore, that Perry G. Holden has been called the father of Iowa extension.

At the time Holden and his colleagues from Iowa State were providing instruction through extension programs, other movements aimed at spreading agricultural information and knowledge were taking place. For example, M. L. Mosher, a farm crops specialist at the college, was advocating that existing county extension directors be paid by the separate counties and that county agents should work more closely with the Extension Service of the college. In his view, this arrangement would provide "coordination and prevent duplication."

Back then, county extension directors in Iowa were paid partly by local private organizations and partly from funds out of treasuries of emerging farm groups like the one in Clay County, where members paid dues of $2 each, with membership available for any resident over sixteen years of age. In 1913 the Iowa General Assembly passed legislation authorizing county supervisors to levy a tax for the support of such organizations, and this legislation encouraged formation of county farm improvement associations, which in turn led eventually to the state Farm Bureau organization.[6]

In December 1918, one month after hostilities in Europe had ended, Iowa farmers, with strong encouragement from extension officials at Iowa State College, met to form a new organization; they called it the Iowa State Farm Bureau Federation. The creation of this Farm Bureau Federation and its fund-raising methods cemented a three-way relationship among the Farm Bureau, county extension directors, and the Extension Service at Iowa State College. Since county extension agents and Farm Bureau personnel often shared the same office, the public tended to think of the two groups as a single entity. Indeed, some county agents did refer to themselves as Farm Bureau agents.

The linkage of the Farm Bureau with personnel at Iowa State College was similarly evident. Ralph K. Bliss, who served as extension director at Iowa State from 1912 until 1946, considered it "an honor and a privilege" for his organization to work closely with Farm Bureau personnel, and he frequently pointed out that Farm Bureau memberships added considerable funds to extension's coffers. In 1924, for example, Bliss estimated that Farm Bureau's membership contributed approximately a third of a million dollars for the development of agriculture within the state. Bliss went further to say: "The county farm bureaus have made possible the extension of education work into every community in the state. They have been a constructive force for agricultural improvement and better living on the farms of Iowa."[7]

A reorganization of the agricultural curriculum at Iowa State also helped solidify the relationship between extension and Farm Bureau. Patterned after changes already made in the experiment station in Ames and at the Department of Agriculture in Washington, D.C., Iowa State College in the spring of 1921 shifted a curriculum formerly known as "farm management and marketing" into a new section named "agricultural economics and rural sociology." The new section, along with established activities within extension proper, worked ever more closely with existing Farm Bureau officers, but while the close relationships generally proved beneficial to both extension and Farm Bureau, there were drawbacks.

The biggest single drawback evolved from the question: Can a person take part in extension activities without being a member of the Farm Bureau? Home economics specialists coming from the college's Extension Service said yes, but that wasn't enough to dispel the common belief, and the resultant misconception kept many farm women from attending extension programs. Furthermore, most Farm Bureau leaders liked the cozy relationships between their organization and Iowa State's extension staff, so the common belief grew stronger.

Criticisms of the linkage between extension and the Farm Bureau mounted. With considerable justice, other farm organizations, particularly the Farmers' Union, objected to its rival's profiting from such close association with a college supported by state and federal tax dollars.

Robert Parks was no stranger to the history and problems of extension when he became president of Iowa State in 1965. As a youth growing up in rural Tennessee, he knew how that state's extension programs had helped his father as well as neighboring farmers. As a lad, Robert had been an avid 4-H club member, and like most youths in the organization, he had an individual project. Seventy years later he explained his choice:

> My project was to raise tobacco on one-quarter of an acre my father set aside for me. Tobacco was the best cash crop in rural Tennessee at the time. I don't think the project would be so popular today, but it was then. Tobacco crops from 4-H kids were a big thing; buyers from national corporations like American Tobacco Company or Liggett Myers would come in and bid up prices. I think I made $40 one year—maybe more—but that was a lot of money for a kid in those days.[8]

Parks's major studies in college had drawn him somewhat away from American history and more toward agricultural economics. Then his work with the Land Economics Division within the Department of Agriculture put him close to problems of farmers in the states where he interviewed them and conducted detailed analyses. Instructing graduate students at the University of Wisconsin, he was deeply involved in such matters as crop production, land treatments and protection, animal husbandry, farm demographics, and nearly every other subject related to farm living. In all such endeavors, extension programs from various land-grant colleges were crucial elements.

Thus Parks was familiar with the strengths as well as the criticisms leveled against extension. There was duplication within extension divisions; too many areas overlapped while others were neglected; and there were not clear enough lines of authority among administrative personnel. Other charges were that experiment stations in most states conducted research on a long-term, project-by-project basis and thus were handicapped when it came to making adjustments needed in a rapidly changing society. Research in the experiment stations, he thought, ought to be more flexible.

Did the emergence of the United States as one of the world's two superpowers bring added responsibilities to extension? Parks believed it did. He praised the federal government for initiating such programs as Point Four and the Peace Corps. International programs, he insisted, were here to stay, and land-grant colleges, with their pools of knowledge and talents, should contribute more to them.

In 1963, while he was vice president for academic affairs, Parks was asked to be visiting critic for a seminar held at Colorado State University. The central purpose of the gathering was to study and analyze problems of agricultural administration in the land-grant college system. It was a rather late invitation, so Parks had little time to prepare his remarks; however, his grounding in rural economics and land-grant colleges enabled him to capture the mood of the meeting and to extend a pertinent criticism:

> I am very much concerned about the typical county extension organization, which usually contains "a man," "a woman," and "a youth agent." The man is usually trained in general agriculture, the woman in home economics, and the youth agent generally is trained in agriculture also. It is very possible that this type of county organization is becoming outmoded in many parts of the nation. Should we not give serious consideration to modifying this organizational pattern ... by going more toward an area basis of field administration with appropriate meaningful specializations?
>
> Remember that we have today essentially the same organiza-

tional arrangement in the counties that we had back in 1925 when we weren't yet daring to span the Atlantic Ocean through flight.[9]

Two years after giving this address, Parks became president of Iowa State and was even more convinced that extension programs needed better coordination. Extension constituted a huge branch of the university's overall operations, but the growth had come helter-skelter. Like Topsy, extension had "jist growed" and now included four major but different areas: the Cooperative Extension Service (largely agricultural and home economics specialists), the Engineering Extension Service, the Center for Industrial Research and Service (CIRAS), and the Agriculture Short Course Office. Each of these branches had its separate director, budget, and staff.

There is no evidence that while he was vice president, Parks ever suggested to President Hilton that extension administration at Iowa State should be revamped. In all likelihood Parks thought it should be, but he probably realized that Hilton was too much of a traditionalist to accept any recommendation in that regard.

Two months after taking office, Parks began talking privately with personnel and directors of each of the four Iowa State programs mentioned above, seeking their opinions as to strengths and needs in their respective endeavors. He was especially impressed with what he heard from Marvin Anderson, who at the time was associate director of ISU's Cooperative Extension Service. Anderson had been a 4-H club agent and an area soils specialist and had risen through academic ranks from associate in 1942 to full professor in the Department of Agronomy. Parks asked Anderson to put his opinions on paper and submit them to him privately.

Anderson drafted an eleven-page confidential memorandum that first traced the background and history of extension at Iowa State. The paper continued by noting that some states already were moving toward broadening extension so that it included more of the university structure, specifically regular curricular teaching and research, thus being organized so that "the total knowledge resources of the university can be extended to the people."

Next, Anderson described objectives of a coordinated university-wide extension service:

1. To extend the resources of the total University to the citizens of the state interested in a program of continued learning.
2. To provide more highly specialized University-level educational services.
3. To assist the University in making fuller use of the most effective educational philosophy and methods of teaching adults.
4. To strengthen the position of the University in obtaining and using funds from governmental and foundation sources in support of extension programs.
5. To assist the University in creating internal efficiencies in the use of staff and resources for off-campus education.[10]

Anderson's memo went further and advocated putting the Cooperative Extension Service, Engineering Extension, CIRAS, and the Short Course Office under a single administrative officer, who in turn would be responsible to either a vice president or the president. The memo also suggested formation of a University Extension Council to be comprised of the proposed administrative officer, the dean of each of the colleges, and the director of university relations.

Parks called Anderson in several times to talk further about the long-range goals of the reorganization proposal, and he also discussed it with Hilton (who upon retirement had been named president emeritus), George Christensen, and J. Boyd Page, who as vice president for research had the experiment station under his general surveillance. All thought the plan workable, and in effect, Parks accepted Anderson's recommendation. With only a few emendations the proposal was put on the docket for regents' approval.

In March 1966—the month in which Parks was formally installed as president of Iowa State—University Extension was officially established. This action by the Iowa Board of Regents provided that (1) The new university-wide extension would include the Cooperative Extension Service, the Engineering Extension Service, the Center for Industrial Research and Service, and all other such units of Iowa State that then or in the future would engage in extension activities. (2) A dean of university extension would be selected and charged with responsibility of employing personnel, directing the extension programs, and allocating resources available for these purposes. Funds allocated for and generated by extension programs would be received, budgeted, and approved for expenditure by the dean to be selected. (3) "Subject-matter" specialists engaged in extension work would have the status of regular members of the appropriate academic departments, and employment of such staff members would need to have joint approval by the dean of university extension and the dean of the appropriate college.

The last-named provision was mildly controversial, especially among some long-time extension workers, who under the former arrangement had enjoyed considerable autonomy. For years they had only to give evidence of satisfactory reception of the various programs offered and to stay within budget limitations that came along with funds from federal, state, or county sources. Under the new plan, all extension personnel would be responsible not only to a dean of university extension but also to a dean of a resident academic department. "Why in the world," asked critics of the revision, "would you want to give up your independence and accept supervision from an additional boss who is to be given control over your appointment, salary, and performance?"

These were precisely the reasons Parks had sought better organization. Moreover, his own background had made him aware of how rapidly agriculture in America was changing. He knew, for example, that the number of farms in the country had shrunk from two hundred thousand in the leanest years of the Great Depression to slightly less than half that number in 1965. New crops had been introduced along with hybrid seed corn that produced a fantastic number of bushels per acre if compared with yields of earlier years. Powerful weed killers and potent synthetic fertilizers were available, and better transportation had opened wider markets for livestock and crops. Hard work from dawn to darkness no longer was enough for a farm family that expected to compete with changing economics. The modern farmer had to be better informed and more strongly motivated to use existing knowledge and technologies.

Some extension methods and practices were similarly outdated; these simply had to be revised and better organized if society's needs were to be met. Moreover, according to Marvin Anderson, Parks wanted to loosen the bond between extension and the Farm Bureau.[11]

Although the Farm Bureau's marriage with extension had broken up by the time Parks became ISU's president, there remained in his mind a small measure of discomfort over the continuing cozy relationship enjoyed between some extension personnel and Farm Bureau leaders.

Extension services from Iowa State needed better coordination and overall management. "Extension," he maintained, "is the most distinguishing feature of land-grant universities, and my biggest role is to reorganize extension's structure."

It was no great surprise when he recommended that Marvin Anderson be named dean of university extension. After all, Anderson was more or less godfather of the new organization—the man Parks had entrusted with major responsibility for developing better procedures, integrating instructional programs, tightening budgeting practices, and establishing clearer lines of authority.

Anderson had been in extension work ever since 1939 and thus brought to his new post more than a quarter-century of experience. He once commented upon aspects of Iowa extension he had observed during that time:

> When I first started in extension work, you had to prove to farmers that you knew something useful—not just that you were a college graduate but that you could offer something practical. You had to sell that point.
>
> Then came a period of tremendous expansion in knowledge about agriculture—knowledge about seed corn, new varieties, crop rotation and soil protection, fertilizers, scientific livestock breeding, leaner meat-type hogs and cattle, marketing strategies,

and so forth. Farmers were hungry for information; we just couldn't give them enough.

Then, too, there were economic and social dimensions of changes taking place in rural America. The farmer and his family no longer lived an isolated life. They had modern equipment and conveniences; they came to the city for groceries and necessities. The number of school districts in Iowa dropped from over 900 in the 1960s to about 450, so farm kids and urban kids went to school side by side.

And there was always the cost of machinery and new technologies to consider, availability and effects of loans and mortgages, the decreasing number of farms, and the trend toward corporate farming.

I'm sure these were some of the factors in Dr. Parks's mind when in 1966 he made Iowa State Extension a university-wide service.[12]

Knowledge gained from the experiment station as well as offerings from other branches of extension had swelled to immense proportions by 1965, when Parks was selected to head the institution, but even greater growth lay ahead. Anderson began his deanship by assuring his coworkers, "Extension will continue to do what it has always done, but we will do more of it and do it better."

Even while president of Iowa State, Parks continued to take keen interest in 4-H clubs with their various projects ranging from calf raising to boys' camps. In Iowa for years there had been boys' 4-H clubs and girls' 4-H clubs. Offerings for girls usually were presented by specialists from the College of Home Economics and included such topics as textiles and clothing, food preparation and storage, or matters of home decoration. Programs for boys were encouraged and directed mainly by specialists from ISU's College of Agriculture. Individual clubs held Dad's Night Out for the boys and Mother-Daughter Teas for girls. Girls in some areas held their own rallies, and boys had basketball tournaments.

With encouragement from Dean Marvin Anderson and President Parks, in the mid 1960s extension personnel began promoting more combined programs for boys and girls. One extension director in Franklin County responded to the encouragement by writing: "Whenever possible, subject matter materials are being prepared that can be used by both boys and girls either jointly or separately."[13]

Within established programs such as 4-H clubs and others like the Future Farmers of America, there began to be other changes in emphasis. Whereas many a farm boy or farm girl had taken pride in winning blue ribbons at the local fair, youth leaders started stressing tangible economic rewards. Livestock specialists in the beef industry, for example, urged 4-H boys and girls to think more about commercial markets and profitability.

Another change in extension practices appeared shortly after Parks had appointed Anderson as dean. That change concerned the state's division into supervisory areas. Preliminary work on the area concept had begun as early as 1961, when ISU faculty, extension personnel, and business and community leaders from ten southern Iowa counties had set up a loosely organized confederation. The purpose of the alliance, quickly given the acronym TENCO (representing the number of counties involved), was to examine economic problems in the region and to search for solutions.

In that southern section of the state, business activities had dropped alarmingly: coal mining had declined 50 percent in ten years, agriculture employment by 35 percent, and business repair services by 33 percent, and it was estimated that the school population in the affected counties would decline by more than four thousand students in the coming decade. As an extension-sponsored program, TENCO was so successful that Parks and Anderson wanted to see similar approaches spread throughout Iowa.

Agricultural and home economics subjects continued to draw the lion's share of ISU's extension programming, but under Parks and Anderson, other problems not so clearly linked were addressed through the revised extension services.

Both on and off campus, for instance, instructional programs were offered dealing with such matters as community land zoning, industrial development, recreational uses of farmland, public schools, taxation seminars, estate planning, workshops for municipal workers, and a host of subjects hitherto not considered within extension's traditional province.

An educational program on local government was started in 1967 after a survey had helped determine specific problems. A series of off-campus short courses based upon the results of this initial survey was arranged and staffed. Again, the new venture was so successful that by 1970, Dean Anderson could report that "7,740 government leaders, community influentials and citizens studied and discussed present-day problems of local government for about 15 hours."[14]

Extension services also had begun responding to needs of another clientele, namely people in the lowest income brackets. The federal government was giving increased attention to better nutrition for low-income people at the same time ISU personnel were researching problems of poverty and welfare within Iowa. Whereas many people believed that poverty was primarily an urban blight, an ISU study brought out the fact that more than 460,000 people in 180,000 households in the state were similarly disadvantaged.

The findings helped spark a plan for a statewide educational program on poverty and welfare. Initiated by extension personnel, the venture was a cooperative one that involved the three state schools: ISU, the University of Iowa, and the University of Northern Iowa. Staff members from these three schools held three-day conferences or workshops in forty-four locations with more than 3700 people taking part. A workshop might center on helping make the home more convenient for the physically handicapped or the elderly. Or it might focus on young, low-income homemakers, with the program using lessons prepared by ISU home economists—lessons designed to help women better understand the basics of good nutrition, ways to stretch their food dollars, ways to make food more appealing, and methods of food preservation.

Iowa's efforts through extension coincided with action in Washington that provided more federal funds for establishing better nutritional programs for low-income citizens. In 1968 the U.S. Department of Agriculture received $10 million from Congress to initiate the Expanded Food and Nutrition Education Program (EFNEP). In the following year, ISU, through its extension services, assigned twelve home economists on its staff to supervise and administer such programs in twelve different locations within the state.

There was a related development on campus that made significant contributions to extension's success in addressing problems of poverty and welfare. For many years, Iowa State had been preparing teachers of vocational agriculture and home economics, but under the Parks administration teachers were also prepared and certified in elementary education, mathematics, biological or physical sciences, physical education, or English and speech. The need for more teachers in Iowa was becoming more critical each year, and faculty members at ISU strongly urged giving the school's teacher-training programs higher recognition—a move that won Parks's enthusiastic endorsement.

Accordingly, in September of 1968 the Iowa Board of Regents approved creation of a College of Education—the first major addition to the academic structure at Iowa State since 1913, when the home economics and graduate colleges (then called divisions) were established. While home economists still presented material on sewing and cooking, trained elementary teachers from the College of Education joined in the government's Headstart programs for pre-school-age children.

As ISU's president, Robert Parks was more than a silent witness to tremendous changes taking place in the school's extension services. Only on rare occasions did his schedule permit him to be an active member of a seminar or discussion group, but he was forever prodding the extension staff toward expanding their offerings, and when those were developed, he was ready to suggest ways of increasing fundings, getting wider publicity, or garnering support for follow-ups. Moreover, on numerous occasions when a short course or conference was held on campus, he was the one who showed up to welcome attendees and help heighten their interest.

His greetings were apt to be short, frequently amusing, and always friendly. He tried to make visitors feel that they were vital members of the university community, and he usually made a point of complimenting colleagues on the staff by telling attendees that these were "the best the college had to offer" or that the participating faculty members had "escaped" from classrooms and "had come to be challenged by peers and people of their own age." He wanted visitors to feel at home, enjoy their stay, and partake of whatever the university had to offer. Such expressions were not shallow sentiment on his part, for he truly believed that the school was a people's college and that every citizen had a stake in its successes or shortcomings.

As a speaker, Parks forte was in extemporaneous remarks. His demeanor at the rostrum was decidedly different from that of his immediate predecessor. In large part, of course, this was due to the differing personalities of James Hilton and Robert Parks. In front of groups, Hilton seemed somewhat uncomfortable and tended to appear officious; in reality, he was anything but that. Nevertheless, his rhetorical strengths lay in establishing rapport with one or two individuals at a time. In those instances he was on common ground and could share homespun, down-to-earth camaraderie. This asset enabled him to win approval from legislators and alumni whenever he met them on a one-to-one basis or in small, informal gatherings. At such times he seemed to come down to the level of his companions and to be one of them.

By contrast, Parks persuaded by means of subtle respect and authority. Marvin Anderson, who was a friend and coworker of both Hilton and Parks, once contrasted the two:

> One day I was in Hilton's office talking with him about some matter when Roberta [Roberta Vance, Hilton's administrative secretary] knocked on the door and announced that a friend from southern Iowa wanted to see him.
>
> Jim apologized to me for the interruption and said to Roberta, "Fine. What's his name? "
>
> Roberta answered, and Hilton said, "I don't remember him, but show him in anyway."
>
> Well, in came a middle-aged man dressed in a plaid shirt,

jeans, and suspenders. He also was wearing buckled overshoes, the kind most farmers wear around the barnyard.

"Hello, Jim," the farmer said, sticking out his hand. "Nothing particular on my mind, but I had to come to Ames to see about some fertilizer. Just wanted to stop in and say hello."

Jim Hilton and the man talked for a few moments just like they were the oldest of friends. A minute earlier Hilton hadn't recalled even the man's name, but that's the kind of man Hilton was.

I couldn't imagine such an incident ever happening in Dr. Parks's office.[15]

Parks's friendliness showed itself in a different way. Whereas Hilton's affability showed best when he was amidst a small group gathered around him, in the judgment of most friends Robert Parks came off as a man who won respect without realizing he was doing so. He had talents of which he himself was unaware, and his messages were inspiring, even if his listeners did not realize it at the time. Parks's ability to motivate people came not from coming down to the level of others but by subtle appeals to the highest instincts in human nature. He made listeners feel they were capable of doing better in whatever particular endeavor was under discussion. Strangers, acquaintances, and friends were apt to respond with special efforts because that is what this likeable evangel from the "people's college" expected of them.

From his presidential vantage point, Parks saw extension services as a major channel through which academic talents and knowledge could help bring about changes in society. Furthermore, it was part of his job to help effect such changes—to assist extension wherever possible in forming linkages with public and private organizations at local, state, and national levels. His credo had evolved through years of experience, beginning with being a member of a Tennessee 4-H club and progressing to the presidency of the nation's first land-grant college. His faith in education through such institutions never faltered and was expressed in numerous speeches, perhaps nowhere better than in his summary remarks to the Colorado seminar on the land-grant system:

> We should not underrate the great prestige, public stature and influence of our land-grant institutions. Whenever we know what should be done and when we present our case honestly, thoroughly and forcefully, I think we will be listened to. ... I sincerely believe that our colleges ... have a great future. Their distinguished past can even be dwarfed by their future if we are only wise enough to visualize it—and brave enough to bring it about.[16]

CHAPTER 9

Parks and Intercollegiate Athletics

The real justification for playing football on such a grand scale is that it brings out the herd instincts, better than anything I've ever seen, in a school's students, staff, alumni and fans.

W. Robert Parks

 Physical sports have been a part of academies ever since organized education began. Such training was in the core curriculum for boys of the privileged classes of Greece during the Hellenic Age when youths spent their whole time in a continuous course of instruction that started with three basic areas: (1) grammatistes, which included reading, writing, and arithmetic, (2) citharistes, made up of music, poetry, dance, and related arts, and (3) the palaestra. The last-named category was taught by paedotribes (from whence comes our modern word pedagogues) and included sports such as gymnastics, wrestling, boxing, running, jumping, and throwing the javelin.
 The training of athletes in ancient Greece involved both physical and spiritual preparation. Trainees were expected to live a celibate life in outdoor camps, devoting weeks and even months to arduous preparation for the Olympic games—popular contests that began as early as 776 B.C. Held in the summer every four years in honor of

the Olympian god Zeus, these contests in boxing, wrestling, running, and chariot races were the greatest festival in the Greek world.

The Romans, who came later and admired nearly everything about Greek culture, also put sports into their schools and training programs. A complete education for the young Roman rested upon the concept *Mens sana in corpore sano—a sound mind in a sound body*—and from the days of the Greeks and Romans until the present, that slogan has been the raison d'être of physical education.

No one has ever been able to figure out how old the sport of football really is; some claim to have traced its origin as far back as 478 B.C. Others say that it didn't start until four centuries later, when Julius Caesar came upon Teutonic tribesmen kicking and running with an oval-shaped object that vaguely resembled a football. However, closer inspection revealed that it wasn't a ball; it was the freshly severed head of an enemy soldier! Skeptics usually add to the anecdote by saying that this was the first time anyone lost his head over a game of football.

The basis for the fable may be questionable, but it is indisputable that Caesar and his Romans put heavy stress on sports. As early as the fifth century B.C., there was a division of Roman athletes into amateurs, who competed for the love of the sport, and professionals, who used their talents as means of earning a living. The most famous class of professional athletes, of course, were gladiators, who fought in arenas.

The history of athletics between the fall of Rome in the fifth century and the nineteenth century is quite sketchy. Sports such as archery, shooting, riding, and hunting were encouraged by rulers because of their value in war. Moreover, religious festivals during the Middle Ages were sometimes accompanied by crude ball games between rival towns and guilds. These contests were forerunners of the great spectator sports of the twentieth century, namely, baseball, football, basketball, soccer, hockey, and tennis.

The Industrial Revolution in the mid–eighteenth century and the later introduction of sports as a regular activity in English public schools (c. 1830) provided a spur that led to increased emphasis on sports during the Victorian age in England. Indeed, it was sports training that prompted Arthur Wellesley, Duke of Wellington, to declare in an earlier decade, "The battle of Waterloo was won on the playing fields of Eton."

Colonial Americans faced a hard life, with little time for such luxuries as recreation and games. Consequently, the first schools put their full attention upon the fundamentals of reading, writing, and mathematics. If a young man were lucky enough to go to college, he would likely be doing so in order to become a lawyer, doctor, or minister. Before the opening of the nineteenth century, curricula in New England colleges began expanding to include courses in practical arts like surveying, navigation, anatomy, and geography.

Collegiate athletics began as unorganized student pastimes, and the few sports played on colonial campuses were intramural. Participation in them was not a meaningful part of campus life until about the second decade of the nineteenth century. By the 1820s, however, certain contests had assumed some importance in the establishment of class honor. For example, at Harvard the freshmen and sophomores competed in an annual game of "kick-ball."

Thirty years later, Yale rowing crews challenged Harvard men "to test the superiority of the oarsmen of the two colleges." Harvard won the first contest, but a rematch was scheduled for 1855, and intercollegiate competition in other sports as well as involvement with additional eastern schools soon followed.

If Joe Citizen living during the opening of the twentieth century in Iowa, Indiana, Illinois, or other parts of the Midwest wanted to read about college sports, he would be apt to find only sporadic reports from prestigious eastern schools like Yale, Harvard, and Princeton. Sportswriters and college football fans referred to these schools as the Big Three. It was Yale that drew the public's interest in athletics when newspaper coverage of its teams combined with mass circulation of the fictional "Frank Merriwell at Yale" stories. These tales, tailored mainly for juveniles, captured the American boy's imagination and glorified the collegiate ideal as a culture hero. During the years between 1890 and 1915, for example, the dime novel Merriwell stories had average weekly sales of over two million copies.[1]

In 1896 the defunct Olympic games were revived in Athens, and despite world wars and numerous minor hostilities, interest in competitive sports continued to grow. The twentieth century also saw the creation of athletic associations that have increasingly controlled intercollegiate athletics in the United States.

Chief among these controlling groups is the National Collegiate Athletic Association (NCAA), which was founded in 1905 at the urging of President Theodore Roosevelt as an advisory body for collegiate sports at a time when a move to abolish football had been started because players were being injured and killed. For nearly three decades, members of the NCAA paid little if any attention to administrative control or to the structural and financial place of college sports within American universities. Instead, members debated methods of standardizing the *style* of play, that is, restrictions on such aspects of football as blocking, passing, and kicking. Then in 1948, the NCAA adopted a so-called "sanity code" to regulate excesses in college recruiting policies, and since that date the NCAA has become increasingly powerful in regard to nearly all phases of intercollegiate sports.

The development of athletics at Iowa State followed the national pattern. For the first score of years in the school's history, organized sports were nonexistent; in fact, there were few recreational activities of any sort, although beginning in the 1880s the departments of engineering, veterinary medicine, and domestic science started forming glee clubs and a college band.

Also, oratorical and literary exercises, very similar to adjuncts of the curricula in colonial colleges, were parts of the required program at Iowa State. The school's only intercollegiate rivalry in those years came in the form of oratorical contests. An Iowa oratorical association was formed in the 1870s and held annual state contests in which the winner would participate further in an interstate gathering. With that kind of entertainment and because of the school's rigorous physical and intellectual demands, there was almost no time or need for sports.

The absence of sports did not trouble the faculty because most educational authorities in the Midwest frowned upon such games as youthful, frivolous, and distracting from the real purposes of college. Some of the college boys in Ames might gather on a Saturday afternoon for a pickup baseball game since that was supposed to be the national sport, but there was no class or interscholastic competition. Football attracted almost no attention, although reports filtered in to the effect that across the country the new game was weaning interest away from baseball. It was further said that at some schools even members of the faculty were participating in the novel sport.[2]

The year 1895 stands out in the annals of Iowa State athletics, for that year marked the first time an organized football team representing the school moved beyond the state's borders to play. The season's schedule showed games with the following universities: Montana, Northwestern, Minnesota, Purdue, Iowa, and Wisconsin. The schedule was largely the product of Glenn "Pop" Warner, the legendary coach who came to the Ames campus for about six weeks and helped drill the football team. The team's record that year was 3-3-0—a record that earned a nickname when the *Chicago Tribune* featured the contest with Northwestern and referred to the Iowa State team as the devastating "Cyclone" that came out of the West.

In the years following 1895, the record of Cyclone football teams against interstate rivals was not outstanding or noteworthy. The University of Iowa handily won the sobriquet as the state's "football school" while Iowa State became the "cow college," known for its technical and scientific training.

Considerable lustre of the athletic program at the University of Iowa was rubbed off later during the years of the Great Depression, however. The NCAA already had set forth commendable principles but was unable to enforce its rules largely because it was a voluntary organization and because it failed to win strong support from the historic eastern universities. A movement for reform of intercollegiate sports was instigated by the Carnegie Foundation for the Advancement of Teaching, and in 1929 the movement culminated in a volatile report labeled "Bulletin Number Twenty-three."[3]

This report attracted widespread interest and became a vanguard of small movements for reform in intercollegiate sports. The bulletin alerted readers to a "curse of bigness," in which flagrant abuses were concentrated in a handful of "big time programs." Unfortunately, the University of Iowa was among the schools cited for violations of procedures and conference rules. The report charged Iowa's athletic department and alumni groups with operating outside the university administration's control; other allegations were that "athletes were given a share of commissions on sale of yearbooks," along with "utilization of a businessmen's slush fund to subsidize teams, refund of tuition fees, and failure to certify athletes as bona fide students." Soon after the report was released, the Big Ten Athletic Conference became the Big Nine when the University of Iowa was expelled for violating conference rules.[4]

Athletic conferences, however, had given themselves power to reinstate as well as to suspend institutional members, and accordingly the Big Ten a few years later returned the University of Iowa as a member in good standing, although it was not clear whether this was done because the institution had corrected the abuses or because Iowa alumni "had come up with charges against all nine other Big Ten schools that sounded uncomfortably like the charges that had been used to suspend Iowa from the league."[5]

The history of intercollegiate sports after World War II is largely an account of three distinct groups competing for control, namely, educational institutions, athletic conferences, and the NCAA. Under the NCAA constitution, the institutional president "has ultimate responsibility and final authority for the conduct of the intercollegiate athletic program," but while this point would seem unequivocal, in practice it is not followed, and presidents who have tried to do so have soon found themselves out of office. A university's losing athletic record can wash out all other presidential accomplishments and become an insurmountable factor in determining presidential tenure, which according to many writers is an average of something less than five years.[6]

A university president wears many hats, some of which are extremely attractive, and others less so. Among the attractive ones are peer recognition, salary, and perquisites of office, but most satisfying of all is the realization that by helping provide educational opportunities for the nation's youth, the university president is playing a key role in developing the country's greatest natural resource. Few experiences can be more rewarding than that. Although an occasional faculty member may regard students as necessary nuisances, most teachers appreciate them and understand that they are the real reasons for a university's existence. A successful president remembers that fact and enjoys a measure of pride in watching the institution's graduates take their places as effective members of the country's economic, social, and political networks.

University presidents like to think of themselves as intellectual leaders of their faculties, but in reality the demands of administration severely limit contacts with active teachers and researchers. A president's relationships with the teaching faculty, therefore, are usually through vicarious persons such as provosts, deans, directors, and department chairs.

A university president presides over a huge business corporation worth millions of dollars and supervises the work of an administrative staff that seems to bulge more each year. Furthermore, the president serves more or less as an executive secretary to a governing board, usually made up of trustees or regents. In addition to carrying out policies set by such governing boards, the president of a state university has to be the main link with the governor and key members of the state legislature.

Added to these demanding duties is one that has become sine qua non for the modern university president, namely, fund-raising. It was an aspect in which Robert Parks excelled. Iowa State had long been touted as "the people's college," and as such a great many persons felt that they owned the institution, so naturally, they wanted to find out what the person at the helm of their school was like. Parks was asked to appear before alumni meetings, leading civic clubs, chambers of commerce, church groups, various clubs, and other organizations. His natural talent for public speaking coupled with experiences in the classroom made him effective on the dais, where he could be entertaining as well as enormously persuasive.

Often the early portion of a university president's tenure is spent traveling around in order to meet new constituencies and establishing relationships with the faculty and other administrators. This was not the case with Robert Parks; in 1965 he had the advantage of being well-known on campus and throughout Iowa. By then, however, the NCAA along with the Big Eight Athletic Conference and similar groups had become aggressive in wresting control of athletics away from the institutions within their domains. Moreover, the NCAA and the various athletic conferences had entrenched themselves with both media and citizenry.

There is no question that Parks himself was a sports buff, his interests being traceable back to his years as a high schooler and later playing baseball and basketball at Berea College. As a professor, one of his favorite "nights out" was slipping away with a couple of close friends like Matty Matterson and Elroy Peterson to watch the Ames High School Little Cyclones play football. There were fewer free nights after he entered the presidency, but on a half-dozen autumn Saturday afternoons, a familiar sight was the tall, silver-haired man walking across the ISU campus to meet with a cheering crowd of ISU football fans.

When he was sixty-four, Parks reminisced with a reporter about his long-standing interest in sports:

> Whenever I didn't have to be doing work on the farm I had a football or basketball in my hand. I don't do much participating any more, but I've always enjoyed any kind of athletics. I find it relaxing and maybe a chance to become a child again for awhile on Saturday afternoons.[7]

In accepting the presidency of Iowa State, Parks took over leadership of a school with an undeniable record for academic excellence; a similar rating could not be accorded its record in all intercollegiate athletics, particularly the so-called major ones. The picture of ISU athletics was not entirely dark, for there were outstanding achievements in such non–revenue-producing sports as baseball, wrestling, and gymnastics.

Leroy C. "Cap" Timm is the person most likely to be remembered in the history of baseball at Iowa State. Cap and his wife "Tippy," an ever-friendly coordinator of student activities at the Iowa State Memorial Union, were a couple who gave their best to the college and to the Ames community. Cap coached baseball from

1938 until his retirement in 1974, and under his guidance Cyclone teams captured three Big Eight titles and won berths in two College World Series.

Timm's career mark of 340-375-5 doesn't accurately reflect his importance to intercollegiate sports. His attitudes, work habits, and philosophy had lasting effects upon young persons fortunate enough to come under his guidance. To athletes who played for him, he was recognized as a father figure, serving the college well by being the primary educator and counselor for those who might be inclined to belittle the academic aspects of the school.

Timm had been an all-around, home-town athlete before going to the University of Minnesota, where he played baseball and football and was the blocking back for the legendary running back Bronco Nagurski. Timm earned his M.A. in 1933 and came to Iowa State College in the 1930s as athletic trainer and assistant football coach.

There are bushels of anecdotes recounted by athletes who played for the colorful Timm. One of his sayings most often recalled is a warning he gave players at the beginning of each season: "If you chew tobacco, sit on the end of the bench, and make sure the wind is not blowing toward me."

Gary Thompson, who won All-American honors in basketball and also played shortstop on Cap Timm's 1957 varsity team, penned a tribute that embodied reasons athletes revered Timm: "Playing for Cap was a great experience because of his concern for the players. Cap never left anyone stranded on base. He was always there to share your personal problem or to give some fatherly advice."[8]

When Timm retired from active coaching, he was given the customary testimonial dinner, and at this affair held on May 18, 1975, President Parks quoted from a commendation he had written Timm several months earlier:

> Your tenure of thirty-six years in a profession not known for the long tenure of its coaches, sums up more than anything else could, the respect with which you are held here at Iowa State University and throughout the baseball profession. I am honored to join in this personal tribute to Cap Timm.[9]

The wrestling program at Iowa State likewise had its share of triumphs, some of the greatest coming in the period Harold Nichols was coach. During his tenure, ISU wrestling teams were always among the nation's best. From 1965 to 1973, for example, Nichols's squads compiled an amazing five NCAA titles and three runner-up finishes.

Nichols was named successor to Hugo Otopalik in 1954 after serving as the head coach at Arkansas State. Under Nichols, Iowa State wrestlers captured seven Olympic medals, three of which were earned at the 1972 Olympic Games in Munich, where Dan Gable and Ben Peterson won gold medals and Chris Taylor added a bronze. In all, Nichols's wrestling teams racked up six NCAA titles and seven Big Eight championships and produced thirty-eight NCAA individual champions.

In gymnastics, Ed Gagnier's teams usually outshone rivals in the Big Eight Conference. For example, in the third year of his presidency, Parks had the pleasure of congratulating Gagnier and his teams for winning their fourth Big Eight title in six years. Gagnier's most renowned gymnast was Ron Galimore, who won two individual NCAA titles and was honored nine times as an All-American gymnast.

Despite Ed Gagnier's excellent record as a gymnastics coach, another performance gained him more recognition. For more than a score of years, thousands of Iowans knew Gagnier as the man, often in clown's garb, who rode a unicycle out onto the basketball court of Hilton Coliseum during halftime of home games and then presented a person chosen at random from the crowd to compete in a highly popular "shoot-five-for-five" contest.

Notwithstanding the achievements of ISU athletes in the so-called minor sports, when Robert Parks came into the presidency, the Cyclone athletic program was considered dismal because of the records of the big sports: basketball and football. The football team had not won a conference title since 1912. A half-century and four years later, the team won only two out of its ten games, and it would be ten more years before it could boast even a winning season.

The basketball record was somewhat better, but not until

1985–1986 and 1986–1987, when Parks was approaching retirement, could Iowa State be considered a bona fide contender in the Big Eight Conference.

Parks's contributions to ISU athletics rest mainly upon his success in building better physical facilities. There were manifold problems with intercollegiate sports at Iowa State when he first took office, and no one could deny that the school's facilities for football and basketball then were well below those of other schools in the conference.

Football was played on Clyde Williams Field—a gridiron named in honor of a graduate of the University of Iowa, who in his time had an outstanding record in football and baseball as well as experience in professional baseball. In 1906 Williams had been chosen as Iowa State's first full-time football coach and was selected later as its athletic director. In the year Parks was chosen as Iowa State's president, seating capacity at Clyde Williams Field was slightly more than twenty-five thousand, but flagging enthusiasm usually drew five thousand less than that.

The basketball team played home games in the Armory, which had been built in 1921 and partially destroyed by fire a year later. The Armory had been renovated numerous times, but by 1965 it still was poorly ventilated and had only uncomfortable, bleacher-type seating.

Spirits on the athletic staff at Iowa State were correspondingly low. Some persons in the department looked through the money lens and saw the odds as insurmountable. For example, Gordon Chalmers, athletics director, declared it was reasonable "to assume that ISU would never win a conference championship" because the school's athletic program did not have adequate financing. In his opinion, the games did not attract big enough crowds to bankroll sufficient expenditures for athletics, nor did the institution provide enough money to recruit the required numbers and quality of football players.[10]

Fans everywhere are quick to blame the coach for the school's losing record, so Iowa State had earned dubious distinction as being a graveyard for sports mentors. In the twenty years between the end of World War II and 1965, for instance, there had been five different football coaches. In the same period, there were four basketball coaches, and there would be five more during the twenty-one years Parks was in office.

Parks sympathized with those who pled for better athletic facilities, but at first about all he could do was to reiterate that help was on its way. As a new president he tried to assure everyone that ISU teams were certain to improve in the very near future, and he had reason for painting a rosier picture. While the football team won only two games in 1966, the basketball team under Coach Glen Anderson was doing better and won more games than it lost during its 1966–1967 season.

Fortunately, Parks's immediate predecessor, James Hilton, had the foresight to set up a special fund-raising organization. In 1958, the year he lured Parks from Wisconsin back to Iowa State as dean of instruction, Hilton had urged creation of the Iowa State College Foundation, a nonprofit group established by alumni and friends of the school. The primary purpose of the foundation was "to accept, hold, administer, invest and disburse, for educational and scientific purposes, such funds as may be given to it by any person, firm or organization."

As early as 1954 President Hilton had conceived the idea for a complex of buildings for the performing arts, continuing education, and athletics, so by 1960 the foundation, now called the Iowa State University Foundation, was actively planning for a $7.5 million multipurpose project that was to be called the Iowa State Center. C. Y. Stephens, a 1925 alumnus, was named national chairman of the fund-raising organization, and a year later he was the person who gave the huge campaign its start by contributing a million dollars for the first building.

The basic plan for the center was accepted by the regents in 1965 when Hilton retired, but it was up to Robert Parks to raise the bulk of the money to bring his predecessor's concept into reality. Athletics facilities were not the first item on either Hilton's or Parks's agenda for improvements. Instead, the first building to go up in the Iowa State Center was one for performing arts. Ground-breaking ceremonies for it were held on October 30, 1965, as part of that year's Homecoming celebration. The building, named the C. Y. Stephens Auditorium in honor of the man who made the initial contribution, opened officially at the beginning of the fall term in 1969 with a series of five concerts by the New York Philharmonic Orchestra under the direction of world-renowned Seiji Ozawa.

Almost immediately after the opening of Stephens Auditorium, a second building got started—a building meant to serve as a coliseum mainly for basketball games. In the year Parks became president, plans to replace the Armory as home court for Cyclone basketball teams already were showing up on drawing boards, and the new president quickly threw enthusiastic support to this second project. Several nonuniversity meetings were held in the building before its formal opening on December 2, 1971, as James H. Hilton Coliseum. On that date, the Cyclone basketball team played the University of Arizona. It was a contest that happily Iowa State won by a score of 71–54 and was the first public exposure of the impressive new facility.

By the time the Iowa State Center was completed, it included, in addition to Stephens Auditorium and Hilton Coliseum, a 44,500-seat football stadium, Fisher Theater, and the Scheman Continuing Education Building. The center also offered a lighted, paved parking lot with a capacity for four thousand vehicles.

Hilton Coliseum cost $8,165,000, raised largely through a $6.8 million bond issue backed by student fees and gifts from alumni. In addition to the playing court for basketball and a seating capacity for fourteen thousand fans, the coliseum boasts four dressing rooms, varsity locker rooms, and a state-of-the-art training area. The coliseum also is the site of many NCAA and Big Eight championship events and is home for Cyclone wrestling, volleyball, and gymnastics as well as commencements, concerts, assemblies, rock groups, and conventions.

The building of the football stadium at the ISU Center was not without controversy. But even before arguments about a new stadium became full-blown, another matter fueled passions of Cyclone fans. That matter was resumption of football competition with the

Hawkeyes at the University of Iowa. The more rabid sports fans were hair shirts to Robert Parks and Sandy Boyd, his counterpart at the University of Iowa, and although both deemed the football issue only tangential to other items on their agendas, each had to deal with the firestorm that developed over it. The University of Iowa had earned national rankings and had exclusive "bragging rights" as the best football team in the state. ISU, on the other hand, had a poor win-loss record, but it played in the tough Big Eight Conference and was committed to upgrading its facilities. ISU, therefore, had much to gain from games with its powerful in-state rivals, while University of Iowa supporters were less enthusiastic.

The two schools had played each other until 1934, when further games were dropped because the rivalry got out of hand. As the 1970s opened, enrollments at the two schools were becoming more evenly matched and their respective athletic programs larger than ever. After intense debate throughout the state and as a result of unrelenting pressure from sportswriters and especially Iowa legislators, annual games between the schools were resumed in 1977.

Putting the University of Iowa back on the annual schedule helped raise the spirits of Cyclone football fans and gave more momentum to the drive for a better stadium, but the stadium idea, too, brought controversy. Some people thought a new one ought not be a high priority when Clyde Williams Field was seldom filled. Indeed, considerable improvements had been made to Clyde Williams Field as late as 1961, when a new press box had been built on the west side of the stadium and four thousand additional seats had been installed on the east side.

An element within the faculty was very disturbed over what was seen as an "overemphasis" on athletics to the disadvantage of more fundamental purposes of the school. A football stadium, said the dissenters, should not be an item of high priority at a time when so many academic needs existed. Among the critics were some of Parks's staunchest supporters, and several of them began writing open letters or approaching influential persons like regents and legislators. The charges got on the agenda for the Faculty Council several times before Parks faced the group in a meeting during January

1972. He reiterated arguments that the present stadium was too small and that the cost of making it "minimally operable" would be more than $1.5 million. Then he took aim at allegations of "overemphasis" and "high priority":

> The question of building a new stadium is not a matter of "overemphasis" or "under-emphasis" on football. It is simply a matter of economics. If resources can be brought together to build a new stadium, we believe that good economics dictate that we build a new stadium. We do not think it good economics to continue ... to spend large amounts of good money after bad in an attempt to make the present stadium into an adequate one. ...
>
> In regard to the more involved question of whether a public drive to underwrite the costs of constructing a stadium might be interpreted as a statement of the top priority of the University, I have made it clear on numerous occasions that my number one priority for the University is better salaries and wages for academic and non-academic employees. ... A public drive for a new stadium would certainly not replace that top priority, nor would it be competitive to it in any sense of the word.
>
> In a real sense, a public drive for funds is tantamount to stating that the project being funded is <u>not</u> [*sic*] a top priority item in accomplishing the University's primary mission. If it were a top priority need (such as faculty and staff salaries and academic buildings) the state legislature would be asked to meet it. Therefore, a state university, whose main functions are supported by the state legislature, customarily employs the public drive as a means of obtaining "desirable extras" for the university, i.e., buildings and programs which in reality the legislature cannot, and perhaps should not, be expected to finance. The buildings which constitute the Iowa State Center, as well as a new football stadium, fall into that category.[11]

Both on campus and beyond, football fans were well aware of ISU's poor record in that sport, and many remained unconvinced that a new field would do much to improve it. Parks had to rebut their arguments every time he went out on the fund-raising trail, so he needed all his platform skills whenever he attempted to raise private moneys.

The proposal for a football stadium had to clear an additional hurdle because of a brouhaha over what it should be called. It should be remembered that in the 1970s when moneys were being solicited for new construction, the ISU campus and the city of Ames were being wracked by racial protests. It was not surprising, therefore, when a group of students, faculty, and staff mustered a campaign to name the stadium after Jack Trice, an African-American athlete who died from injuries suffered in one of the school's intercollegiate games.

Three decades after George Washington Carver's enrollment at Iowa State College, Jack Trice, another black student, gained an important niche in the school's history. In October of 1923, Trice played football against the University of Minnesota, one of the very few schools that would agree to schedule a game against an "integrated" team. Early in the game, Trice broke his collarbone but continued playing until he was more seriously injured. Then he was carried from the field and rushed to a Minnesota hospital. Doctors there said that he could make the return trip to Ames, and upon arrival in Ames he immediately was admitted to the local hospital. There he developed respiratory and stomach problems, so a Des Moines specialist was called in for consultation. This specialist advised that an operation would be too risky in the patient's condition, so surgery was postponed. The next day, October 8, 1923, Trice died of hemorrhaged lungs and internal bleeding throughout the abdomen.

Two days later the school's newspaper, *The Iowa State Student,* ran the headline "Ames Mourns Jack Trice." The accompanying story read in part:

> In a spirit of reverence, the student body of Iowa State gathered near the Campanile yesterday to pay a last tribute to its silent dead at the short funeral service for Jack Trice, tackle on the football team, who died Monday.

College classes were suspended at 2 P.M. and nearly three thousand people formed a semi-circle in the northwest of the memorial tower while those who knew the star gridiron player best told the simple story of their friend's life. Before the wooden platform rested the gray casket with an Ames blanket of cardinal and gold covering it.

Following the invocation, President R. A. Pearson said something of the football star as a student at Iowa State and closed by reading a letter written by Jack Trice the night before the Minnesota-Ames game, his first big college football conflict. The letter was read with the consent of Trice's widow and is to be preserved as a college document.[12]

The letter was indeed preserved and half a century later became a cause célèbre in a long-running dispute over what to call the new football stadium at Iowa State. The letter Trice wrote reads as follows:

Oct 5, 1923

To Whom it may Concern:

My thoughts just before the first real college game of my life: the honor of my race, family, and self is at stake. Everyone is expecting me to do big things. I will. My whole body and soul are to be thrown recklessly about the field. Every time the ball is snapped, I will be trying to do more than my part. Fight low, with your eyes open and toward the ball. Watch out for crossbucks and reverse end runs. Be on your toes every minute if you expect to make good.

(meeting) :8: 7:45—
Jack.[13]

The Trice story was largely forgotten until a plaque honoring him was discovered in a university gym in the early 1970s—about the same time President Parks set out on the fund-raising trail for the new stadium. While students and some faculty argued that naming the stadium after Trice would show a commitment to healing racial wounds, potential donors to the project, including some of the biggest, let President Parks know in no uncertain terms that the stadium should bear a more generic name because many people, not just one, had contributed to the school's history. Cyclone Stadium was the name endorsed by the Athletic Department and favored by most persons opposed to naming it after Trice. That name, they argued, would honor all donors and athletes.

Disagreement over the name of the structure went on even after it was built and the first game played in it during the fall of 1975. Unlike most other big building projects, the stadium had no single major donor; instead funds came from an accumulation of thousands of names. Money, therefore, helped justify postponement of its naming.

Carl Hamilton, vice president for public relations, advised President Parks that selecting a name should wait until the stadium was paid for and it became official university property. Furthermore, the influential Hamilton deemed it wise to hold the matter of a name out as a carrot just in case someone might be willing to make a gigantic donation. Indeed, several potential donors were approached with specific guidelines as to what appeals might be most persuasive.[14]

The controversy rose higher. In 1976, when the editor of the *Iowa State Daily* leveled a series of charges to the effect that (1) the university was spending general funds to the disadvantage of enrolled students, (2) students were ignored by the Special Events Committee because important decisions were postponed until the summer, when most students were away from campus, (3) the administration was "handpicking" students to serve on advisory committees, and (4) student wishes to name the stadium after Trice were being thwarted.

Hamilton attempted to rebut the attacks with a far-ranging open letter to the editor of the student newspaper. First, he denied the charge that students were disadvantaged by measures enacted in behalf of persons taking courses in the continuing education program or through extension. The latter persons, he insisted, were not "external" but were the equal of all other students even if perhaps a little older. Second, he explained that President Parks had created the Special Events Committee for the express purpose of bringing more students into the decision-making process and that Parks had insisted the committee should be cochaired—one student and one faculty member or administrator.

It was the fourth charge, however, that fueled the most argument—the controversy over whether the stadium should be named after Trice or the Cyclones. That matter had been taken to the regents only because the Government of the Student Body and the Faculty Council had asked that it be done at once. In his refutation of the charges, Hamilton cited Parks's decisions:

> The President said, pick a name, get it done before the end of the school year—while students are still here—and I will take the name to the Board of Regents after I have cleared it with the stadium owner, i.e., the Board of Governors. He did just that and made a special effort to take it to the Regents at their May meeting, so students could make their voices heard.[15]

Hamilton wrote further that he recognized the vigorous—and "in no way inappropriate"—campus campaign that students and some staff members were waging to name the stadium after Jack Trice. That name, he said, had great emotional appeal, but he wanted students to bear in mind that generations of alumni had rallied to cries like "Go Cyclones, Go!" It was only natural that many of them would be for a Cyclone name rather than one honoring a single person:

> The only thing that is certain is that the issue should be settled. To think that viewpoints will change is pretty unrealistic. In the

meantime, it will simply fester. And, after all it is hardly the largest question in higher education these days![16]

Ground-breaking ceremonies for the new "no-name" football stadium had been held in October of 1973 with hopes of having it ready for Homecoming on the next year's schedule. That goal, however, could not be met, and the Homecoming game of 1974 was played on Clyde Williams Field.

When the first football game was played on the new field in the fall of 1975 against the Air Force—a game ISU won 17 to 12—people commonly referred to the new facility as the Cyclone Stadium. For the next two years, there continued to be passionate speeches for and against naming the stadium after Jack Trice. In 1976 the Board of Regents passed a motion that postponed naming the facility until the stadium was paid for. The intervening years failed to cool the dispute, and in 1984 the regents finally adopted Parks's attempt at a compromise: the *building itself* should be called Cyclone Stadium and the *playing surface* Jack Trice Field.

The compromise seemed to be the best solution at the time, but it failed to halt the debate, which would simmer for another decade and a half. After the stadium was paid off, passions cooled but did not disappear; there was a lingering feeling of sympathy for the Jack Trice name. Indeed, a statue honoring Trice had been placed in front of Carver Hall on central campus, and in the fall of 1997 this statue was moved to the northeast corner of the Olsen Building, just north of the football stadium. In a dedication ceremony just prior to a game against Oklahoma State on August 30, 1997, the stadium and field were named officially the Jack Trice Stadium.

On another occasion, a milder controversy somewhat related to athletics confronted President Parks. The issue was forced largely by George Christensen, Vice President for Academic Affairs, who had become concerned about how the university could better serve students taking courses in physical education.

The school had a Department of Physical Education for Men and a Department of Physical Eduction for Women. The men's department was in the College of Sciences and Humanities while the women's was in the College of Home Economics, so the two departments were totally separated. Christensen believed that, from an academic standpoint, the quality of instruction would be improved if the separate departments were combined. He amassed his data and arguments before submitting the recommendation to Parks along with his suggestion that the revised single department be put into the new College of Education. Parks liked both aspects of the proposal and said, "Let's go for it."

Hoping to prevent a firestorm over the anticipated move, for several weeks Christensen shuttled back and forth between meetings with the respective staffs trying to win acceptance for the intended change. He might meet with the men's group at one time and an hour later find himself presenting the same arguments to the women. The common denominator was that neither group trusted the other on the matter of scholastic standards. Both departments thought the other less dependable. Women were worried that football coaches would want special compensation for their athletes, and on the other side Earle Bruce, football coach, feared that under the proposed rearrangement athletes might be held to standards higher than those the NCAA had established.

The two staffs were not entirely mollified, but after Christensen completed a series of meetings and reaffirmed his recommendation, President Parks announced that he was accepting it and that the merger was going to happen providing he could get the Board of Regents to approve it.

The rationale he presented to the board revolved around the following points: (1) the trend at comparable institutions was toward such a merger, (2) the needs of students majoring in physical education no longer fell into traditionally male or female programs, and (3) the philosophy of physical education was changing as a result of changing societal concepts of male and female roles.

The board approved Parks's request, so his next step was to find a person qualified to lead the combined department. Christensen explained what happened:

We set out on a nationwide search, one of the first times we had done so because such practices weren't often done at that time [1974]. In our search we discovered that Barbara Forker [already serving as head of the Department of Physical Education for Women at ISU] was one of the top candidates; in fact, after studying the credentials of all candidates, it seemed clear to us that she was *the* [emphasis supplied by Christensen] top candidate. From that point on, I don't recall any friction or dissension beyond what might be expected in any department.[17]

By appointing Barbara Forker to head the new and larger department, President Parks and his administrative team had taken a giant step toward bringing more women into the power structure of the university. It was another instance when his orientation and problem-solving action were well ahead of the usual practices.

No other aspects of a university stirs public emotions as quickly or raises them to a higher pitch than does intercollegiate athletics, and because a president is the titular overseer of this extensive branch of university living, he cannot remain aloof from whatever criticism develops. Parks was no exception. While he might decry malfeasance whenever and wherever it occurred, he seldom retreated from defense of athletic programs if properly run. He saw sports as rallying points that brought people together and helped support programs beyond the realm of athletics. Always careful to avoid the shibboleths that athletic competition molds character, instills discipline, and promotes leadership, he said repeatedly:

> You can't justify a multimillion-dollar athletic program on the basis of molding character. The only way an institution of learning can explain 50,000-seat stadiums, artificial surfaces and weight-training coaches ... is that all of these things generate money for areas that, frankly, are more important to a university's mission.[18]

Parks had little patience with colleagues who approached problems with their minds unbuttoned. To him athletics was an asset to higher education regardless of how tainted the programs occasionally were because of commercialism and the insatiable quest for victory. He was steadfast in believing that an ISU athlete should be a bona fide college student eligible to play on university teams as long as he or she maintained satisfactory scholastic standing while making normal progress toward a degree. When badgered about scandals reported in athletic programs across the country, Parks would say that sports at ISU ought to be like Caesar's wife—above suspicion. As long as he was in charge, he meant for ISU to play by the rules.

During the first half of his presidency, Parks relied upon Arthur Gowan, dean of admissions, for interpretation of an athlete's eligibility. After Gowan's retirement, Parks turned over such matters entirely to Gowan's successor, Fred Schlunz, who gave this testimony:

> President Parks never put pressure of any kind on me regarding athletics, and I cannot even imagine that happening. During most of my years working with athletes' eligibility, Arch Steil was the liaison between our admissions office and the coaches. If a coach had a problem, he'd first take it to Arch, and Arch then would bring it to me. I'd read the proper sections of the Big Eight Rules and the huge NCAA rule book along with any parallel NCAA cases. Then I'd give my opinion as to how the rules applied to our situation. That would be the end of it.
>
> I think the biggest reasons for Parks's success as president were his great class and the fact that his confidence in colleagues and subordinates was such that he did not feel it necessary to rule supreme.[19]

There were times, however, when incidents in athletics programs at Iowa State were real cause for embarrassment, and in those instances, Parks found that he was holding a bear by the tail; his only choice was to hang on and try to tame the beast or to let go and run for cover. It was against his nature to run, so he usually chose the first option.

He was realist enough to understand the prominence given to athletics and that a president's control over intercollegiate sports was limited because of public attitudes and NCAA regulations. He agreed with intimates in academia who deplored the excesses of football and basketball, but he would remind them that alumni and public sentiment were tolerant and usually fell in line behind coaches rather than university administrators when disputes between the two factions arose. Then he was apt to resort to a limerick:

> *There was a young lady from Kent*
> *Who knew what it always meant,*
> *When men took her to dine,*
> *Bought her cocktails and wine.*
> *She knew what it meant—*
> *But she went.*

One power Parks did retain and use was approval of head coaches. He was enough of a fan to want team victories, but he recognized the pressure put upon coaches to produce wins. He predicted that such pressures would mount as revenues, particularly those that came with ever-increasing television coverage, continued to swell.

The football program at ISU was in the doldrums when in 1968 Parks helped recruit a fellow Tennessean, Johnny Majors, as coach. Majors had had a brilliant career as a player at the University of Tennessee and was rapidly making a name for himself among the nation's younger coaches. Majors would stay at Iowa State a mere four years and have only one winning season, but there is no question that he did a great deal in raising enthusiasm for football at ISU.

Even the most popular coach receives criticism, however, and it was not unusual for a fan to send complaints about a coach's behavior directly to President Parks. Parks once received a letter concerning Coach Majors, who sometimes could get fired up enough over a game to lose his temper. Majors did that at a game in Colorado in 1972. A spectator wrote Parks, who felt that he had to respond in some way so as not to appear as if he condoned his coach's outburst. So with tongue-in-cheek Parks sent the football coach a reprimand:

October 16, 1972

Mr. John T. Majors
Head Football Coach
Iowa State University
Campus

Dear Johnny:

I've just visited with your mother. We simply can't understand where you learned those words you used on the referee out in Colorado. Nice young men who grow up in Lynchburg and Huntland just don't talk that way.

We do hope that you at least remembered to address the gentleman as "Sir" before you aimed those strange remarks in his direction!

Disappointedly yours,

W. Robert Parks
President

P.S. Your mother and I feel that the Astro-turf was partially to blame for your words with the referee. With synthetic turf, there is no longer any way for a concerned coach to follow the time-honored practice of kicking a little dirt on an erring referee. All in all, however, we think it would have been better if you had just stepped on the referee's foot and then properly apologized for your clumsiness.[20]

The mildly chastised Majors received the message and replied in similar style four days later:

October 20, 1972

Dr. W. Robert Parks
President's Office
Iowa State University
117 Beardshear Hall

Dear Dr. Parks:

    Frankly, I wish I had been smart enough to think of an ingenious way to stop the Colorado game and postpone it until we had a ruling interpretation on the disputed call (I knew the referee had made a poor call and tried to tell him so at the time—he made an error that could be the biggest factor in the ball game). When that was to no avail, I then gave him some choice words I had heard my daddy use on the sideline a long time ago. However, I assure you I did not make any remarks about the referee's mommy or about his extraction.

    I am tired of losing and hope to get back on the right track.

Meekly yours,

John Majors
Head Football Coach[21]

Majors was followed by the capable but less charismatic Earle Bruce, who stayed five years at ISU and garnered three winning seasons. On the fund-raising trail, President Parks was lavish in his praise for each of these two coaches, although he wasn't above taking an occasional humorous swipe at coaches in general. It's common practice for speakers to use humor at the beginning of their talks, and Parks often did that. One of his favorite anecdotes went as follows:

We once had a football coach—a man I hasten to say is no longer with us—who was a pretty good coach except when it came to public appearances. His appearances on television were disasters. TV endorsements were just becoming popular, and Wisconsin cheese manufacturers persuaded our coach to help promote their product. The sponsors assured him all he had to do was read cue cards held below the camera.

When it came time to shoot the scene, the announcer asked, "Coach, what do you like best about ———————— cheese?" Our coach dutifully read from the card: "That tangy, delicious taste."

Next, the announcer asked, "Do you prefer the brick or individual slices?" Again our man read the card: "I usually buy a little of both."

The final question was: "And, coach, what's your favorite brand of cheese?"

So the coach faithfully read the words: "Ad lib."[22]

Parks also lent support to recruiting a basketball coach, Johnny Orr, from the University of Michigan. Orr did in basketball what Majors had achieved in football, namely, revive flagging spirits of ISU fans. In 1981, Orr was brought to Ames with the hope of boosting attendance at Hilton Coliseum, where attendance had fallen to only about half its capacity. In the 1979–1980 season, for example, the average attendance for basketball games was only 6470 in a coliseum intended for well over 12,000.

The colorful and controversial Orr helped bring in more fans, for in his first year at ISU, attendance at games climbed more than a third. It would be another year before the team could post a winning season, but more fans began showing up, and by 1983 attendance had risen to over 12,675 and thereafter never fell much below that figure.

While Parks along with most presidential colleagues in such organizations as the National Association of State Universities and Land-Grant Colleges and the Association of American Universities deplored the seedy aspects of commercialism in big-time athletics, he joined with those who said, like it or not, intercollegiate sports had grown to the point of being so widely accepted by the public that institutional presidents had little choice but to cooperate. Schools had been given a responsibility that they could not abdicate, and after all, colleges and universities traditionally have provided public entertainment in the form of musical concerts, recitals, lectures, or dramas. Why not do it, too, with intercollegiate sports?

He was ever-quick to defend athletics on economic grounds. Even though in many instances athletic programs might not pay for themselves, athletic teams, he maintained, became magnets for attracting greater financial support for the university:

> There are lots of people whose original interest in this place [ISU] is spurred by athletics. How many times do I get on a plane, and the first question is, "How's your football team going to be this year?" Or, "Is Johnny Orr going to have anything in basketball?"
>
> I think oftentimes it is the original spark of interest which then develops into a much broader interest in the university. I would make the general statement that those who are the largest contributors to our athletic programs happen to be our most reliable contributors for the academic purposes of the university. In other words, hook 'em on scoring drives and interceptions, then land 'em on library books and laboratory equipment.[23]

Money, in Parks's judgment, dominated athletics, and the main culprit was television—network, cable, and subscription. Television, he warned repeatedly throughout the 1980s, would soon be attracting so many more viewers to college football and basketball games that present ones by comparison would seem like intramurals.

During the time he was president of the National Association of State Universities and Land-Grant Colleges, Parks acknowledged there was little administrators could do to diminish the prominence of athletics. Rather than play King Canute and try to hold back that tide, university presidents, he insisted, ought to collaborate in establishing reasonable rules that might help ease what he said were "incredible pressures" on athletic departments and coaches. When a school becomes successful in building huge, financially productive athletics programs, coaches become legendary folk heroes and much stronger than the president. The situation, he said, was not healthy, for athletics programs soon developed into "rich, bloated enterprises," impossible to control and separated from the rest of the university.

An unusually pragmatic administrator, Parks looked at intercollegiate sports as something to be dealt with and controlled, not abolished. Athletics programs required restraint, but when kept in proper perspective, they could be rallying forces that brought university supporters together. He might worry about excesses and scandals—including questionable academic achievements—or that athletes were spending ever-increasing chunks of time on their respective sports. Nevertheless, he believed that if a university were to attain its fullest potential in teaching, research, and service, it needed successful athletic programs. Therefore, whenever he reached the bottom line on his athletics balance sheet, Parks found himself siding with sports.

CHAPTER 10

Building and Funding Iowa State University, 1965–1986

But it is pretty to see what money will do.

Samuel Pepys
Diary

Lofty goals are easier to state than to achieve, and no university can grow without adequate financing. A quality university, moreover, is forever short of funds, and its chief fund-raiser, the president, is always on a treadmill striving but destined never to reach the promised land of fiscal abundance. Money is the Aladdin's lamp that makes wishes come true. Yet costs of operating and expanding an already large state university are only vaguely interesting to most people, somewhat like reading minutes of city council meetings held in a distant town.

The cost of going to college anywhere in America began climbing in the early 1960s. Federal spending, triggered in part by Sputnik's success in 1957, shot upward. Throughout the 1960s and well into the 1970s, a spate of Great Society financial-aid packages permitted universities to launch mammoth building and hiring programs at a time when prices for innovative technologies and equipment were skyrocketing. High-rise dormitories were constructed along with new classrooms and laboratories.

As prices for attending college rose, so did America's ability to pay. With considerable evidence, parents came to feel that a college diploma was a necessity, a direct conduit to a high-paying job. Some observers estimated that a student with a degree from a top-notch university might earn as much as 56 percent more than one with only a high school diploma. Easier financial credit enabled parents to borrow money, and doing so to meet college costs became socially acceptable. Along with parental money came increases in the amount and number of financial aids available to students.

Iowa State was typical of what was happening in higher education elsewhere. Spiraling enrollments demanded expansions in faculty and services along with more buildings and additional equipment for laboratories and classrooms. To meet these needs, ISU relied on three primary sources: state appropriations, tuitions, and private gifts. It wasn't enough for President Parks to articulate a vision of Iowa State as a broad-based university with excellence in science and technology; it would take unrelenting fund-raising on several fronts if the university was to move toward goals he had expressed in his New Humanism speech.

At the December 1964 meeting of the Board of Regents when it was announced that W. Robert Parks had been selected as ISU's next president, the regents also approved an operational budget of $46 million for Iowa State, including appropriations for the Agriculture and Home Economics Experiment Station and extension services. The capital improvements request for the institution that year was $16.5 million. The board was warned by Governor Harold Hughes that it could count on those requests being cut before he submitted them to the legislature.[1]

In 1965 the ISU campus covered one thousand acres of gently rolling prairie in the northwest sector of Ames, a city that then had a population of approximately thirty thousand, including students. The campus had been carefully developed to provide a pleasant, naturalistic setting with conveniently located facilities. In addition to holdings on the Ames site, the university owned and operated farms and research areas nearby or scattered across the state in strategic locations.

Acquisition value of ISU's physical plant was estimated to be in excess of $80 million, and the anticipated expenditure for the academic year 1965-1966 was set at $58 million, of which state appropriations were expected to provide one-third. The remainder would come from tuitions, fees, contracts, sales, private gifts and grants, or federal funds and endowments.

The school's catalog for the year totaled 409 pages, and slightly more than fourteen thousand students enrolled for the fall term. An undergraduate living in a residence hall was charged $1675 for the year (three quarters), broken down into the following order: registration fee, $345; tuition, $495; board and room, $735; and books, supplies, and equipment estimated at $100. The existing six colleges offered degree work in more than 115 different fields, and 2119 degrees had been conferred the previous year. The university faculty numbered 1500.[2]

Twenty-one years later when Parks left the presidency, the university had changed from the quarter to the semester system and was publishing its catalog every two years rather than annually. The *General Catalog for 1985-1987* numbered only 269 pages, but that figure is deceiving because in contrast with earlier editions the newer catalogs were full-size (8 × 11 inches) rather than three-quarter size and also used smaller print. More pertinent comparisons show that the university was awarding more than 4500 degrees each year—double the number in 1965—and had a student enrollment of more than twenty-six thousand—a jump of nearly 86 percent. The number on the faculty had increased to just over two thousand. In other words, compared with twenty-one years earlier the school had one-third more faculty and nearly twice as many students.

The university had grown in other ways, too. Rather than the six colleges that comprised the university in 1965, there now were nine. Parks had helped add three new ones: business administration, design, and education. In addition to belonging to the National Association of State Universities and Land-Grant Colleges, Iowa State University under Parks had received recognition and membership in organizations such as the National Council for Accreditation of Teacher Education and the Association of American Universities, a long-standing group usually linked with prestigious schools in the East.

Growth did not come without costs, however, and forces that drove up the price of attending Iowa State were fundamentally the same as those of other large state universities. In the first ten years of Parks's presidency, for example, heat and electricity costs for the school rose more than 300 percent.

From the outset of his presidency, Parks made clear his vision of Iowa State as a broad-based university, and this widening of opportunities and curricula almost certainly helped spur an ever-rising number of students coming to the Ames campus. By far the most formidable weapon he carried in his rhetorical quiver was the obligation to meet the needs of these ever-mounting numbers, and throughout his term of office he used the argument with maximum effectiveness. As a result, regents and state legislators were inclined to endorse most of his recommendations.

By far, the largest portion of the university's income, approximately 66 percent, came from state funds, and each year it was up to Parks and his lieutenants to make the case for adequate appropriations, first to the Board of Regents and then before various committees of the Iowa house or senate.

Legislators usually looked very favorably toward the three state universities, but exceptions to this habit surfaced in the 1970s when protests over Vietnam and civil rights erupted. Even old friends and staunch supporters in the senate and house began questioning needs for increased expenditures for campuses where "radicals" were reported to be disrupting the educational process. Critics complained that university authorities were "not doing enough" to quell the disturbances. Wayne Moore, former vice president for business and finance at ISU, put it bluntly:

> In the late 1960s and the early 1970s, the attitude of the legislature changed considerably because of student unrest. So for a few years, the Board of Regents instead of being a favorite of the legislature became a target for criticism. Legislators in general were

quite upset about the failure of the institutions to handle what they called "campus uprisings."[3]

Although the state appropriated more money with each passing year, those funds never quite matched Iowa State's phenomenal growth. Students were rightly concerned with rising tuition and housing costs, but despite attempts for restraint made by Parks and his administrative colleagues, student expenses went up dramatically. In 1986, for example, an undergraduate student from Iowa who chose to come to ISU was expected to pay tuition of $1304 for two semesters (up $809 from the $495 charged in 1965); board and room expenses showed even greater increase. It cost $910 per academic year to live in a double-occupancy room in one of the university's dormitories, where a meal plan could be purchased for $1048.[4]

To an executive, a budget is what health is to an athlete, absolutely necessary before the race can be run. Robert Parks's experiences with the Land Economics Division of the Department of Agriculture in Washington, D.C., proved invaluable in helping train him in the complexities of understanding and developing budgets for a huge and costly educational institution.

A few stabs at ISU's budget for the forthcoming year usually were taken as soon as Parks and his family returned from a week or two at Cape Cod during the summer, but budget preparation couldn't begin in earnest until the all-important figure for fall enrollment became available.

The basic unit within a university is the department, and this is where ISU's internal budgeting process began. A department is administered by a head, chairperson, or executive officer—whatever title is chosen—and departments are grouped together to form schools or colleges; the distinction is not always clear. A dean is the administrative leader of a college. He or she is responsible to a vice president or provost, and, finally, to the president.

Parks believed very strongly that it was a dean's prerogative and indeed responsibility to determine the appropriate budget for his or her college. That was not the practice of all his predecessors, however. He liked to tell the story of an exchange between him and Dean Helen Hilton, nee LeBaron, who had been appointed in 1952 by then President Charles Friley. Parks's version of the conversation went this way:

> Once we were talking about the old days, and I said to Helen, "You know, when I was on the faculty a lot of good people thought Friley was pretty dictatorial, arbitrary, and so forth and so on. Was he that way with his administrative colleagues?"
> And she said, "Was he ever!" She recalled that the very first budget hearing she had with him was really not a hearing. Mr. Friley told her, "Look, Helen, all you do is write in the names of your people on a piece of paper, and I'll write in the salaries."
> So I said to Helen, "That isn't the Helen LeBaron I know. Why in the world did you put up with that?"
> And she said, "Well, I knew he'd be here for only another year or two, and I thought we'd get a better president after he left."
> And in view of what happened later when she married that other president* [James Hilton, who succeeded Friley], I guess she was right.[5]

At Iowa State under Parks's administration, preparation of the annual budget began with a chairperson making his or her request for next year's funds to the college dean. Nearly two-thirds of the requested amount would be for faculty salaries.

Beyond the several deans, the persons most directly responsible for Iowa State budgets during the years Parks was in office were George Christensen, Wayne Moore, and Parks himself, although it should be noted that in the later years of Parks's presidency Warren Madden was given many of Wayne Moore's responsibilities.

Under Parks's administration, there would be several private exchanges with individual deans before the next step occurred when Christensen and Moore, Vice President for Business and Finance, would meet with the respective college dean and the chairperson of the department under review. Occasionally President Parks would

---

*On May 24, 1970, Helen LeBaron and James Hilton were married in Charlotte, North Carolina.

attend such budget sessions, which he referred to as the "dog and pony show," but knowing he would have the final approval, he usually left active questioning in these preliminary sessions up to the lieutenants.

After the hearing with departmental heads, each dean would present his or her budget to the Deans' Council—a group made up of all the deans and vice presidents and Parks. The council was chaired by George Christensen, and according to him it was here that Parks began to take a more aggressive role. His probing usually gave the deans cues as to what they could or could not expect when the total budget finally reached his desk—a destination where sometimes the most severe cuts had to be made.[6]

While authorities at ISU could predict with considerable accuracy funds that would be coming from student fees and subsidiary sources, the lion's share, namely, state appropriations, depended upon moods and actions of the legislature, and during months that ISU administrators were putting together a budget for the next year, the Board of Regents as well as committees within the state legislature were making their respective plans.

Each of the three state universities had lobbyists and supporters within the legislature, and the regents usually would be first to come up with a tentative figure. Wayne Moore, who in addition to his role as vice president for business and finance was given responsibility for supervising budgets for security and the physical plant, explained the practice:

> The regents usually gave us a total figure that we were expected to stay within. One or two times, I remember that we had our budget prepared before getting a figure from the regents. In any case, my main responsibility in attending the budget review sessions was to see that requests from departments and whatever allocations were given to them stayed within the totals set by the university for each college.[7]

In Parks's first full-time year as ISU's president, the university's receipts for current operating funds reached $56,301,148, and expenditures were $55,334,829. Total value of loan funds went up to $2,068,183 largely due to the creation of new funds and enlarged contributions from government sources. Endowment funds were $1,707,462, and the value of the physical plant of the university was set at $74,720,594.

The story of bulging enrollments, expanded curricula, new buildings for dormitories, classrooms, and laboratories is told in the university's annual income. The spectacular growth in enrollments demanded huge rises in incomes and expenditures—rises that can best be seen by comparing the school's total income in 1964–1965 with that of 1985–1986 (Tables 10.1 and 10.2).

From the $19,191,950 that the school received in 1965, the dollar amounts from all sources soared to $338,278,080 in 1985–1986, approximately 176 percent, which could be translated into an average of 8.4 percent for each year of Parks's administration.

During the years Parks was at the helm, the annual *operating budget income* for the institution rose from $18,731,950 in 1965 to $188,430,848 for 1985–1986—an increase of $169,698,898, or

TABLE 10.1. Sources of Iowa State University income, 1964–1965

	General university
State appropriations	$11,758,950
Federal funds	320,000
Endowment interest	28,000
Student fees	4,140,000
Sales and miscellaneous	360,000
Overhead	950,000
Engineering extension fees	75,000
Balance brought forward from 1963–1964	1,100,000
Total operating budget	$18,731,950
Repairs, replacements, and alterations	460,000
TOTAL BUDGET INCOME	$19,191,950

Source: *ISU Financial Report, June 30, 1965, Iowa State University Archives, Parks Library.*

slightly more than 900 percent. The average jump in the operating budget for each of his twenty-one years was slightly more than 43 percent.

For the first ten years this phase of the budget climbed steadily, but as Figure 10.1 shows, in 1975 its increases became more steep with each passing year.

The biggest expense category in the budget of a major university is faculty salaries, and this item was always the most important one to Parks. He repeatedly said that faculty salaries were his first budget priority. Willard Boyd, Emeritus President of the University of Iowa, said that on this score the presidents of the three state universities presented a solid front: "Faculty salaries were always Dr. Parks's first order of priority. That also was mine, and it likewise was true for Dr. Maucker at the University of Northern Iowa."[8]

TABLE 10.2. Sources of Iowa State University income, 1985–1986

	General university	*Extension and research*	*Total budget*
State appropriations	$101,988,514	$22,816,875	$124,805,389
Comparable worth	547,000	165,043	712,043
Federal funds	50,000	11,191,416	11,241,416
Student fees	46,777,000		46,777,000
Other income	3,601,000		3,601,000
Sales and services	1,150,000	144,000	1,294,000
Total general operations	$154,113,514	$34,317,334	$188,430,848
Restricted program operations			
Contracts and gifts for special purposes			36,348,631
Auxiliary enterprises			113,498,601
TOTAL INCOME			$338,278,080

Source: ISU Financial Report, June 30, 1986, Iowa State University Archives, Parks Library.

Parks had the philosophy that ISU had to meet the competition from the best universities in the Midwest. Salary levels in lesser schools were irrelevant, so he backed up his arguments with data on salaries at Indiana, Purdue, Illinois, Minnesota, Michigan, Michigan State, and the University of Iowa. His perseverance toward salary improvement for faculty and staff laid the foundation for Iowa State's successful expansion.

At teaching and research universities such as Iowa State, addi-

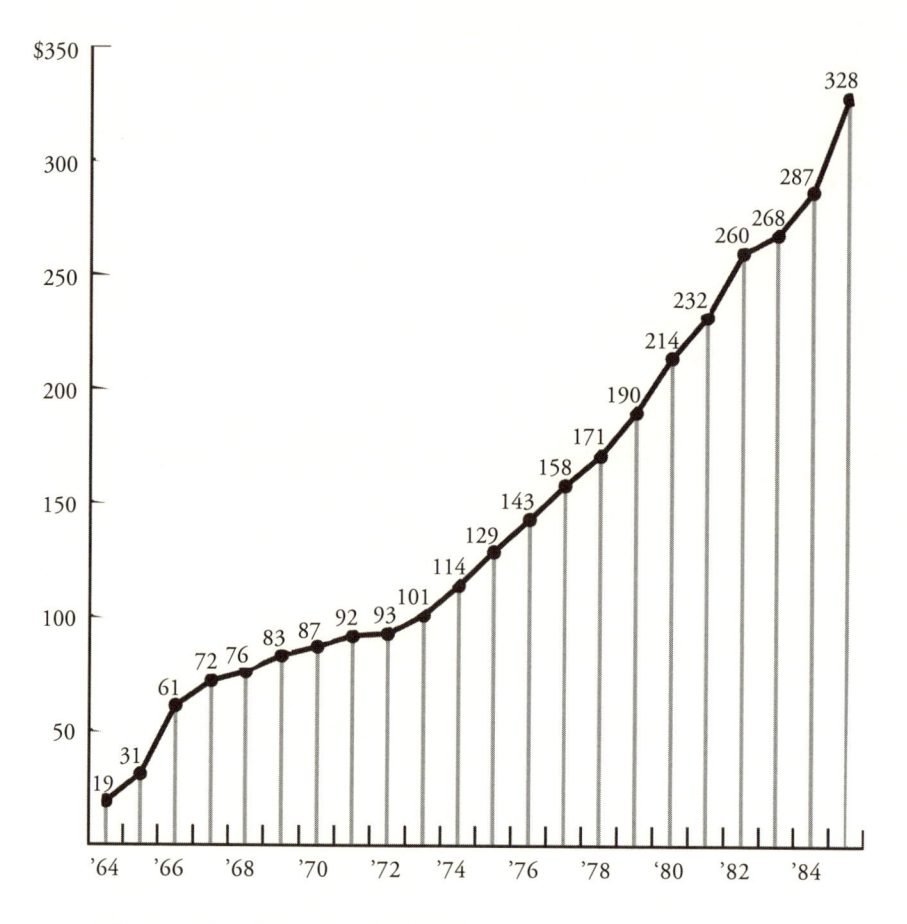

FIG. 10.1. Total operating budgets for Iowa State University, 1964–1985 (rounded to nearest million). *Data from Financial Reports for 1965–1986, Iowa State University Archives, Parks Library*

tional faculty were hired because some individuals were paid from federal grants, but total funds available for salaries were never adequate in the judgment of Parks and his colleagues. Graduate students and adjunct faculty members increasingly shouldered the teaching load, but competition among universities for teachers grew ever-more keen. If it were to compete, ISU had to recruit and keep the best teachers it could muster in order to meet a demand by students for more course choices and more access to professors.

The State of Iowa assumed an ever-larger share of the university's expenses, contributing 29.65 percent in 1965 as compared with over 36.4 percent in 1985. In that span of years, the percentage received from student fees went up from 7.76 percent to 10.7 percent. The tidal wave of students coming to ISU buttressed Parks's arguments for more funds, and each year he put more and more dollars into the instruction category. The first budget submitted under his name showed $11.9 million for instructional purposes, and his last one requested $79.4 million (Fig. 10.2).

Even though the dollar amounts for a teacher's salary went up dramatically during Parks's tenure, the percentage of the school's revenue that went directly into instruction remained about the same. In 1965, for example, 60.72 percent of the expenditures was spent for salaries, and twenty years later (1985) that category was 61.4 percent. In Figures 10.3 and 10.4, incomes and expenditures are presented for each of these years.

The growth in faculty salaries may be demonstrated in part by the median incomes for each of the four major academic ranks: professor, associate professor, assistant professor, and instructor (Fig. 10.5). One must be cautious in examining data of this sort, however, because there are numerous variables such as differences in levels of expertise within a department; what constitutes the pay period, that is, twelve months (A basis) or nine months (B basis); higher costs for graduate instruction; and personnel changes due to retirement or resignations. Also, beginning in the 1980s, the university began making many adjunct appointments, and since such appointments did not lead to tenure, these salaries tended to be less than average and skewed the data.

Nevertheless, we can better understand the incremental increases in earnings of teachers at Iowa State by looking at an individual department. The English department, for example, had the largest number of faculty members. The year Parks accepted the presidency, the department's median salary for each academic rank was professor—$14,700, associate professor—$11,000, assistant profes-

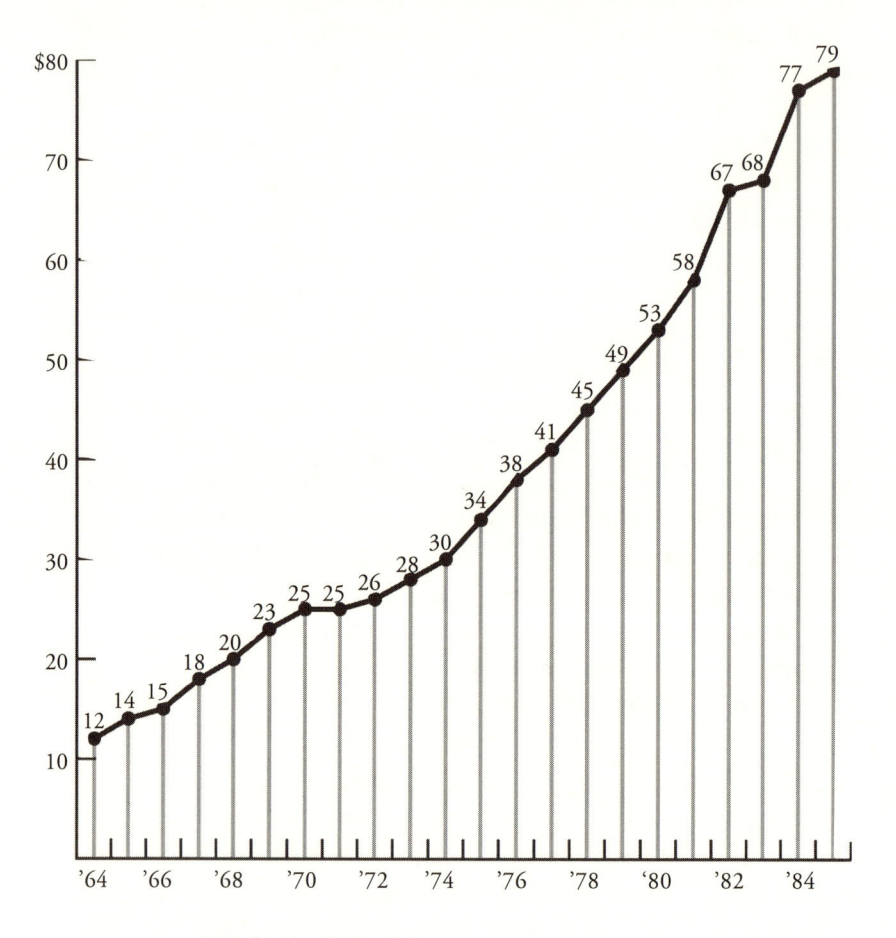

FIG. 10.2. ISU funds allocated for instruction, 1964–1985 (rounded to nearest million). *Data from Financial Reports for 1965–1986, Iowa State University Archives, Parks Library*

BUILDING AND FUNDING, 1965–1986 241

sor—$7800, and instructor—$6650. These dollar figures would almost treble in the next twenty-one years.

Linked with salary increases was the vital matter of providing physical resources: classrooms, laboratories, and equipment. The outdated library was one of his highest priorities, and Parks was adamant in insisting that if ISU was to fulfil its true purpose, it

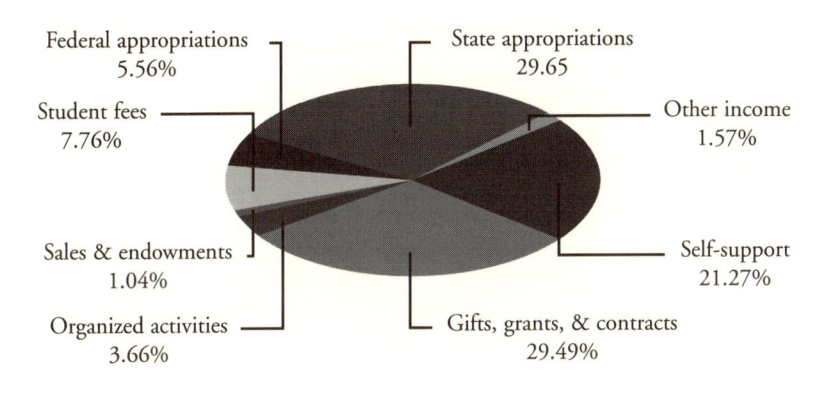

Federal appropriations 5.56%
Student fees 7.76%
Sales & endowments 1.04%
Organized activities 3.66%
State appropriations 29.65
Other income 1.57%
Self-support 21.27%
Gifts, grants, & contracts 29.49%

SOURCES

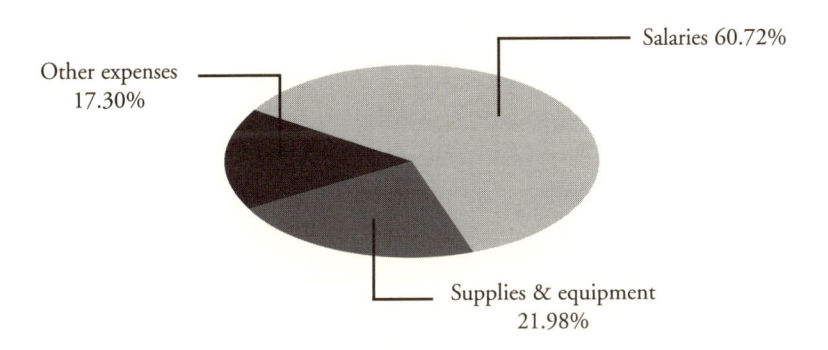

Other expenses 17.30%
Salaries 60.72%
Supplies & equipment 21.98%

EXPENDITURES

FIG. 10.3. Allocation of the ISU dollar, 1965. *Data from Financial Report for 1965, Iowa State University Archives, Parks Library*

must have a library equal to those at established universities in other parts of the country.

The building program initiated by President Hilton accelerated beyond all predictions in the years President Parks led Iowa State. Alumni who came back to visit Iowa State after an absence of a few years nearly always expressed amazement at the number and size of new buildings on campus.

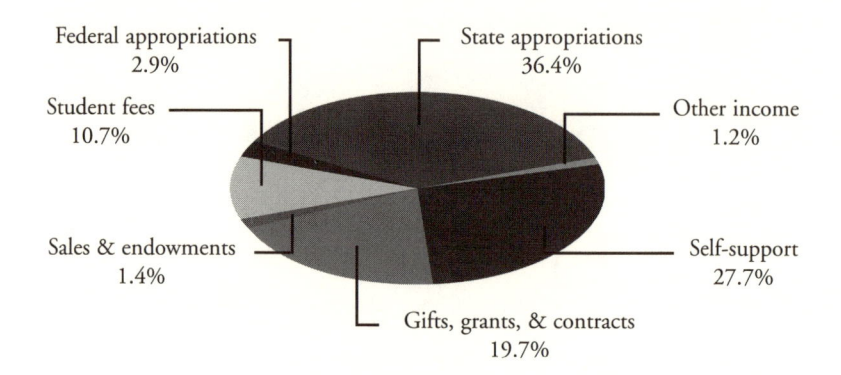

SOURCES

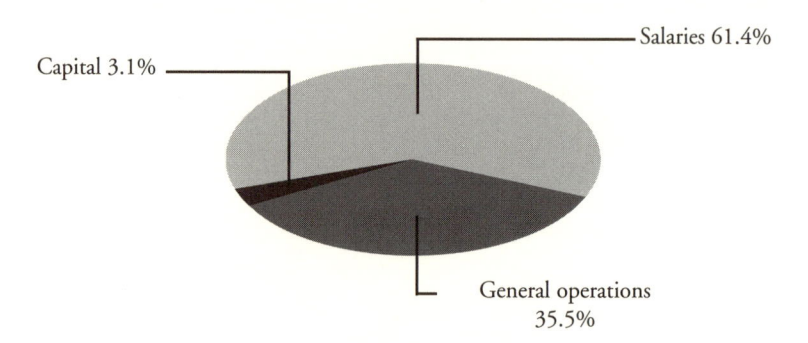

- Federal appropriations 2.9%
- State appropriations 36.4%
- Student fees 10.7%
- Other income 1.2%
- Sales & endowments 1.4%
- Self-support 27.7%
- Gifts, grants, & contracts 19.7%

EXPENDITURES

- Capital 3.1%
- Salaries 61.4%
- General operations 35.5%

FIG. 10.4. Allocation of the ISU dollar, 1985. *Data from Financial Report for 1985, Iowa State University Archives, Parks Library*

BUILDING AND FUNDING, 1965–1986   243

Several buildings conceived during Hilton's administration were completed during Parks's first year as the university's president. At the beginning of the fall quarter in 1965, for instance, a contingent of three hundred men moved into the initial complex of the Towers, a men's new dormitory on Storm Street, six blocks south of central campus. Construction of the high-rise dormitory had been delayed because of a workers' strike, and it would be another three months before a second group of three hundred students could move into the finished building.

In the same year, married students moved into the first one hundred units of University Village, residences that had been constructed north of the Chicago and Northwestern tracks and east of Stange Road. Construction of a four-lane bridge over Squaw Creek on Stange Road also was completed as was a sizable addition to the northeast side of the Memorial Union.

An impressive ground-breaking ceremony was held on the morning of October 30 as part of that year's Homecoming celebration

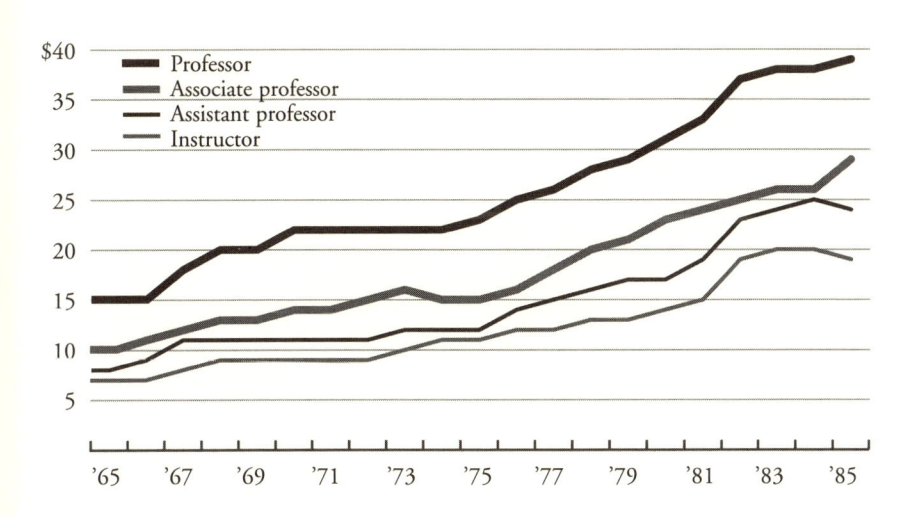

FIG. 10.5. Growth in faculty salaries, 1965–1985 (in thousands of dollars). *Data from Iowa State University Budgets, 1964–1986, Iowa State University Archives, Parks Library*

when Mrs. C. Y. Stephens, whose late husband had served as chairman of the Iowa State Center and had made the first major contribution, grasped a silver shovel and turned the first dirt.

Meanwhile, the new administrative team under the leadership of Robert Parks was bombarding the Board of Regents with askings for new buildings. Accordingly, the board approved and let contracts for construction of a plant sciences building, another women's residence hall, renovation of the third floor of the chemistry building, and a parking ramp at the Memorial Union, and the board approved a project budget for remodeling Building 3 of the Veterinary Medical Research Institute for a microbiological laboratory.

Conditions at the state's three institutions of higher learning would be extremely crowded, and no school ever had a surplus of buildings, yet some observers believed that Iowa had parochial attitudes that at times worked to advantage for its separate institutions. For example, Wayne Moore said that an unwritten political rule seemed to exist in the legislature requiring that when one state university got a building, the other two did as well. This occurred even if most of the new construction needs existed on only one or two of the campuses.[9]

John W. Pace was appointed assistant director of admissions and records in the fall of 1965 and for the next twenty-four years was responsible for compiling data on university buildings, spaces, and schedules. Pace's meticulous records show that under the aegis of Robert Parks more than 120 separate buildings or renovations were recommended to the regents and subsequently approved and constructed. Constructions ranged from buildings that cost millions of dollars and were as large as the 166,256-square-foot Bessey Hall, the 132,247-square-foot Carver Hall, the 447,416-square-foot Veterinary Medicine Central Building, or the 153,790-square-foot College of Design to smaller buildings such as sheep barns, pump houses, and sheds for storage of university-owned cars.[10]

Iowa's farm crisis that began in the late 1970s and continued well into the early 1980s shook the state to its roots. Newer farmers who had started up in the heady days of farm prosperity during the

1960s or early 1970s were the first casualties when boom turned to bust. Within the space of ten years, the number of Iowa farms dropped by more than 10 percent. Farmers were pushed off their land; mortgage holders were driven to the edge of bankruptcy, and Main Street businesses were plowed under.

The downturn cut deeply into the state's economy and reverberated throughout the state's house and senate chambers. Legislators, many of whom were victims of the debacle, were reluctant to spend money on buildings for the future; instead, available funds had to go into current operations to help university administrators retain the best teachers, who frequently were tempted to switch to more remunerative pursuits.

Those lean years were reflected in budgets at Iowa State, where hopes for new buildings had to be put on hold. For example, in 1973 the only construction was an addition to the General Services Building; the following year showed the nadir of frugality when only a golf maintenance shed and a storage building could be built. Even when odds for approval were against him, however, Parks kept pressing regents and legislators for buildings he knew were needed, and the campus showed indisputable evidence of his persuasions. Pace, the most knowledgeable person about space and schedules at ISU estimated that "74% of all the structures in active use on campus in 1986 were built after 1961 and almost entirely during the Parks administration. Moreover, anything that went up within the following five years was likely to have been planned and funded by President Parks."[11]

One of Parks's related challenges in the presidency was to bring more of the fine arts into the university. It was a challenge because it meant persuading the faculty, regents, and legislature that new academic programs were necessary, more faculty with backgrounds in the liberal arts had to be hired, and, of course, new physical facilities would have to be built. If such goals were to be realized, funds allocated to them would compete with those needed for scientific and technical training—traditional areas in which the school had earned its standing.

Despite snide references to Iowa State as being bereft of culture, the campus could boast of certain original artworks, particularly in painting and sculpture. Under the inspiration and effort of President Raymond Hughes, a smidgen of progress even during the lowest point of the Great Depression had been accomplished. Hughes had succeeded in bringing scattered samplings of the visual arts to the school, and with the strengthening of the nation's economy, in September of 1935 he could report a total acquisition of 271 pictures and prints, including 17 originals by Iowa artists. Grant Wood, Iowa's foremost contemporary artist at the time, had been commissioned to paint large impressive murals on the walls of the entrance hall and stairway to the library.[12]

President Hughes also hired the school's first artist-in-residence, Christian Petersen. The Danish-born sculptor was paid a token annual salary; actually, his monthly pay for both teaching and sculpting was approximately $150—less than the salary of the most unskilled laborer on campus. Nevertheless, Petersen created hundreds of works of art during his years at Iowa State, his most well-known ones undoubtedly are two that are installed on opposite sides of the stairway in the Parks Library and the equally famous *Gentle Doctor*.

The two life-sized, fired-clay statues that grace the library are of a young man and a young woman; each is seated and casting a furtive look at the other, instead of reading the book each holds. Petersen's whimsy in this work would please thousands of students and visitors for generations to come.

Petersen's second work that became notable is his *Gentle Doctor*—another life-sized statue made in terra cotta, sculpting material both beautiful and inexpensive. Petersen used it after salvaging and grinding old firebrick from a razed heating plant on campus and then combining the substance with native Iowa clay. This work shows a tall doctor cradling a hurt puppy and is an artistic creation that would be reproduced in murals and pictures the world over as a symbol of veterinary medicine.[13]

The opening of C. Y. Stephens Auditorium—a building first conceived by President James Hilton, Parks's immediate predecessor—was of enormous importance in bringing more performing arts to Iowa State. First approval for what eventually would be called the Iowa State Center was given by the Board of Regents for one of Hilton's last and most significant proposals.[14]

When Stephens Auditorium opened as the first unit of this remarkable concept for a cultural center, it immediately became a magnet, attracting performing artists otherwise not seen in Iowa or perhaps anywhere in the Midwest. It was Hilton's inspiration, but it was up to his successor to raise enough money to complete the project. Parks was four years into his own presidency before Hilton's hope would become a reality.

The new auditorium faced competition from facilities in cities like New York and Los Angeles, but now students and visitors could enjoy the performance of a world-famous musician or a Broadway touring company. Orchestras such as the Chicago Symphony and the London Philharmonic and musicians such as Andres Segovia and Itzhak Perlman displayed their talents in the acoustically superior auditorium. Performers were delighted to appear on-stage in Stephens because the building featured a masterful blend of beauty and theatrical function.

All of the buildings constituting the Iowa State Center—Stephens Auditorium, James H. Hilton Coliseum, the Scheman Continuing Education Building, and Fisher Theater—were built under the aegis and through the money-raising talents of President Parks.

Parks was an eminently practical administrator with enough of the scientific method in his work habits to insist on facts and results. In high school and later in his college training, he had not participated in any extracurricular activities that involved the fine arts of music, painting, dance, or drama. Nor did he play any musical instrument, but he enjoyed listening to a few favorite classical composers, particularly when he was in his study or alone at home. His voracious reading had acquainted him with the lives of some of those composers as well as artists like van Gogh, Rembrandt, da Vinci, and Titian. Although he and Ellen might enjoy an evening watching dance performances at Iowa State, dance as an art form still held many mysteries for him. There is no record that he ever appeared on stage in a dramatic production or aspired to do so; however, he and his wife seldom missed a performance of the Iowa State Players under the direction of the imaginative and tireless Frank Brandt, Iowa State's "Mr. Theatre."

Parks became very sensitive to charges that Iowa State was a "cow college" even though in earlier years he had used the sobriquet himself. He came to resent the charge because it conjured up an image entirely out of place in his vision of a true university.

Other than rhetorical skills, there was nothing in his background that showed talent in any of the arts, but he developed genuine appreciation for them, and the higher he rose in administrative positions, the more he saw how the arts added perspective to his vision for the university. He committed himself, therefore, to bringing more drama, painting, sculpture, dance, and music, including symphonies and opera, to the school where in 1948—seventeen years before he became its president—he had cast his lot.

Despite the dearth of construction during the economic crisis in rural America, Ross Hall was completed in 1973. President Parks took justifiable pride in the classroom building named in honor of the senior professor in the department he had joined when he first came to Iowa State College. Years later, Parks commented on how the name happened to be selected:

> The person I remember with great affection was Earle Ross. He was the best scholar in the department and took an interest in us younger fellows. One of the real satisfactions I got in being president was that I was able to pull whatever strings had to be pulled and to name that building for Earle Ross and to do it just before he died. I was able to tell him on the telephone that the building was going to be named after him.[15]

It was fitting that the last major construction project on which Robert Parks stamped his presidential approval was an addition to the library. By 1986—the year in which he retired—the university library had grown from its sparse holdings twenty-one years earlier to more than two million volumes. According to George Christensen, during the long time they served together, Parks repeatedly said that "a library is the very heart of a university." With that conviction, it is understandable that while in the presidency he never turned down a request for enlarging or improving the library or its facilities.[16]

CHAPTER 11

W. Robert Parks: A Reckoning

The final test of a leader is that he leaves behind him ... the conviction and the will to carry on.

Walter Lippmann

Every great university is more than "the lengthened shadow of one man," and thousands of men and women have contributed to Iowa State's past. What niche, therefore, should we accord to W. Robert Parks in the institution's history?

Before attempting to answer the question, we will do well to remember that no other position is quite comparable to that of being president of a major university. College or university presidents (the terms can be used interchangeably) simply do not conform to any single stereotype. As leader of an academic community, a university president belongs in part to many different groups and yet cannot be a full-fledged member of any one of them. He or she lives in isolation and loneliness, apart from coworkers, friends, and former colleagues.

Today, there are approximately 3200 accredited senior colleges and universities in the United States, and a person chosen to lead one of them serves several constituencies—students, faculty, regents or similar governing boards, as well as the citizenry at large. These constituencies often have conflicting interests, so the institution's president treads a narrow path, always under unrelenting pressures of time and crisis. Small wonder, therefore, that the average tenure of a university president is less than seven years.

Clark Kerr, president of the University of California from 1958 until 1967, described the roles a modern university president must play:

> These multiple-constituency leaders are politicians who also administer, administrators who also preach, preachers who also must balance accounts, accountants of finance who must simultaneously balance the books of personal relations, human affairs accountants who must survive today and tomorrow, planners of the future whose own careers have an uncertain future. They are the glue that holds their communities together, the grease that reduces friction among the moving parts, and the steering mechanism that guides any forward motion.[1]

There has not been another time in our nation's past when American colleges faced problems of the sort encountered in the 1960s and 1970s. Campuses across the country were rocked by angry protests over Vietnam and civil rights. There were violent riots that closed down university classrooms and offices, set fires to administration buildings, and in some instances necessitated calling out the National Guard to maintain order and protect public property. University presidents, many of them good, capable, and tolerant people, were harassed and driven out of their offices.

Yet this was precisely the period when Robert Parks was establishing his reputation. Observers of ISU's history agree that his political skills, good judgment, and innate character had a great deal to do with enabling the institution to escape the riots and violence that erupted at such universities as Columbia, California, Wisconsin, Maryland, Michigan, and Kent State.

The log of Iowa State, however, reveals that Parks did much more than keep the ship afloat during troubled times and difficult passages. A university president always risks having too many rules, some of which may be entirely unenforceable, or not enough that clearly and specifically prohibit certain actions. In this regard, the president is forever sailing the straits between Scylla and Charybdis.

On numerous occasions Parks's course would be through troubled waters and into the face of gales from the past, yet his twenty-one years as captain at Iowa State show that he was able to navigate between the rocks and the whirlpool time after time with nothing worse than a few scratches or a small dent well above the waterline.

Under Parks's twenty-one-year guidance the university's enrollment doubled, the staff grew by a third, and three new colleges were created. Extension administration was reorganized and was providing research-based information to Iowans in every part of the state as well as in numerous cooperative programs with overseas agencies. At home, extension programs were enlarged so that they addressed topics such as community development, agricultural profitability, environmental concerns, management of natural resources, nutrition, health, and family development.

A successful university president grows while on the job, and Robert Parks was no exception. He came into office with all the qualifications one could expect from a fledgling president. After all, no one can prepare for a university presidency in the way a dentist or a lawyer can train by several years of practice to extract a tooth or build a legal case. Parks had been a graduate instructor, had held a responsible post in the Department of Agriculture, had been a university professor, and then in succession had become a dean and a vice president. Although by 1965 not a green newcomer to multilayered administration, he had yet to prove himself capable of leading the university.

It was not his nature to rule by virtue of authority alone; he wanted people to sit down together first to try to reach a consensus. He had seen the approach used successfully by administrators he admired, one of whom was Clarence Dykstra. Dykstra was president of the University of Wisconsin while Robert Parks and Ellen Sorge were graduate students there, and one evening he met with a small group of students. Neither Robert nor Ellen ever forgot thoughts Dykstra had expressed at that evening meeting. Robert Parks recalled:

I was a lowly graduate student at Wisconsin in political science, and Clarence Dykstra had been experienced in a field where political science people were much needed—that is, in local governments and city managers.

So we invited Dykstra over to speak to us, and we graduate students asked him, "What do you see is the difference between being a city manager and being president of a large university?"

And this was his answer, which fits my view just as well as it did his. He said, "As a city manager you order, and you make other people do things, get out there, put in a new water line, a different crosswalk, fix that sanitary sewer or whatever it is that isn't working, but in a university you work for your colleagues."

So that was always my philosophy. I saw myself only as first among peers.[2]

As contrasted with industrial corporations where decisions made by upper-level managers or chief executive officers are passed down to workers, Parks viewed university administration as quite different. Within industrial corporations decisions can be made with slight or no input from workers, but Parks said that a university faculty simply could not be treated in that way. Upon occasion he would compare a university to a large medical center, whose top administrator would never presume to tell a doctor how to treat a patient but would instead be concerned with efficient organization, providing adequate facilities, and financial matters. Like the superintendent of a medical center, a university president, he maintained, presides over professional personnel.

Looking back, he gave his own modest appraisal,

I can't think of very many things that were really worthwhile that I did all by myself. It would have been impossible. There were always other people involved in this administration business, and I also made the statement—which I still subscribe to—that in order for a university to be good, excellent, or even adequate you have to have good people throughout the organization, people who will do their jobs if there were no president at all. So I don't consider a president really that fundamental to everything within a university.[3]

Parks's method centered on getting people to sit down together to work out common problems. Nothing could illustrate that preference better than his refusal to take hasty actions during the tumultuous protests over Vietnam. He related a minor controversy at Iowa State during those tense times:

> Another incident that was sort of amusing to me during this trying period of student protests occurred in the year that Jerry Schnoor was president of the student body. There was a big hassle one morning when the peaceniks weren't going to let people raise the flag. And the ROTC boys were equally determined to raise it. So Jerry, looking for peace, talked leaders of each group into coming to my office. And I suggested a solution which was pretty crazy.
> I said, "Raise the flag, but do it upside down."
> That was a compromise which each group agreed to, and they actually did it for that day. I never heard any more about it, but Jerry said they really did it. I'll always say that I don't know it was the best way because it violated every rule I know about flag etiquette, but on that day it lessened tensions.[4]

The contretemps might seem trivial, but it was another example of Parks's preference for compromise. Moreover, whenever feasible he strove to bring students into the decision-making process.

The ability of a university president to win and retain the confidence of students can be a major factor in determining how long he or she will stay in office. This was particularly true in the latter half of the twentieth century because of the large numbers of students enrolled and the wide range of backgrounds from which they were drawn. Whether or not campus unrest develops is often beyond prediction because it may arise from local controversies, passions over athletics, social or political dissatisfaction in the state or nation at large, or perhaps even an excess of youthful exuberance. The only constant is that if a major disturbance breaks out, the president of the institution will be held responsible.

Among Parks's strengths as an administrator were his understanding of human motivations and his skill in analyzing problems. He attacked controversies first by insisting upon knowing the facts of the situation. Then before making a decision he would search out possibilities for common ground. This talent for finding compromise carried over even after his retirement from the presidency.

In retirement he was continually called upon for an endless variety of enterprises, local, state, and national: heading up community chest drives, Christmas Seals, veterans' fund drives, Boy or Girl Scouts, chambers of commerce, natural resource conservation, educational societies, agricultural groups, and municipal improvements. A prime example of the last-named category occurred in 1986—the very year he retired.

At that time citizens of Ames were embroiled in an argument of several years' standing. Municipal authorities and commercial businesses had long debated the best methods of controlling traffic on the narrow downtown main streets. One plan, developed at considerable expense, involved razing the old city hall and turning several blocks surrounding it into a pedestrian shopping mall. The Ames Chamber of Commerce endorsed the proposal that in effect meant closing to vehicular traffic the north half of the block facing on Fifth Street between Douglas and Kellogg avenues. The plan also called for constructing a new hotel, city hall, civic center, and business block.

Proponents of the plan trumpeted that it would be the greatest improvement that had ever been attempted in the city, but opponents were equally vehement in arguing that the plan was too costly, some businesses would have to relocate, and several existing buildings that were in good condition would have to be destroyed. Among the buildings to be razed was the former high school, later a junior high, which was only a block and half away from the old city hall. Finally, the issue was put to a public referendum and was defeated amidst bitter controversy.[5]

Shortly after the public vote, Paul Goodland, Mayor of Ames, telephoned Parks, saying, "I hear you're out of a job and looking for work." Goodland persuaded the emeritus president to come out of retirement long enough to take on the chairmanship of a task force charged with responsibility for recommending what should be the next step.

Parks helped select responsible civic leaders for the committee, and for the next several months the group under his leadership analyzed the problems. When the task force's final recommendations came out, they were clearly stated: (1) abandon the concept of a downtown mall closed to vehicular traffic, (2) convert the old city hall into offices for youth and shelter activities, and (3) most important, refurbish the structurally sound old high school so that it could become a spacious and useable new city hall.

The recommendations were so simple and so far less costly that they seemed to please nearly everyone; even die-hard critics were placated when the downtown area remained open and refurbishings of the former school proved so attractive. Again, Parks had helped release tensions and avoid prolonged controversy.

Parks's desire for efficient organization became legendary; some thought it amounted almost to a passion. His zeal for strong organization was apparent at the outset of his presidency when as one of his first administrative actions he decided to restructure the disparate system of cooperative extension.

Zeal for better organization also helps explain many academic changes he led within the university. He pushed hard to get the B.A. approved and advocated new curricula and graduate programs, which he insisted on having in place before he would seek degrees, particularly graduate ones, or ask for certification from national accrediting associations. His strong endorsement won regential approval for three new colleges, and behind all such moves was his conviction that it was necessary to unite disciplines of sciences with those of the humanities.

There also was the phenomenal growth in physical facilities: completion of the ISU Cultural Center, modern facilities for research and training in the College of Veterinary Medicine, new classroom and office buildings, improvement for athletics facilities, and gigantic upgrading of the library. The last named was always highest on his priority list. Former vice president George Christensen said, "I don't recall that we ever cut back on library allocations even at a time when other extremely important programs had to be sliced."[6]

Whenever accomplishments were praised, Parks was quick to give credit to colleagues, and indeed he did have a knack for picking able subordinates—notably Christensen, Moore, and Hamilton. In examining the history of Iowa State University during the years Parks was president, one is reminded of Machiavelli's dictum:

> The first impression that one gets of a ruler and of his brains is from seeing the men that he has about him. When they are competent and faithful one can always consider him wise, as he has been able to recognize their ability and keep them faithful. But when they are the reverse, one can always form an unfavorable opinion of him, because the first mistake that he makes is in making this choice.[7]

Knowing that the quality of a university rests upon the merits of its personnel, Parks gave great attention to selecting the right persons for administrative positions. When asked about which "advisors" he relied upon most heavily throughout his tenure, Parks responded:

> Well, I guess I don't particularly go for the term "advisor." Mine was more of a collegial administration. "Advisor" was too formal for what we were trying to do. I wasn't trying to depend upon advisors, but I worked very closely with people you'd expect me to work with. Those were the vice presidents—Carl Hamilton had a good view of public relations; George Christensen—always a rock, with good solid understanding and practical sense. And there was Bill Layton because of his position as vice president for student affairs. Art Sandeen, Dean of Students, was an excellent person in that position, and there were people on the faculty whom you could always depend on. So we were never alone in what we were trying to do.
>
> Another example was Shorty Schilletter in the residence halls,

who was with me for a few years. And we had many good people in admissions and registrations who were always dependable and understanding—people like Dean of Admissions Art Gowan, who was a real brick, as was his successor, Fred Schlunz.[8]

Beyond the levels of administration, when it came to appointing or promoting faculty members, Parks was not so directly involved. Although not obliged to follow every recommendation from a departmental chairperson or dean, he usually tried to do so. Only in rare instances would he turn down a recommended candidate in favor of someone else. Usually, he asked for two or three persons listed in no order or rank. He had served on enough committees to realize that there is a tendency for such groups to try for a unanimous opinion or to submit a majority report without detailing a minority point of view that might be important. He believed it was his responsibility to appoint only candidates to the faculty who gave every indication of being contributing members in a community of scholars charged with a high degree of responsibility for self-governance and for maintaining academic standards in such matters as student relations, admission requirements, courses, curricula, and graduation requirements.

In an endeavor as large as Iowa State, there were instances, of course, when an individual did not live up to what was expected of him or her. If such lack of performance was significant enough, Christensen, under Parks's direction, might talk with the person privately. If it was a senior professor, Parks himself met with the individual behind closed doors, but such instances were rare. Parks made it a point never to embarrass anyone publicly. Usually the message of dissatisfaction could be transmitted by payroll means. There were cases when no salary increases were given to nonperforming individuals even when the average increase for the year was as high as 10 percent.

Christensen said that he never saw Parks lose his temper, although on occasion he might be visibly upset. Profanity was a rarity; once in a while in private consultation with one or two close colleagues Parks might slip in a mild expletive like "damn" or "hell."

Actually, he paid careful attention to language and said that to him habitual profanity indicated paucity in a person's vocabulary.

His final commencement speech at ISU was given in the spring of 1986 and appropriately enough was entitled "A 'New Humanism' Revisited." In it he challenged the school's newest alumni not to let difficult economic times and pressures from outside the university "siphon off those resources so needed by the total university into narrow, single-purpose programs." Again, it was a talk into which he put great effort, and he linked it with the other given twenty-one years earlier.

> The two speeches—"New Humanism" and "New Humanism Revisited," my convocation talk in 1986—were very, very important to me. They really are the bookends of my philosophy and my vision of what Iowa State should become.[9]

Careful reading of these two addresses reveals ideas and attitudes that Parks had been developing through more than fifty years of life in academe—from his days as a student at Berea College through his presidency of Iowa State. The thoughts were not just abstract generalities but rather the harvest of his own homestead, grown from seed planted by his education-minded parents, nurtured by extensive study, and pruned through experience, including occasional sparrings with colleagues or resistant students.

As years passed he had become ever more convinced that there was a dangerous lag between scientific knowledge and society's ability to use it. He could cite numerous examples, one of which occurred eleven years after he left office. In 1997, for the first time, British researchers successfully cloned an adult mammal. The scientists slipped genes from a six-year-old ewe into unfertilized eggs, then impregnated those eggs into other sheep. The result: a lamb that was a genetic copy of the ewe. It was an astonishing scientific landmark that raised the unsettling possibility of making copies of humans.

Parks, well into retirement years, related the new threat to what he had talked about in his "bookend" speeches:

> This is a perfect example of what I call the cultural lag—the lag between invention and scientific advance—which comes at such frightening speed—and society's ability to handle it. It's something I have no clue as to how you do it, but I think at least with the education of our students these days we should try to integrate science with the human and the humane. I don't think science can be neutral or unconcerned; scientific education should bring along with it some knowledge of the social impact which it has.[10]

There were numerous other examples that illustrated Parks's concern about technology getting ahead of humanity's capacity to deal with its findings. By the time the twentieth century was approaching its end, scientists had created new terrors in biological warfare, had developed nuclear power capable of wiping out whole civilizations, and had brought in vitro fertilization to a level where it seemed that there might be the possibility of offering women the ability to freeze their ova, thus lengthening their reproductive years. The prospect of storing unfertilized human ova for later use transcended time and raised the specter of babies born of mothers long deceased. Each new development seemed to bolster Parks's call for better integration of ethical judgments and technology.

Robert Parks served his final day as president of Iowa State University on June 30, 1986. The next morning the man who had been the institution's prime administrator longer than any of ten predecessors said farewell to his office and began moving personal files and books from Beardshear Hall to a small office set aside for him and Ellen—his scholar wife—in the building that bears their names: the William Robert Parks and Ellen Sorge Parks Library. Both stated that of all resolutions, testimonials, and tributes given them, none could be more fitting than naming the "heart of the university" in their honor.

Within a few days after official retirement, Robert and Ellen Parks moved from the Knoll to a home they purchased two miles south of central campus. The home had a spacious garden area where he could enjoy one of his favorite pastimes—gardening. It was an activity his neighbors appreciated, too, for he usually kept many of them supplied with fresh tomatoes, sweet corn, and other vegetables most of the summer. He also spent leisure hours in the office reserved for him in the library, where he read mostly historical or biographical works. In that study office and at home, he and Ellen pursued literary interests they had put aside for two decades in favor of the more pressing duties of the president and first lady.

For nearly thirteen years, Robert and Ellen enjoyed their retirement, and then on May 9, 1999, the marriage that had lasted fifty-nine years ended when Ellen, suffering from pneumonia and related disorders, passed away quietly at home.

Well before Ellen's death, however, the couple became grandparents and behaved accordingly. Robert showed the deep affection for his grandchildren that had characterized the home he and Ellen had established as well as the strong ties his own parents had maintained. He liked to read aloud to the younger grandchildren, choosing stories like *The Grinch Who Stole Christmas*, *Winnie the Pooh*, and Dickens' *Christmas Carol*.

At a time when he was finishing his own doctorate at Harvard University, one grandson, Robert Parks Van Houweling, remembered his grandfather's camaraderie with young people:

> One summer when I was quite young, he had me and one or two of my cousins in the car with him. We were going to Cape Cod for some vacation time, and like all kids, we got antsy in the car. There were a lot of roses climbing on trellises in yards of cottages we passed, and my grandfather began singing "Rambling Rose" just to keep our minds occupied, I guess. He taught us the words, and pretty soon we all joined in; we must have tried to sing that song for miles—all the way to the cottage.[11]

Scholars seldom put university administration into the category of either science or art, yet it is an endeavor that demands combining some of the best skills necessary in each. By the very nature of the job, a university president has to be its number one problem solver. The person also must possess enough intellectual ability and judgment to understand human behavior in order to work within its capacities and confines.

At the time he retired, Parks was asked by reporters to discuss his years as president of Iowa State. Among his reflections, he said that he hoped people would remember his administration as one which broadened the base of the university. He went further to explain,

> I think the biggest change has been programmatic. We have broadened the base of the university, accomplishing a full flowering of the liberal arts and the fine arts. I think we've come a long way toward the blending of the physical sciences, the social sciences, and the humanities. ... There are new colleges, a tremendous number of new majors and degree programs like the bachelor of arts, master of arts, bachelor of music, bachelor of liberal studies. All of these are new degrees which we didn't have before.[12]

Parks was not alone in making his judgment, for there was near unanimity from all persons acquainted with Iowa State that his greatest single contribution was transforming the institution into a broad-based university aimed toward excellence while science and technology were balanced with the arts.

Willard Boyd, President Emeritus of Iowa University, phrased it well when asked what he considered Parks's accomplishments. Boyd stated:

> First, there was his broadening of the institution. The university that had as much science as ISU needed to have the arts as well in order to have a balance in its educational offering. Therefore, he succeeded in bringing in more liberal arts to achieve that balance at the same time he was helping maintain and even improve the excellent science programs and instruction.
>
> Secondly, there was his commitment to the library over there. On several occasions we talked about books, and both of us agreed that the library is the real heart of a university.[13]

Robert Parks had vision and leadership that helped Iowa State change more in twenty-one years than it had done under ten predecessors in the previous century. Sometimes the progress was distressingly slow, but his goal was a broad university noted for academic excellence, and he would not be deterred. He never wavered from his aim of bringing together the disciplines in the sciences, in technology, and in the humanities in a common concern for the human and the humane—a concern he believed should be at the core of Iowa State's philosophy of education.

The American credo passed on to Robert Parks by loving parents was that education is the magic process through which betterment of individual life and human society are built. That principle was emphasized in 1986 at the end of his presidency and was substantially the same one with which he began it in 1965. The credo had stood the tests of time, and so had he.

CHRONOLOGY

The Presidency of W. Robert Parks, 1965–1986

1965

1. In December 1964, the Board of Regents announced that W. Robert Parks, Vice President for Academic Affairs, had been selected as the eleventh president of the university, effective July 1, 1965.

2. March 1965, the regents approved appointments of George Christensen as vice president for academic affairs and Carl Hamilton as director of university relations.

3. The animal industries building was named Kildee Hall in honor of Dean Emeritus H. H. Kildee.

4. The graduate dormitory was named Buchanan Hall in honor of Dean Emeritus Robert Buchanan.

5. The regents approved establishment of master of science and doctor of philosophy programs in computer science, effective July 1.

6. Iowa State led the Big Eight Conference in the enrollment of Merit Scholars.

7. All-time high enrollment figures were reached for each quarter: 12,256 for winter, 11,602 for spring, 7906 for summer, and 14,014 for fall.

8. Short course attendance in 1965–1966 was 22,941, a gain of 2349 over the previous year.

9. The Iowa General Assembly passed a bill authorizing the Board of Regents to grant leaves of absence with pay for further study or research to faculty members at the three state collegiate institutions.

10. Ground-breaking ceremonies for the Iowa State Center were held October 30 as a part of the Homecoming celebration.

11. The first one hundred units of University Village were occupied on November 24.

12. Three hundred men moved into the first complex of the Towers, the new men's dormitory on Storm Street.

13. The regents approved construction contracts for the following buildings or renovations: (1) a new plant sciences building, (2) a new women's residence hall to be located north of Lincoln Way and east of Wallace Road, (3) remodeling of the third floor, northwest wing of the chemistry building, (4) construction of a four-lane bridge over Squaw Creek at Stange Road, (5) a Memorial Union parking ramp, and (6) remodeling of a microbiological laboratory at the Veterinary Medical Research Institute.

1966

1. President W. Robert Parks was inaugurated on March 22 on the 108th anniversary of the founding of Iowa State University.

2. Wayne Moore was appointed vice president for business and finance.

3. Extension work at Iowa State was reorganized into a single administrative unit with Marvin Anderson named dean of university extension.

4. Regents approved four advanced degree programs: doctor of philosophy in forestry, master of forestry, master of science in the history of science and technology, and master of science in industrial relations, all effective June 1.

5. Regents accepted a $595,300 grant award for a library addition from Title 1, Higher Education Facilities Act of 1963.

6. ISU became a member of the Universities Research Association—an organization of forty-six leading research institutions.

7. The National Aeronautics and Space Administration (NASA) awarded fifteen more traineeships to Iowa State.

CHRONOLOGY 267

8. Iowa State's Cyclone Computer, one of the first in the nation, was dismantled ten years after the date of its initial construction.

9. The American Council on Education made an assessment of quality in graduate education among 106 institutions. Thirteen out of sixteen eligible departments at ISU attained high ratings. The departments cited were chemistry, entomology, chemical engineering, economics, civil engineering, electrical engineering, mechanical engineering, botany, zoology, physics, biochemistry, bacteriology, and physiology.

10. All-time high enrollment figures were reached: 13,594 in winter quarter, 12,987 in spring, and 15,183 in fall. Record enrollments also were attained in summer school, with 4922 in the first session and 3662 in the second.

11. Nearly 7000 students were enrolled during fall quarter in twenty-two courses utilizing closed television.

12. A policy statement of the Human Relations Committee applying to social fraternities and sororities was approved.

13. A no-hours policy for senior women and women over twenty-one went into effect on February 9.

14. The regents awarded the following contracts: (1) construction of the Iowa State Center theater-auditorium, (2) a steam generator and related equipment in the power plant, (3) enlargement of the football stadium at Clyde Williams Field, (4) construction of a Fire Service Extension Building, (5) improvements of the university parking lots, (6) extension of street lighting on Stange and Bissell roads, (7) remodeling for Building 4 at the Veterinary Medical Research Institute, (8) alteration of the Knoll, home of the university president, and (9) resurfacing of Union Drive.

1967

1. The regents approved establishment of a design center operated by faculty members from three departments: applied art, architecture, and landscape architecture.

2. President Parks authorized combining the Departments of Home Management and Household Equipment into the new Department of Family Environment.

3. The regents approved four new degree programs: bachelor of science in computer science, music, and philosophy, and the master of science degree in English—all beginning in the fall of 1967.

4. Regents approved development of a two-year Technical Institute in Agriculture, effective June 1967. The agriculture program was in addition to existing programs in chemical industries technology, construction technology, engineering, electronics technology, food service management, and mechanical technology.

5. ISU ranked twentieth among the nation's universities in research expenditures.

6. The National Academy of Sciences reported that ISU ranked twenty-fifth in the United States in awarding doctorates in science during 1960–1966.

7. NASA awarded ISU nine three-year doctoral traineeships beginning in the academic year 1967–1968.

8. All-time enrollment figures were reached: 14,641 in winter quarter, 14,047 in spring, and 16,481 in fall. Record enrollments were reached in summer school also, with 5294 in the first session and 4013 in the second session.

9. The Council on Instruction recommended a "pass-fail" system in which students who have earned at least sixty credit hours and who are not on temporary enrollment may take a maximum of two such courses—neither of which can be in the student's major field—in a given quarter.

10. The self-limited residential hours policy for women was extended to sophomore and junior women with the provision that women under twenty-one received parental permission.

11. The Memorial Union opened a forty-car parking ramp.

12. The regents approved contracts for the following: (1) upgrading of parking lots, (2) sale of 240 acres at the research farm near Ankeny to the Area XI School District for a community college, (3) construction of the second unit with a commons at the new women's residence complex, north of Lincoln Way and east of Wallace Road, (4) construction for Carver Hall, classroom and office building, (5) fourth Towers unit and commons at the men's residence complex on Storm Street, (6) the second addition to the library, with a total projected

budget of $2,670,000, (7) construction of two hundred married student housing units at University Village, (8) construction of a computer laboratory with a projected budget of $1,066,975, (9) improvements in the power plant amounting to a total cost of $1,209,273, (10) renovation of women's residence halls amounting to $483,000, and (11) construction of a printing services building for $165,150, renovation of a portion of Friley-Hughes Hall for the sum of $200,000, an addition to the Insectary to cost $192,000, remodeling of the dairy and food industry building with a projected budget of $96,805, and remodeling of the university hospital with a total cost of $278,698.

1968

1. The new College of Education was established on September 1.

2. The Order of the Knoll, a new organization to assist the advancement of the university, was formed. Eighty-one charter members signified their intention of contributing a minimum of $1000 a year for ten years.

3. A special pilot program for seventeen disadvantaged students, primarily black, from Chicago's inner city and Iowa was undertaken during the fall quarter.

4. The Board of Regents adopted a resolution in February relating to disruptive acts at regent institutions.

5. Regents approved the purchase of fifty acres at the site of the new horticulture farm from the ISU Research Foundation.

6. The physics building addition was dedicated in April. The addition, built with $1,461,000 from state appropriations and a $1,106,000 grant from the National Science Foundation, included four undergraduate teaching laboratories as well as fifty-six graduate research laboratories and offices.

7. The Board of Regents approved the following contracts: (1) a two-phase $16 million plan for new veterinary medicine facilities to be located on South Beach Avenue, (2) project budgets totaling $2,234,379 for improvements or additions to the heating plant, (3) a project budget of $544,000 for construction of chilled water distributing mains, (4) construction of a third tower at Larch Hall to cost

$1,434,510, (5) renovation of the chemistry building with a projected cost of $81,318, (6) relocation of the horticulture gardens, (7) construction of the observatory building on a fifty-acre site southwest of Boone to house the physics department's telescope and the electrical engineering department's radio telescope equipment, and (8) relocation and construction of the varsity and freshman baseball diamond on the old horticulture farm south of the campus.

1969

1. The Department of History, Government, and Philosophy was divided into three departments: the Department of History, Department of Political Science, and the Department of Philosophy. In similar action, the Department of English and Speech was divided into two departments. All divisions became effective July 1.

2. All-time high enrollment figures were reached: 17,201 in the winter quarter, 16,417 in spring, and 19,172 in fall. Record enrollments were reached in summer school also, with 6018 in the first session and 4663 for the second.

3. Numerous new majors were authorized by the Board of Regents. New undergraduate majors were anthropology; biology and meteorology; French, German, Russian, and Spanish—which replaced the former foreign language major; and public service and administration in agriculture. The undergraduate major in genetics was dropped, and new graduate majors were offered in both biomedical engineering and immunobiology. The five-year bachelor of architecture was eliminated in favor of a revised curriculum that included a four-year program leading to the bachelor of arts degree, a year of cooperative studies with industry, and a two-year graduate program leading to the degree master of architecture.

4. The Dairy Sales Room was closed, ending over-the-counter sale of cheese.

5. The U.S. Office of Education allocated eighteen new National Defense Education Act graduate fellowships, making a total of 101 NDEA fellowships at ISU.

6. C. Y. Stephens Auditorium was formally inaugurated on September 9 with a series of five concerts by the New York Philharmonic Orchestra under the direction of Seiji Ozawa.

CHRONOLOGY 271

7. The Board of Regents approved naming of the following buildings: (1) the electrical engineering building was named Coover Hall in honor of Mervin S. Coover, Dean Emeritus of Engineering, and (2) the service building was named Snedecor Hall in honor of George W. Snedecor, Professor Emeritus of Statistics.

8. The ISU gymnastics team won its fourth Big Eight Conference title in six years, and the ISU wrestling team won its second national championship in four years at the NCAA tournament.

9. Regents approved actions or contracts for the following changes or new construction: (1) authorizing sale of revenue bonds totaling $1,155,000 for construction and equipping of the new engineering building and the addition to the science building, (2) a project budget of $4,702,100 for a second addition to the science building, (3) a project budget of $3,375,000 for a new engineering building to house the Departments of Civil Engineering and Aerospace Engineering, (4) a project budget of $2,585,000 for an addition to Larch Hall, (5) a project budget of $2,024,000 for an addition to East Hall, (6) $1,120,517 for remodeling and renovation of Birch, Welch, and Roberts Women's Residence Halls, and (7) a project budget of $359,642 for construction of buildings at the new horticulture farm six miles northeast of Ames. Other projects authorized and completed during the year were the Printing and Publications Building, enlargement of the capacity of the electric distribution system, construction of a car pool garage, and constructing a new water supply well.

1970

1. President Parks appointed a multidisciplinary Environmental Council to study and seek solutions to long- and short-range environmental problems.

2. The General Faculty adopted recommendations of the Council on Instruction pertaining to the pass-fail system beginning in fall quarter.

3. The Iowa State Center coliseum was dedicated on June 5 as James H. Hilton Coliseum in honor of President Emeritus Hilton.

4. Carver Hall was dedicated on September 27 in honor of George Washington Carver. The Black Cultural Center, 517 Welch Avenue, was formally dedicated on the same day.

5. The ISU wrestling team won its second straight national championship, and the ISU gymnastics team won its fifth Big Eight Conference title in seven years and its second in a row.

6. The Board of Regents awarded the following contracts: (1) purchase of 7.7 acres of land southeast of the research reactor at a cost of $22,000 to provide a "buffer zone" between the reactor and nearby residences, (2) construction of a third classroom and office building with a project cost of $3,156,000, (3) an addition to the women's physical education building with the total cost expected to be $2,759,422, (4) authorized sale of 230 acres of land in Keokuk County for the sum of $132,250, (5) improvements at the Bilsland Swine Breeding Research Center near Madrid with an estimated budget of $232,000, and (6) facilities at the Animal Reproduction Station, two miles south of Ames, with an expected cost of $104,910.

1971

1. Maurice John, basketball coach at Drake University for thirteen years, was named head basketball coach, succeeding Glen Anderson, who had been head coach since 1959.

2. The College of Home Economics celebrated its one hundredth anniversary, and as part of the ceremonies President Parks spoke on "A Look at the Past, and a Plan for the Future."

3. The Department of Music offered a bachelor of music degree beginning in fall quarter.

4. According to a national report, the ISU Department of Statistics ranked first in the number of Ph.D. degrees granted in probability and statistics during the last three years.

5. The Technical Institute in Agriculture as well as the Technical Institute in Engineering were discontinued because it was felt that the vocational-technical programs were available through other curricula.

6. President Parks established a Special Events Committee, responsible for coordination of musical, lecture, dramatic, dance, and other cultural events, and named Vice President Carl Hamilton as its chairman.

7. All-time enrollment figures were reached: 18,627 in winter quarter, 17,089 for spring, and 19,724 for fall. Summer session enrollment dropped for the first time since 1959.

8. In December, a formal opening of Hilton Coliseum was held prior to the basketball game with the University of Arizona. The fall quarter class that year was the first to graduate in the new Hilton Coliseum.

9. The football team compiled the best record of any ISU football team in modern history (eight wins and three losses) and earned an invitation to its first postseason bowl game—the Sun Bowl in El Paso, Texas.

10. The Philadelphia Orchestra under the direction of Eugene Ormandy gave a series of five concerts in C. Y. Stephens Auditorium.

11. The regents approved the following: (1) sale of $2,445,000 in academic revenue bonds, (2) a general contract for a physical plant and central stores building, a three-station two thousand–foot television tower near Alleman, (3) a general contract for an office building on State Avenue north of the ISU Press warehouse with a project budget of $160,000, and (4) a general contract for a beef research barn with a project budget of $70,472.

1972

1. Earle Bruce became head football coach at ISU, succeeding John Majors, who resigned to assume the position of head football coach at the University of Pittsburgh.

2. The College of Education was certified for full accreditation by the National Council for the Accreditation of Teacher Education.

3. With a grant of $112,303 from the federal Department of Health, Education, and Welfare (HEW), a new Iowa Head Start Training Office operated by the Department of Child Development opened in Richards House on campus.

4. The regents granted permission to award a bachelor of arts degree in applied art, and the residence requirement for the master's degree programs was waived at the request of the graduate faculty.

5. For the first time in more than ten years, the annual enrollment figure dropped; the enrollments were as follows: 18,249 for winter quarter, 17,388 for spring, and 19,206 for fall.

6. Summer orientation programs brought 3473 students and 2551 parents to the campus between June 5 and July 11.

7. Draft beer began being dispensed in the Trophy Tavern of the

Memorial Union after the Iowa legislature lowered the age for adult rights from twenty-one to nineteen years.

8. W. Robert Parks was installed as president of the National Association of State Universities and Land-Grant Colleges on November 15.

9. In sports, ISU's football team, which had compiled a record of 5-6-1, played in the Liberty Bowl at Memphis, ISU wrestlers won medals at the Twentieth Olympics in Munich, West Germany. Dan Gable and Ben Petersen won gold medals, while Chris Taylor was a bronze medalist, and ISU gymnasts placed second in the National Collegiate Athletic Association finals, which were held in Hilton Coliseum.

10. Actions by the regents during the year included (1) authorizing sale of $6,485,000 in building bonds to cover a portion of the cost for new veterinary medicine facilities and certain upgradings of the power plant, (2) awarding a general contract for construction of the first phase of the veterinary medicine facilities (this phase was expected to approach $14.3 million, which included a federal grant of $6.8 million), (3) approving a new two-story addition to the Memorial Union, (4) awarding a contract for a Little Theatre (later named Fisher Theater) at the Iowa State Center, (5) approval of plans for a new continuing education building at the Iowa State Center, and (6) approval of a contract in the amount of $174,000 for five additional units in the married students' housing project.

1973

1. The Alvin Edgar Fund for the Performing Arts was established in honor of Dr. Alvin R. Edgar, emeritus concert director at ISU.

2. Two ISU scientists were recipients of the Award of Merit given by the Iowa Academy of Sciences. Henry Gilman was cited for "outstanding contributions in the field of organic chemistry," and Robert Buchanan was cited for "outstanding contributions in the field of bacteriology."

3. Doctoral programs in aerospace and mechanical engineering were approved by the Board of Regents.

4. At the commencement in May the university awarded degrees to 2263, the largest-ever class of graduates.

CHRONOLOGY 275

5. Project 400, the program of university commitment to minority student recruitment and development, was implemented in August.

6. The millionth paying spectator at the Iowa State Center attended the March 31 concert of the London Symphony Orchestra in James H. Hilton Coliseum.

7. The London Symphony Orchestra presented concerts March 27–April 2, and the Leningrad Philharmonic performed November 8–11.

8. A charter of Phi Beta Kappa, oldest honorary fraternity in the nation, was granted to the College of Sciences and Humanities.

9. A federal grant to assist in renovating the Farm House, a national historic landmark on campus, was received by the university.

10. Classroom Building 3 was officially named Earle D. Ross Hall at a dedication in June, Engineering Building 2 was named in honor of George R. Town, and the chemistry building was renamed Henry Gilman Hall.

11. Ground-breaking for ISU's new stadium was held in October. No tax funds were to be used in construction of the stadium.

12. The Board of Regents took the following actions: (1) approved sale of 187 acres of farmland in Page County at a sale price of $105,635, (2) issued contracts for completion of eleven modular housing units in University Village, (3) approved plans for a student services building to house the Health Service, Counseling Service, and the Dean of Students Office, and (4) approved razing four campus buildings as well as Kildee Cottage, built in 1901.

1974

1. President Parks was elected chairman of the executive committee of the Association of American Universities.

2. Gateway Center, Ltd., a private corporation, announced plans to develop land at the intersection of Elwood Drive and U.S. 30. The land presently was owned by the Alumni Achievement Fund.

3. Fisher Theater, the third unit in the Iowa State Center, was dedicated in January by President Parks. The theater was named for J. W. Fisher of Marshalltown, whose $325,000 contribution provided the impetus for the campaign, which raised $900,000 for construction of the building.

4. The Campanile received a face-lift, which included painting, sheetmetal work, and tuck-pointing of the bricks.

5. The Iowa General Assembly appropriated $6.49 million for construction of the design center at ISU.

6. The Departments of Physical Education for Men and Physical Education for Women were combined into a single department.

7. The Department of Zoology and Entomology was separated into three departments: zoology, entomology, and animal ecology.

8. A no smoking policy was adopted for most areas of the university.

9. The ISU-Nebraska football clash was the last ISU game to be played at Clyde Williams Field, which was scheduled to be retired the next year, when the new stadium south of the Iowa State Center would open.

10. Alumni and friends of ISU contributed a record $1.23 million to the 1974 Alumni Achievement Fund.

11. The Board of Regents took the following actions: (1) approved a budget of $2.8 million for a Meat Laboratory, (2) approved ISU's purchase of 424 acres of farmland in Lucas County, (3) accepted from Jessie V. Coles a gift of 285 acres in Hamilton County, (4) officially renamed the new married housing area north of University Village as Schilletter Village in honor of J. C. Schilletter, Director of Residence from 1946 until 1967, and (5) approved a budget of $110,000 for renovation of the Horticulture Greenhouse, damaged during a hailstorm in June.

1975

1. The fall enrollment of 19,914 students included men and women from every state in the union and from sixty-eight foreign countries.

2. ISU's new football stadium with seating for forty-two thousand fans was opened when the Cyclones played the Air Force Academy's football team on September 20.

3. Also on September 20, the $5.3 million Scheman Continuing Education Building was dedicated.

4. The ISU Library acquired its one millionth book, which was Leonardo da Vinci's Trattato della Pittura, a famous treatise on painting.

5. The slide rule, long a fixture slung on the hip of engineering students, began disappearing in favor of smaller electronic calculators.

6. The Boston Pops Orchestra under the direction of Arthur Fiedler gave concerts in James H. Hilton Coliseum.

7. In the spring quarter ISU set its all-time record enrollment of 21,205 students, of whom 40 percent were women. In 1962–1963, years earlier, just 22 percent were women.

1976

1. According to a national survey, ISU ranked sixth in the nation among all public colleges and universities in total alumni-giving in fiscal 1973–1974.

2. The Brunnier Gallery on the top floor of the Scheman Building was officially opened with a collection of dolls and art objects from the Fisher Foundation.

3. An extensive refurbishing of the original Farm House, the first building constructed on the Iowa State campus in 1861, was completed.

4. The New York Philharmonic, which had presented the spectacular opening festival of concerts in 1969 to open C. Y. Stephens Auditorium, returned for two appearances—this time in Hilton Coliseum.

5. The veterinary medicine college—founded in 1879 and the oldest state college of veterinary medicine in the United States—moved to its new location two miles south of central campus.

6. The World Food Conference of 1976 was held at ISU and attracted more than 2600 participants and visitors.

7. Enrollment at ISU for spring of 1976 reached 19,464—highest ever for a spring session.

8. The housing crunch at ISU continued as the Department of Residence announced in March that no more housing contracts could be offered for men in the fall because all available spaces were taken. A similar announcement regarding housing for women soon followed.

1977

1. ISU enrollment reached 20,000 for the first time in any spring quarter—an increase of 507 over the same period last year.

2. A study of more than two hundred thousand freshmen in 393 colleges and universities across the nation showed that 64 percent of students entering ISU chose the school because of its good academic reputation.

3. ISU ranked eighth in the nation in the total number of doctoral degrees awarded between 1964 and 1974, according to a U.S. Office of Education report.

4. W. Robert Parks was elected president of the Association of American Universities, succeeding Kingman Brewster, Jr., of Yale, who was appointed U.S. ambassador to England.

5. The Board of Regents approved establishment of a College of Design, which became the seventh undergraduate college and the second one created under the administration of President Parks.

6. A new design center building on the west side of the campus was erected at a cost of $7.4 million. The center would house the Departments of Architecture, Applied Art, and Landscape Architecture.

7. The Iowa Public Employee Relations Act of 1974 permitted state employees to begin collective bargaining June 1, 1976.

8. More than two hundred scientists from around the world came to ISU in order to attend the first International Conference on Iceberg Utilization. "Over 2/3 of the world's supply of freshwater," said Paul Barcus of ISU, "is in the form of icebergs."

9. Nearly 1200 students from eighty-three countries were enrolled at ISU this year.

10. An average of 975 persons per week participated in extension courses and conferences at ISU during the past year. More than 45,490 persons took part in the 410 programs offered.

11. Football rivalry between ISU and the University of Iowa was renewed after a hiatus of forty-two years. The Hawkeyes won the game by a score of 12–10.

1978

1. Twenty-one academic departments began offering evening and Saturday classes.

2. The north wing of Friley Hall underwent a $500,000 remodeling and renovation project.

3. Governor Robert Ray in his budget message delivered to the Iowa legislature asked for an additional $1 million special appropriation for ISU in light of its rapid enrollment growth.

4. A change from the quarter to the semester system was recommended by the faculty and approved by President Parks. The new semester system would take place beginning in the fall of 1981.

5. The Cyclones' forty-eight thousand–seat football stadium was sold out for the season.

6. The ISU Memorial Union held a week-long celebration of its fiftieth anniversary.

7. The Iowa State University Foundation's campaign to raise funds for the library got off to a fast start when members of the Board of Governors personally pledged $100,000 at their meeting in September.

8. The football game between ISU and the University of Iowa brought joy to Cyclone fans when the Cardinal and Gold won with a score of 31 to 0.

9. Cyclone footballers dropped a Hall of Fame Classic game against Texas A&M on December 20, 1978, at Birmingham, Alabama, by a score of 28–12.

1979

1. The Financial Aid Office at ISU reported that it had dispensed $11,708,671 in student support for the fiscal year of 1978.

2. The Stars over Veishea production was Rodgers and Hammerstein's wartime musical, *South Pacific*.

3. ISU's enrollment for the fall quarter climbed to an all-time high of 23,056 students at a time when its voluntary financial support figures also were rising.

4. The ISU Achievement Fund increased by almost $1 million over the previous year and reached $2.6 million; the ISU Foundation received $1.5 million in gifts, maintaining a decade average of over $1 million in annual support for the university.

5. A new $4.6 million building—long a dream of ISU musicians and music lovers—began rising on a wooded hillside overlooking Lake LaVerne, just south of Carver Hall.

6. Pope John Paul II visited Iowa and toured Living History Farms. On six hundred acres just south of Des Moines, Living History Farms are closely linked with ISU. Professor William G. Murray was a prime mover in the project, and President Parks had been a member of the Living History Farm Board of Governors from the outset.

7. The Dresden State Orchestra, founded in 1548 and now the world's oldest orchestra, gave a concert in Stephens Auditorium marking the tenth anniversary observance of the Ames International Orchestra Festival.

1980

1. ISU retained its title as the state's largest university, edging the University of Iowa for the third straight year.

2. The Cardinal Keynotes, a small pop-oriented ensemble, toured the country during the Christmas holidays and capped their performances with a concert before an enthusiastic ISU alumni crowd in the Denver area.

3. President Parks emphasized on several occasions before regents and legislative committees that a substantial increase in salaries for faculty and other employees was ISU's number one budget priority.

4. A dance marathon held in Hilton Coliseum set a goal of $100,000 for muscular dystrophy, but student organizers were pleased when the marathon surpassed that goal and raised $104,000.

5. A Guthrie Theater's touring group presented a production of Tennessee Williams' *The Glass Menagerie* in Stephens Auditorium.

6. President Parks announced that ISU received an appropriation from the state of $22 million for capital improvements—by far the largest ever for that category.

CHRONOLOGY 281

7. The College of Veterinary Medicine celebrated its one hundredth anniversary.

8. Changing class schedules was expedited by the use of computers installed in the Memorial Union. The newer system replaced the older one of checking card files to see if a class was open. Officials said that in a typical day during enrollment times there were as many as four thousand schedule changes.

1981

1. ISU had a record full-time equivalent (FTE) of 23,272 students. Approximately 74 percent of the students were Iowa residents, 20 percent were from other states, and just under 6 percent were from foreign countries.

2. Greek Week, 1981, joined the ISU Library fund-raising effort with a call-a-thon that netted $30,000.

3. The Faculty Council reported that faculty salaries at ISU lagged more than 20 percent behind the decade's inflation.

4. *The Iowa Stater* reported that all of Iowa's cacao, rice, and bamboo crops were grown in the greenhouse at Bessey Hall.

5. President Parks announced that forty ISU faculty members were granted Faculty Improvement Leaves during the academic year 1981–1982.

6. The Los Angeles Philharmonic gave a concert in Stephens Auditorium. Members of the orchestra as well as the music critic for the *Los Angeles Daily News* praised the building for its splendid acoustics.

7. Due to lack of sufficient faculty or classrooms, a record number of students were shut out of courses they requested.

8. Cyclone footballers celebrated a 23–12 victory over the Iowa Hawkeyes.

1982

1. The ISU Foundation Board of Governors announced a five-year plan to raise $50 million in gifts from alumni and friends "to attain and sustain excellence in all fields at Iowa State University."

2. Approximately 1200 people filled the Great Hall, the South

Ballroom, and the Sun Room to hear Vice President George Bush defend the Reagan administration's economic, social, and foreign policies.

3. ISU officials reported that a higher percentage of the school's students were completing their degrees within a four-year time span than was the case fifteen years before.

4. Despite a sluggish national economy, ISU's alumni and friends established a new record for private giving by contributing more than $7 million in 1982.

5. ISU scientists received half of the awards presented by the Iowa Academy of Sciences.

6. Extensive remodeling of the Veterinary Quadrangle was undertaken in order to provide better facilities for the College of Education.

7. The Office of the Registrar reported 24,906 students enrolled, 704 (2.9 percent) more than in the previous fall and 638 (2.6 percent) more than the previous record set in the fall of 1980.

8. In his fall convocation address, President Parks warned that proposed massive federal budget cutbacks jeopardized the nation's higher-education system.

1983

1. President Parks described Governor Terry Branstad's budget recommendation for ISU for the 1983–1985 biennium as "encouraging."

2. The last of fifteen wooden structures left over from World War II came down, ending the "temporary" chapter in ISU campus building history.

3. A three-day international conference was held at ISU to mark the fiftieth anniversary of the founding of the Statistical Laboratory on campus.

4. The 1983–1984 school year began with a record enrollment of 25,000 students, and applications for the next fall were running ahead of the previous year.

5. ISU ranked fifteenth among the nation's colleges and universities in the number of National Merit Scholars enrolled.

6. The Iowa General Assembly approved issuance of revenue bonds by the Board of Regents. The bonds would provide $30.5 million for an addition to the agronomy building.

CHRONOLOGY   283

7. Regents also approved expenditures of $500,000 for remodeling of McKay Hall in the College of Home Economics.

8. The ISU Library completed an $8 million addition that increased usable space by 40 percent, adding more than 70,000 square feet for book shelving and individual study seats.

1984

1. The U.S. Congress appropriated planning funds for a National Soil Tilth Center, a research establishment, to be located on the ISU campus.

2. President Parks presented the university's highest award to John V. Atanasoff. Atanasoff, who received his M.S. from Iowa State in 1926, invented the digital computer. In 1939, Atanasoff, along with his graduate student Clifford Berry, built the Atanasoff-Berry Computer (ABC) at Iowa State.

3. The playing field in the school's football stadium was named the Jack Trice Field to honor an Iowa State athlete who in 1923 died of injuries suffered in a game against Minnesota. It was hoped that naming the field for Jack Trice would put an end to a long-running controversy over the stadium's official name.

4. On July 1, 1984, the School of Business Administration became ISU's ninth college—the third one created under the administration of President Parks.

5. After undergoing more than $330,000 in remodeling, the Hub on ISU's central campus opened with more upgraded landscaping, vending machines, and outdoor eating areas.

6. The Iowa State University Press celebrated its fiftieth anniversary in book publishing.

7. During Alumni Days in June, the ISU Library, cornerstone of the school's academic and research programs, was officially dedicated and named the William Robert Parks and Ellen Sorge Parks Library.

1985

1. The Board of Regents authorized ISU to begin a $2 million renovation project for Alumni Hall for the purpose of converting it into a complex for student services and on-line computer registration space.

2. More than fifteen thousand persons from across the country

filled Hilton Coliseum for a National Farm Crisis Rally focusing attention on the nation's dire farm economy.

3. WOI-TV marked its thirty-fifth anniversary of telecasting. In February of 1950, WOI-TV went on the air as the first educationally owned television station in the country and the only television outlet in central Iowa.

4. With the announcement from President Parks that he planned to retire June 30, 1986, the Board of Regents authorized formation of a University Presidential Search Committee.

5. ISU ranked number one in Iowa and in the Big Eight Conference in the number of freshmen National Merit Scholars enrolled.

6. The Board of Regents authorized ISU's College of Business Administration to grant a new master of business administration (MBA) degree.

7. The fall enrollment in 1985 was slightly more than 26,000—up 12,000 from the 14,000 in attendance during 1965, when W. Robert Parks became ISU's president. During his twenty-year tenure approximately eighty-three thousand degrees have been awarded.

8. For the fourth time in five years, Iowa's deteriorating economy resulted in state-ordered across-the-board reductions in appropriations. This year's 3.85 percent reduction in state appropriations meant a loss of $3.9 million for ISU's 1985–1986 operating budget.

9. Tragedy hit the campus in November when six student athletes and an ISU pilot were killed when their university airplane crashed in Des Moines.

1986

1. The Board of Regents announced that Gordon P. Eaton would succeed W. Robert Parks, who would retire June 30, after twenty-one years as president of Iowa State University.

2. ISU's metallurgy building, part of the Ames Laboratory of the U.S. Department of Energy, was named the Harley Wilhelm Hall in honor of one of the key persons whose works led to the establishment of the national research laboratory at Iowa State.

3. President Parks, making his final appearance at state legislative budget hearings, emphasized that when ISU faculty received a 2 per-

cent salary increase in 1985, surrounding Midwestern states did considerably better. One result was that ISU lost valuable faculty members. He said that improving salaries for faculty and staff, therefore, was at the top of the regents' priority list for that year.

4. The Cyclones' men's basketball team had another record year, with twenty-two victories, second place in the Big Eight Conference, and another appearance in the NCAA tournament, this time advancing to the third round.

5. More than one thousand friends of ISU's First Family for twenty-one years—W. Robert and Ellen Sorge Parks—attended a banquet in their honor March 22 in James H. Hilton Coliseum.

6. ISU officials reported that two-thirds of all living alumni of ISU earned their degrees during the Parks years.

7. In May, shortly before the end of the school year, ISU students organized a "We Love W. Bob" party at the Memorial Union. The Maintenance Shop was filled to overflowing, and "Bob and Ellen" were greeted with thunderous ovations and cheers from the latest of twenty-one student bodies with which they have been associated.

8. At Alumni Days in June, the Parkses were honored with Gold Medals. The Gold Medals traditionally are given to members of reunion classes of fifty years or more, but this fifty-year rule was waived in view of the fact that Parks has presented more than 3500 Gold Medals to others during his tenure as president of ISU.

9. At W. Robert Parks's final meeting with the Iowa Board of Regents in June, the regents unanimously conferred upon him the title president emeritus, effective July 1, 1986.

NOTES

Chapter 1. Iowa State University
1. Earle D. Ross, *A History of Iowa State College of Agriculture and Mechanic Arts* (Ames: Iowa State College Press, 1942), p. 17.
2. Ibid., p. 28.
3. Ibid., p. 65.
4. *The Iowa Stater,* February 1997.
5. Ross, *A History of Iowa State College,* p. 43.
6. Ibid., 212–213.
7. *Commemorative Papers from the Iowa State College Centennial* (Ames: Iowa State College Press, 1958), pp. 41–42.
8. Interview with W. Robert Parks, January 30, 1997.
9. Minutes of the Iowa Board of Regents, April 9–10, 1959, pp. 357–58.

Chapter 2. 1915–1938
1. As quoted in *The Mark Twain Omnibus,* ed. Max J. Herzberg (New York: Harper and Brothers, 1935), p. 370.
2. Aaron Parks: His Ancestors and Descendants, p. 3. This unpublished genealogy is compiled by Joe Parks of Winchester, Tennessee, and Joe Parks of Austin, Texas.

3. Ibid.
4. Ibid., pp. 19–20.
5. Interview with W. Robert Parks, January 9, 1997.
6. Ibid.
7. *Four Taylor Brothers of Lincoln County, Tennessee*, p. 119. This unpublished genealogy is compiled by Joseph H. Parks.
8. Parks interview.
9. Ibid.
10. Ibid.
11. Ibid.
12. Ibid.
13. Ibid.

Chapter 3. 1938–1958

1. Interview with W. Robert Parks, January 30, 1997.
2. Wayne Cole in a letter to this author dated March 11, 1997.
3. Ibid.
4. Ibid.
5. Ibid.
6. Interview with Ellen Sorge Parks, January 29, 1998.
7. W. Robert Parks interview, March 11, 1997.
8. Interview with Elroy Peterson, M.D., and his wife, Jean, April 26, 1997.
9. Ellen Sorge Parks interview.
10. Wayne Cole in a letter to this author dated March 31, 1997.
11. Petersons interview.
12. John C. McNee, as told to this author on December 15, 1997.
13. W. Robert Parks, *Soil Conservation Districts in Action* (Ames: Iowa State College Press, 1952), p. 189.
14. W. Robert Parks interview, January 30, 1997.
15. Ibid.
16. Ibid.
17. Ibid.
18. Interview with Andrea Parks Van Houweling, January 10, 1997.
19. W. Robert Parks interview, January 30, 1997.

NOTES 289

20. Virgil Lagomarcino, *The Owl, the Elephant, and the Other Side of the Mountain* (Ames, Iowa: Lake March Press, distributed by Iowa State University Press, 1997), p. 71.

21. W. Robert Parks interview, January 30, 1997.

22. Wayne Cole in a letter to this author dated March 31, 1997.

23. Earle D. Ross, *A History of Iowa State College of Agriculture and Mechanic Arts* (Ames: Iowa State College Press, 1942).

24. Ellen Sorge Parks interview.

Chapter 4. 1958–1965

1. Interview with W. Robert Parks, January 30, 1997.

2. Iowa State University Chronology of Important Events, compiled by Dorothy Kehlenbeck but not published, 1961, p. 7.

3. Parks interview.

4. Ibid.

5. Kehlenbeck, p. 5.

6. Ibid., 1963, p. 12.

7. Ibid., 1960, p. 5.

8. *Des Moines Register,* September 22, 1959.

9. *Des Moines Register,* September 23, 1959.

10. Parks interview.

11. Ibid.

12. *Des Moines Register,* September 24, 1959.

13. Ibid.

14. Parks interview.

15. *Ames Daily Tribune,* December 10, 1964.

16. Ibid.

17. Interview with Andrea Parks Van Houweling, January 10, 1997.

Chapter 5. Outset of the Parks Presidency

1. Wayne Cole in a letter to this author dated March 31, 1997.

2. Interview with Andrea Parks Van Houweling, January 10, 1997.

3. Interview with W. Robert Parks, January 30, 1997.

4. Parks File, Folder 2, Iowa State University Information Service, Communications Building.

5. Parks interview, March 11, 1997.

6. Ibid.

7. Parks interview, January 3, 1997.

8. George William Curtis, "The Public Duty of Educated Men," in *American Speeches,* ed. Wayland Maxfield Parrish and Marie Hochmuth (New York: Longmans, Green and Co., 1954), p. 367.

9. Staff Convocation Address, September 7, 1965, Parks Inaugural File 211/9, Iowa State University Archives, Parks Library.

10. *Julius Caesar,* Act IV, Scene III, Lines 219–220, in *Complete Works of William Shakespeare,* ed. Hardin Craig (Glenview, Illinois: Scott, Foresman and Co., 1961), p. 792.

11. Parks interview, January 30, 1997.

12. I. S. U. Bomb, Centennial Album, p. 25, Parks Library Special Collections, Iowa State University, 1993.

13. Interview with Elroy Peterson, M.D., and his wife, Jean, March 11, 1997.

14. Iowa State University Chronology of Important Events, compiled by Dorothy Kehlenbeck but not published, 1964, p. 14.

15. Minutes of the Iowa Board of Regents, March 11–12, 1965.

16. Parks interview, March 11, 1997.

17. Kehlenbeck, 1969, p. 3.

18. Parks interview, March 11, 1997.

19. Ibid.

20. Ibid.

21. Interview with Willard "Sandy" Boyd, President Emeritus of the University of Iowa, September 9, 1997.

22. Parks interview, March 11, 1997.

23. Parks Inaugural File 211/9, Iowa State University Archives.

24. Parks interview, March 11, 1997.

Chapter 6. The Vietnam Issue

1. As quoted by Terry H. Anderson in *The Movement and the Sixties* (New York: Oxford University Press, 1995), p. 122.

2. Survey reported in the *Des Moines Register,* May 20, 1967.

3. Ibid.

4. Interview with W. Robert Parks, May 2, 1997.

5. *Des Moines Register,* March 22, 1967.

6. Parks interview.

7. This account is summarized from several sources, including Anderson, *The Movement and the Sixties,* pp. 351–353; Charles De Benedetti, *An American Ordeal: the Antiwar Movement of the Vietnam Era* (Syracuse, N.Y.: Syracuse University Press, 1990), pp. 279–280; and D. Thorstad, *May 1970: Birth of the Antiwar University* (New York: Pathfinder Press, 1971), pp. 12–13.

8. Interview with Stanley Redeker, April 18, 1997.

9. Ibid.

10. Interview with Willard "Sandy" Boyd, former president of the University of Iowa, September 9, 1997.

11. Interview with Neil Harl, May 19, 1997.

12. Ibid.

13. Interview with George Christensen, October 28, 1997.

14. Harl interview.

15. Interview with Wayne Moore, June 2, 1997.

16. Parks File, Folder 4, Iowa State University Information Service, Communications Building.

17. Harl interview.

18. Parks interview.

19. Interview with Ames police chief Dennis Ballantine, June 17, 1997.

20. Parks File.

21. Moore interview.

22. The author was seated next to President Parks on this occasion and witnessed the incident.

23. *Iowa State Daily,* May 13, 1970.

24. Parks interview.

25. Boyd interview.

26. Redeker interview.

27. Arthur Sandeen, Vice President for Student Affairs at the University of Florida, in a letter to this author dated April 16, 1997.

28. Parks interview.

Chapter 7. Race Relations

1. Alexander Kendrick, *The Wound Within: America in the Vietnam Years, 1945–1974* (Boston: Little, Brown, and Co., 1974), pp. 151–152.

2. Howard Zinn, *A People's History of the United States, 1492–Present,* revised and updated ed. (New York: HarperCollins Publishers, 1995), p. 451.

3. John Milton, *Paradise Regained,* Book IV, Line 220.

4. Interview with W. Robert Parks, January 9, 1997.

5. Ibid.

6. Parks interview, February 1, 1997.

7. Parks interview, March 11, 1997.

8. Interview with Fred Schlunz, former dean of admissions and records, June 20, 1997.

9. *Iowa State Daily,* April 25, 1970.

10. Interview with Judge John L. McKinney on July 2, 1997.

11. Interview with Elroy Peterson, M.D., and his wife, Jean, April 26, 1997.

12. Ibid.

13. *Iowa State Daily,* April 29, 1970.

14. McKinney interview.

15. Interview with George Christensen, October 28, 1997.

16. Ibid.

17. Interview with Wilbur Layton, May 12, 1997.

18. Ibid.

19. Office of the Registrar, Iowa State University.

Chapter 8. ISU Extension

1. Earle D. Ross, *A History of Iowa State College of Agriculture and Mechanic Arts* (Ames: Iowa State College Press, 1942), pp. 101–102.

2. C. Austin Vines and Marvin A. Anderson (eds.), *Heritage Horizons: Extension's Commitment to People* (Madison, Wisconsin: Extension Journal, 1976), pp. 5–6.

3. Ralph K. Bliss, Extension Service Work in Iowa: Agriculture and Home Economics Annual Report, July 1, 1920–June 20, 1921, pp. 20–21.

4. As told by Marvin Anderson to this author on August 18, 1997.

5. Dorothy Schwieder, *75 Years of Service: Cooperative Extension in Iowa* (Ames: Iowa State University Press, 1993), p. 18. This source is a well-written single volume that presents an excellent history of extension at Iowa State.

6. Ibid., pp. 21–22.

7. Ibid., p. 36.

8. Interview with W. Robert Parks, December 11, 1997.

9. "New Dimensions: How Far from Reality?" address given by W. Robert Parks, Vice President for Academic Affairs, Iowa State University, in *The Century Ahead: Proceedings of a Seminar on Agricultural Administration in the Land-Grant System Held June 16–19, 1963, at Fort Collins, Colo.* (Fort Collins: Colorado State University Publication Service), 1963.

10. Confidential memorandum from Marvin Anderson to President W. Robert Parks proposing a university-wide extension service, dated August 8, 1965.

11. Interview with Marvin Anderson, November 18, 1997.

12. Ibid.

13. Annual Narrative Reports from County Extension Directors of Allamakee, Appanoose, and Franklin Counties, as quoted by Schwieder, *75 Years of Service*, p. 170.

14. As quoted by Schwieder, *75 Years of Service*, p. 176.

15. Anderson interview.

16. "New Dimensions," p. 140.

Chapter 9. Intercollegiate Athletics

1. James Cain, "The Man Merriwell," *Saturday Evening Post,* June 11, 1927, p. 129.

2. Earle D. Ross, *A History of Iowa State College of Agriculture and Mechanic Arts* (Ames: Iowa State College Press, 1942), pp. 79–81.

3. Howard J. Savage, *American College Athletics,* bulletin 23. New York: Carnegie Foundation for the Advancement of Teaching, 1929.

4. Mervin D. Hyman and Gordon S. White, Jr., "The Big Ten's Dirty Linen," *Big Ten Football: Its Life and Times, Great Coaches, Players, and Games* (New York: Macmillan, 1977), pp. 30–31.

5. Ibid.

6. See, for example, Wilford S. Bailey and Taylor D. Littleton, *Athletics and Academe* (New York: Macmillan, 1991), pp. 67–68.

7. As quoted in the *Des Moines Register,* September 13, 1981.

8. Letters of Tribute to Cap Timm, compiled by Thad Dohrn. See also Department of Athletics, Iowa State Baseball Media Guide, 1974.

9. Ibid.

10. *Des Moines Register,* December 25, 1966.

11. Parks File, Stadium Folder 1, Faculty Newsletter, Iowa State University Archives, Parks Library.

12. *The Iowa State Student,* October 10, 1923.

13. Jack Trice File, Folder 1, Iowa State University Archives.

14. See, for example, Parks File, Stadium Folder 1, Iowa State University Archives.

15. *Iowa State Daily,* May 16, 1976.

16. Ibid.

17. Interview with George Christensen, October 28, 1997.

18. As quoted in the *Des Moines Register,* September 13, 1981.

19. Interview on June 27, 1997, with Fred Schlunz, Emeritus Dean of Admissions and Records.

20. Athletics Director File, 1972–1973 Folder, Iowa State University Archives.

21. Ibid.

22. Interview with W. Robert Parks, January 30, 1997.

23. As quoted in the *Des Moines Register,* September 13, 1981.

Chapter 10. Building and Funding

1. *Iowa State Daily,* December 12, 1964.

2. *General Catalog, 1965–1967,* Iowa State University of Science and Technology, Ames.

3. Interview with Wayne Moore, August 5, 1997.

4. *General Catalog 1985-87,* Iowa State University Bulletin, Ames.

5. Interview with W. Robert Parks, March 11, 1997.

6. Interview with George Christensen, October 28, 1997.

7. Moore interview.

8. Interview with Willard Boyd, President Emeritus of the University of Iowa, September 9, 1997.

NOTES 295

9. Moore interview, August 8, 1997.
10. Data supplied by John W. Pace, interview on September 24, 1997.
11. Ibid.
12. Arthur C. Wickenden, *Raymond M. Hughes: Leader of Men* (Oxford, Ohio: Oxford Printing Company, 1966), pp. 84–85.
13. *The Iowa Stater*, vol. 23, issue 3, September 1997, p. 11.
14. Minutes of the Iowa Board of Regents, June 23–25, 1965, p. 634.
15. Parks interview, January 30, 1997.
16. Christensen interview.

Chapter 11. A Reckoning

1. Clark Kerr and Marian L. Glade, *The Many Lives of Academic Presidents* (Washington, D.C.: Association of Governing Boards of Universities and Colleges, 1986), xiv.
2. Interview with W. Robert Parks, March 11, 1997.
3. Ibid.
4. Parks interview, May 2, 1997.
5. Farwell T. Brown, *Ames: The Early Years in Word and Picture* (Ames, Iowa: Heuss Printing, 1993), pp. 53–56.
6. Interview with George Christensen, October 28, 1997.
7. Niccolò Machiavelli, *The Prince and the Discourses* (New York: Modern Library, 1940), pp. 85–86.
8. Parks interview, May 2, 1997.
9. Parks interview, March 11, 1997.
10. Parks interview, December 11, 1997.
11. Interview with Robert Parks Van Houweling, February 3, 1997.
12. *Des Moines Register*, July 9, 1986.
13. Interview with Willard Boyd, September 9, 1997.

BIBLIOGRAPHY

Books

Allen, Frederick Lewis. *Only Yesterday.* New York: Harper and Row, 1931.
———. *Since Yesterday—1929–1939.* New York: Bantam Books, 1940.
Amter, Joseph A. *Vietnam Verdict.* New York: Continuum Publishing Co., 1982.
Anderson, Terry H. *The Movement and the Sixties.* New York: Oxford University Press, 1995.
Bailey, Wilford S., and Taylor D. Littleton. *Athletics and Academe.* New York: Macmillan, 1991.
Bliss, Ralph K. *Extension in Iowa: The First Fifty Years.* Ames: Iowa State University of Science and Technology, 1960.
Blue Book of College Athletics for 1977–78. Cleveland, Ohio: Rohrich Corporation, 1979.
Brown, Farwell T. *Ames: The Early Years in Word and Picture.* Ames, Iowa: Heuss Printing, 1993.
Carlson, Kenneth N. *College Football Scorebook,* 2nd ed. Lynnwood, Washington: Rain Belt Publications, 1984.
The Century Ahead: Proceedings of a Seminar on Agricultural Administration in the Land-Grant System Held June 16–19, 1963, at Fort

Collins, Colo. Fort Collins: Colorado State University Publications Service, 1963.

Commemorative Papers from the Iowa State College Centennial (Ames: Iowa State College Press, 1958), pp. 41–42.

Craig, Hardin, ed. *The Complete Works of Shakespeare.* Glenview, Illinois: Scott, Foresman and Co., 1961.

Cross, George Lynn. *Letters to Bill on University Administration.* Norman: University of Oklahoma Press, 1983.

Frey, James H., ed. *The Governance of Intercollegiate Athletics.* West Point, New York: Leisure Press, 1982.

Hacker, Louis M., and Benjamin B. Kendrick. *The United States Since 1865.* New York: F. S. Crofts and Co., 1935.

Halberstam, David. *The Best and the Brightest.* New York: Random House, 1969.

Herzberg, Max J., ed. *The Mark Twain Omnibus.* New York: Harper and Brothers, 1935.

Isaacs, Arnold R. *Without Honor: Defeat in Vietnam and Cambodia.* Baltimore: John Hopkins University Press, 1983.

I. S. U. Bomb: Centennial Album. Parks Library Special Collections, Iowa State University, 1993.

Kendrick, Alexander. *The Wound Within: America in the Vietnam Years, 1945–1974.* Boston: Little, Brown, and Co., 1974.

Kerr, Clark, and Marian L. Glade. *The Many Lives of Academic Presidents.* Washington, D.C.: Association of Governing Boards of Universities and Colleges, 1986.

Lagomarcino, Virgil. *The Owl, the Elephant, and the Other Side of the Mountain.* Ames, Iowa: March Lake Press, distributed by Iowa State University Press, 1997.

Machiavelli, Niccolò. *The Prince and the Discourses.* New York: Modern Library, 1940.

McCallum, John D. *Big Eight Football.* New York: Charles Scribner's Sons, 1979.

Michener, James A. *Sports in America.* New York: Random House, 1976.

Morison, Samuel Eliot. *The Oxford History of the American People.* New York: Oxford University Press, 1965.

Morley, John. *The Life of Richard Cobden.* Boston: Roberts Brothers, 1890.
O'Brien, Kenneth Paul, and Lynn Hudson Parsons, eds. *The Home-Front War.* Westport, Connecticut: Greenwood Press, 1995.
Parks, W. Robert. *Soil Conservation Districts in Action.* Ames: Iowa State College Press, 1952.
Parrish, Wayland Maxfield, and Marie Hochmuth, eds. *American Speeches.* New York: Longmans, Green and Co., 1954.
Pettittt, George A. *Twenty-eight Years in the Life of a University President.* Berkely: University of California Press, 1966.
Podhoretz, Norman. *Breaking Ranks.* New York: Harper and Row Publishers, 1979.
Powers, Thomas. *The War at Home: Vietnam and the American People, 1964-1968.* New York: Grossman Publishers, 1973.
Ross, Earle D. *A History of Iowa State College of Agriculture and Mechanic Arts.* Ames: Iowa State College Press, 1942.
———. *The Land-Grant Idea at Iowa State College.* Ames: Iowa State College Press, 1958.
Schwieder, Dorothy. *75 Years of Service: Cooperative Extension in Iowa.* Ames: Iowa State University Press, 1993.
Sperber, Murray. *College Sports Inc.* New York: Henry Holt Co., 1990.
Summers, Harry G., Jr. *Vietnam War Almanac.* New York: Facts on File Publications, 1985.
Thelin, John R. *Games Colleges Play.* Baltimore: John Hopkins University Press, 1994.
Underhill, Robert. *The Bully Pulpit.* New York: Vantage Press, 1988.
———. *FDR and Harry: Unparalleled Lives,* Westport, Connecticut: Praeger Press, 1996.
———. *The Truman Persuasions.* Ames: Iowa State University Press, 1981.
Vines, C. Austin, and Marvin A. Anderson, eds. *Heritage Horizons: Extension's Commitment to People.* Madison, Wisconsin: Extension Journal, 1976.
Wickenden, Arthur C. *Raymond M. Hughes: Leader of Men.* Oxford, Ohio: Oxford Printing Co., 1966.
Williams, Harry T., Richard N. Current, and Frank Freidel. *A History*

of the United States Since 1865. New York: Alfred A. Knopf, 1966.

Zinn, Howard. *A People's History of the United States, 1492–Present,* revised and updated ed. New York: HarperCollins Publishers, 1995.

Unpublished Sources

Aaron Parks: His Ancestors and Descendants. Compiled by Joe Parks of Tennessee and Joe Parks of Texas.

Annual Narrative Reports of County Extension Agents in Iowa

Four Taylor Brothers of Lincoln County, Tennessee. Compiled by Joseph H. Parks.

Iowa State University Budgets

Iowa State University Chronology of Important Events, 1958-1967. Compiled by Dorothy Kehlenbeck.

Iowa State University Financial Reports

Minutes of the Iowa Board of Regents

Minutes of the Iowa State University Faculty Council

Magazines, Journals, Newspapers

Ames Daily Tribune
Des Moines Register
Green Gander (Iowa State College humor magazine)
Iowa State Daily
The Iowa Stater

Personal Interviews

W. Robert Parks (President Emeritus of Iowa State University)
Ellen Sorge Parks (Mrs. Robert Parks)

Marvin Anderson
Dennis Ballantine
Willard "Sandy" Boyd
George Christensen
Wayne Cole
Neil Harl

BIBLIOGRAPHY

Wilbur Layton
John L. McKinney
Wayne Moore
John W. Pace
Elroy and Jean Peterson
Stanley Redeker
Arthur Sandeen
Fred Schlunz
Andrea Parks Van Houweling
Robert Parks Van Houweling

INDEX

Page numbers followed by n denote references in the Notes section.

Agricultural Adjustment Act (Triple A), 31
Agricultural and Economic Adjustment, Center for, 61
Agricultural experiment station program, 6
Agricultural Wheel, 180
Agriculture
   extension service, 173–197
   Farm Bureau, 183–185
   farm crisis, 244–245
   farm organizations, 179–180
   Populism, 180–182
Agriculture, Department of, 45
Agriculture Short Course Office, 95, 187, 188
Agronomy, Department of, 187
Agronomy building, 282
Alcohol, 28–29
Alger, Horatio, 27
Alumni Achievement Fund, 161, 275, 276
Alumni Association, ISU, 94
Alumni Hall, 283
Alvin Edgar Fund for the Performing Arts, 274
American Philosophic Society, 174
Ames, Iowa
   City Hall bombing, 167–168
   founding of, 5
   protests
      racial, 163–164
      student, 129, 139, 162
   race relations, 162–168
   restoration of downtown area, 256–257
Ames Laboratory, 70, 284
Anderson, Ernest W., 62, 72
Anderson, Glenn, 210, 272
Anderson, Julia Faltinson, xvi
Anderson, Marvin, xvi
   appointment as dean for extension, 94, 266
   contrasting styles of Hilton and Parks, 195–196, 293n
   extension service, 187–188, 190–193, 292n, 293n
Anderson, Terry H., 290n
Andre, Floyd, 12
Animal Reproduction Station, 272

303

Armory, 209, 211
Association of American Agricultural Colleges, 175
Association of American Universities, 225, 232, 275, 278
Atanasoff, John V., 283
Athletics
  conferences, 204, 206
  history of, 199–202
  Iowa State University, 202–203
    baseball, 206–207
    basketball, ISU, 208–209, 210, 211, 225, 272, 285
    eligibility, 221
    facilities, 209–211, 212–218
    football, 208–218, 222–225, 276, 278–279
    gymnastics, 208, 271, 272
    Parks, Robert, 206, 207, 209–214, 217–227
    Physical Education, Department of, 218–220
    Timm, Leroy C. "Cap," 206–207
    wrestling, 208, 271, 272
  University of Iowa, 203–204, 211–212
Atomic research, 70
Automobiles, impact of, 15–16

Ballantine, Dennis, 139–140, 291n
Barcus, Paul, 278
Barnett, Ross, 151
Baroda University, 64
Baseball, 203, 206–207
Basketball, 208–209, 210, 211, 225, 272, 285
Bay of Pigs, 119
Beardshear, William, 86, 182
Bell, William, 160–161, 163
Benbrook, Edward A., 62
Berea College, 24, 32–33
  athletics at, 206
  race relations, 155–156
Berlin Wall, 120
Berry, Clifford, 283

Bessey Hall, 244, 281
Big Eight Athletic Conference, 206, 208, 209, 221
Big Ten Athletic Conference, 204
Bilsland Swine Breeding Research Center, 272
Birch Hall, 271
Black Cultural Center, 160, 271
Black Panthers, 152, 162
Black Student Organization, 160–161, 166, 170–171
Blackwelder, Murray, xvi
Bliss, Ralph K., 51, 178, 184, 292n
Board of Regents. *See also* Chronology of the Parks presidency
  buildings, requests for new, 244
  curriculum expansion, 62–63, 89–91
  departments, division of, 90–91
  football stadium name and, 217, 218
  funding requests, 230, 232, 235
  human rights policy statement, 157–158
  Iowa State University name change, 12
  minority enrollment, encouragement of, 159
  Parks's appointment to presidency, 71–73
  Physical Education department restructuring, 219
  student conduct rules, 138–139
  student protests and, 131–132
  university extension, 188–189
Board of trustees, Iowa State University, 8, 9
Boeke, Robert W. and Roberta, xvi
Bombs, 164–165, 167–168
Book club, 87
Boston Pops Orchestra, 277
Boston University, 129
Bowen, Howard, 73
Boyd, Willard "Sandy," xvii, 290n
  athletics and, 212
  faculty salaries, 237, 295n
  on Robert Parks, 263, 295n
  on Robert Parks's relationship with

INDEX

administrative associates, 144
   student protests and, 131–132, 291n
Brandeis University, 129
Brandt, Frank, 248
Branstad, Terry, 282
Brewster, Kingman, Jr., 278
Brown, Barbara T., xvi
Brown, Farwell T., 295
Browning, George, 72
Brown v. Board of Education, 158
Bruce, Earl, 219, 224, 273
Brunnier Gallery, 277
Bryan, William Jennings, 18, 28, 181–182
Buchanan, Robert, 51, 265, 274
Buchanan Hall, 265
Buildings, construction and funding, 242–249. *See also* Chronology of the Parks presidency
Burch, Maxine, xvi
Bureau of Agricultural Economics, 45–46, 49–50
Burke, Edmund, 80
Bush, George, 19, 282
Business Administration, School of, 283, 284
Butterfield, Kenyon L., 175

Calley, William L. Jr., 146
Cambodia, invasion of, 128–129
Cambridge, Massachusetts, 48
Campanile, 276
Cape Cod, 262
Cardinal Guild, 60
Carnegie Foundation for the Advancement of Teaching, 203
Carter, Jimmy, 19
Carver, George Washington, 156, 271
Carver Hall, 244, 268, 271
Case Western Reserve University, 130
Casey, Judy, xvii
Center for Industrial Research and Service (CIRAS), 95, 187, 188, 189
Chalmers, Gordon, 209
Chicago Tribune, 203

Child Development, Department of, 89, 273
Chisholm, Shirley, 152
Christensen, George
   appointment as vice president of academic affairs, 92–93, 265
   budget process, 234–235
   extension reorganization, 188
   on library allocations, 258, 295n
   Physical Education, Department of, 218–220, 294n
   racial unrest, 169–170, 292n
   reliance upon, Parks's, 258
   student protests and, 134–135, 143, 291n
Christensen, Jack, 67
Chronology of the Parks presidency, 265–285
   1965, 265–266
   1966, 266–267
   1967, 267–268
   1968, 269–270
   1969, 270–271
   1970, 271–272
   1971, 272–273
   1972, 273–274
   1973, 274–275
   1974, 275–276
   1975, 276–277
   1976, 277
   1977, 278
   1978, 279
   1979, 279–280
   1980, 280–281
   1981, 281
   1982, 281–282
   1983, 282–283
   1984, 283
   1985, 283–284
   1986, 284–285
Churchill, Winston, 41
Civil rights, 120, 122, 123, 148, 252. *See also* Race relations
Civil Rights Act of 1964, 152
Civil War, 5, 22
Clark, Mark, 152

Clark University, 129
Clyde Williams Field, 209, 212, 267, 276
Cole, Virginia, 44
Cole, Wayne, 55–56, 288n, 289n
  on Ellen Parks, 44, 56
  on Robert Parks
    appointment to presidency, 76
    intellectual broadness, 56
    political orientation, 38
Coles, Jessie V., 276
Colorado State University, 186, 197
Computer science, 89, 265, 268
Congress. *See* Federal government
Coolidge, Calvin, 19
Coon Rapids, Iowa, 66–67
Cooperative Extension Service, 6, 94–95, 175, 187, 188. *See also* Extension service
Coover, Mervin S., 271
Coover Hall, 271
County extension agents, 176, 182, 183–184
Crabbe, Maurice, 73
Crawford, Reid W., xvi
Crom, Robert, 164
Curfews, 77, 268
Curtis, George William, 81, 290n
Cyclone nickname, origin of, 203
Cyclone Stadium, 218

Dairy Sales Room, 270
Darrow, Clarence, 28
Davey, Hal and Mary, 44, 87
Dayton, Tennessee, 28
Dean's Council, 235
Design, College of, 244, 278
Design center, 267, 276, 278
Des Moines, Khrushchev's visit to, 66
Des Moines Packing Company, 66
Des Moines Register, 123, 183
Detroit, Michigan, 152
Dewey, John, 79
Distinguished Professor program, 62
Donnelly, Ignatius, 180–181

Draft, military, 126, 132
Dykstra, Clarence, 253–254

East Hall, 271
Eaton, Gordon P., 284
Economics, Department of, 90
Eddy, Bob and Barbara, xvi
Edgar, Alvin R., 274
Education, College of, 194, 273
Eisenhower, Dwight D., 19, 66, 70, 118
Emerson, Ralph Waldo, 35, 79
Engineering, 64
Engineering Extension Service, 95, 187, 188
English, Department of, 91, 270
Enrollment. *See also* Chronology of the Parks presidency
  initial, 8, 75
  minority, 159, 172
Environmental Council, 271
Epright, Ercel, 72
Equal Employment Opportunity Commission (EEOC), 152
Erickson, Betty, xvii
Expanded Food and Nutritional Education Program (EFNEP), 194
Experimental station, 179, 191, 230
Extension Act of 1906, 182–183
Extension service, 173–197
  county agents, 176, 182, 183–184
  demonstrations, 177–178
  early years, 173–185
  Extension Act of 1906, 182–183
  Farm Bureau, 183–185, 190
  farm organizations and, 179–180
  Iowa State University
    Anderson, Marvin, 187–188, 190–193
    Bliss, Ralph K., 178, 184
    curriculum expansion, 192–193
    experimental station, 179
    Holden, Perry G., 182–183
    Knapp, Seaman A., 175–176
    Parks, Robert, 187–197

INDEX

poverty and welfare programs, 193–194
reorganization, 94–95, 187–191
TENCO, 192
youth programs, 191–192
short courses, 176–177
Smith-Lever Act of 1914, 175

Faculty
contact with university presidents, 205
departments, division of, 89–91
Distinguished Professor program, 62
exchange program, 159
gathering in the Nook, 54–55
initial, 8
leaves, 159, 266, 281
number of, 231
overseas teaching experiences, 64
Parks, Robert as member, 51–56
promotion, 259
reception for, annual, 83–84
retirement program, 64–65
salaries, 61, 213, 234, 237–241, 243
Faculty Council, 92, 140–141, 212, 217, 281
Faculty Improvement Leave program, 159
Family Environment, Department of, 267
Farm Bureau, 182, 183–185, 190
Farmers' Union, 180, 185
Farm House, 275, 277
Farm organizations, 179–180
Farrar, Floyd, 24
Fayetteville, Tennessee, 30
Federal government
Hatch Act of 1887, 6
Land-Grant Act, 5, 6
New Deal legislation, 31
nutritional programs, 193–194
Privacy Act of 1974, 126
Smith-Lever Act of 1914, 6, 175
Fee, John G., 32
Financial aid, student, 61, 63–64, 230

Fine arts, 245–248
Fire Service Extension Building, 267
Fisher, J. W., 275
Fisher Foundation, 277
Fisher Theater, 211, 247, 274, 275
Football, 203, 208–218, 222–225, 273–274, 276, 278–279
Ford, Gerald, 19
Ford, Henry, 18
Ford Foundation, 61, 64
Foreign Languages, Department of, 81
Forker, Barbara E., xvi, 220
Forsythe, Richard H. and Charlotte L., xvi
Foster, Suel, 7
4-H clubs, 177, 185, 187, 191, 192
Fox, George and Annie Mae, 154–155
Fox, Robert "Spud," 155
Franklin, Benjamin, 174
Fraternities and sororities, 267
Friley, Charles, 52, 83, 84, 234
Friley Hall, 279
Friley-Hughes Hall, 269
Funding, 229–249
Board of Regents and, 230, 232, 235
budget process, 233–235
buildings, 242–249
faculty salaries, 234, 237–241, 243
library, 214–242, 248–249
state appropriations, 230, 231, 232–233, 235, 239
Fund-raising, 61, 205, 213–214, 224. *See also* Funding
Future Farmers of America (FFA), 192

Gable, Dan, 208, 274
Gagnier, Ed, 208
Garcia, Pilar A., xvi
Gardner, Jay, 171
Garst, Roswell, 66–67
Gaskill, Harold, 51
General Assembly of Iowa. *See* Legislature, Iowa
General Services Building, 245
Gentle Doctor sculpture, 246

Gilman, Henry, 274, 275
Gilman Hall, 275
Glanton, Luther, 161, 168
Goldwater, Barry, 122
Goodland, Paul, 256–257
Government, Department of, 123
Governor's Day, 142–143
Gowan, Arthur
   appointment as dean of admissions and records, 95
   athlete eligibility and, 221
   enrollment requirements and, 158–159
   reliance upon, Parks's, 258–259
Graebner, Norman, 55
Grange, the, 179–180
Great Depression, 30, 189
Greensboro, North Carolina, 150
Grosvenor, Dale, xvi
Gue, Benjamin F., 4, 7–8
Gulf of Tonkin Resolution, 121
Gunderson, Marion and Deane, xvi
Gymnastics, 208, 271, 272

Hadwiger, Don, 123
Hamilton, Carl
   appointment as director of university relations, 93, 265
   radio and television stations, 93–94
   reliance upon, Parks's, 144, 258
   Special Events Committee, 272
   stadium naming and, 216–217
   student protests and, 134–136, 143–144
   vice president for information and development, 94
Hamilton, Samuel C., xvi
Hampton, Fred, 152
Hancher, Virgil, 10–11, 12, 63
Hansen, Gilda, 87
Hansen, Robert S., 95
Harding, Warren G., 18
Harl, Neil, 133–136, 138, 161, 291n
Harrington, Fred, 140
Harvard University, 47, 129, 201

Hatch Act of 1887, 6
Hatcher, James, 25
Head Start, 194, 273
Hicks, Ellis and Jo, 87
Hilton, Helen, 233–234. *See also* LeBaron, Helen
Hilton, James, 56–57
   backing of Parks for presidency, 71–73
   building program, 242–243, 246
   on butchering demonstration, 178
   faculty receptions, 83, 84
   fund-raising, 210
   Iowa State University name change, 11–12
   Khrushchev's visit to ISU, 68, 69
   marriage to Helen LeBaron, 234
   retirement, 71
   style, 195–196
Hilton, Lois, 71, 74
Hilton Coliseum, 211, 247, 271, 273
Hiram College, 55
History, Department of, 270
History, Government, and Philosophy, Department of, 50–51, 90, 91
A History of Iowa State College of Agriculture and Mechanical Arts, xv, 287n, 289n, 292n
Hoffman, David and Judie, 87
Holden, Perry G., 182–183
Home Economics
   building projects, 283
   extension programs, 184, 191, 193–194
   Honors Program, 60
   Khruschev's visit and, 68, 69
   short courses, 95, 177
   100th anniversary, 272
Honors Program, 60
Horticulture farm, 269, 271
Hovey, Betsy, xvii
Hughes, Harold, 230
Hughes, Raymond, 72, 246
Humanism, 100–103, 260–261, 264
Human Relations Committee, 157, 267

INDEX

Humphrey, Hubert, 128
Huntress, Keith, 54, 72

Illinois University, 55
Inaugural address of Robert Parks, 98–103
India, 64
Indiana University, 85, 103
Iowa Agricultural College. *See also* Iowa State University
  chartering, 4
  location choice, 4
Iowa Farmer, 7
Iowa Grain Dealers Association, 183
Iowa School for the Blind, 176
Iowa State Center, 210–211, 211, 247, 266, 267, 274
Iowa State College of Agriculture and Mechanic Arts, 9, 10. *See also* Iowa State University
Iowa State Daily, 76–77, 216
Iowa State Foundation, 94
Iowa State Players, 248
Iowa State Teachers College at Cedar Falls, 9, 11
Iowa State University. *See also* Chronology of the Parks presidency
  athletics, 202–203
    baseball, 206–207
    basketball, ISU, 208–209, 210, 211, 225, 272, 285
    eligibility, 221
    facilities, 209–211, 212–218
    football, 208–218, 222–225, 273–274, 276, 278–279
    gymnastics, 208, 271, 272
    Physical Education, Department of, 218–220
    Timm, Leroy C. "Cap," 206–207
    wrestling, 208, 271, 272
  board of trustees creation, 8
  budget process, 233–235
  catalog, 231
  curriculum expansion, 62–64, 89–92, 192–193

enrollment
  1965, 75
  initial, 8, 75
  minority, 159, 172
extension service
  Anderson, Marvin, 187–188, 190–193
  Bliss, Ralph K., 178, 184
  curriculum expansion, 192–193
  experimental station, 179
  Holden, Perry G., 182–183
  Knapp, Seaman A., 175–176
  Parks, Robert, 187–197
  poverty and welfare programs, 193–194
  reorganization, 187–191
  TENCO, 192
  youth programs, 191–192
founding, 4
funding
  Board of Regents and, 230, 232, 235
  budget process, 233–235
  buildings, 242–249
  faculty salaries, 234, 237–241, 243
  library, 214–242, 248–249
  state appropriations, 230, 231, 232–233, 235, 239
growth of, 231–232, 236–237, 257, 263
Khrushchev's visit, 65, 67–70
Land-Grant Act, 6
location choice, 4–5
naming of, 9–13
presidents, 56–57, 62–63 (*See also* Hilton, James; Parks, William Robert)
  Beardshear, William, 86, 182
  Friley, Charles, 52, 83, 84, 234
  Hughes, Raymond, 72, 246
  Pearson, Raymond A., 86, 215
  Storms, Albert B., 86
  Welch, Adonijah Strong, 8–9, 75, 176
race relations
  Black Cultural Center, 160–161

Iowa State University, race relations
    (*continued*)
  Black Student Organization,
      160–161, 166, 170–171
  Carver, George Washington, 156
  director of minority affairs, 160
  Human Relations Committee, 157
  protests, 163, 168–171
  recruitment of minorities,
      158–159, 172
  student protests, 123–127, 129,
      133–146
  teacher-training programs, 194
Iowa State University Foundation, 210,
    289
The Iowa State Student, 214
ISU Achievement Fund, 280

Jack Daniel's Distillery, 28–29
Jack Trice Stadium, 218, 283
Jean, Chuck, 162
Jensen, James
  Distinguished Professor program,
      61–62
  recruitment of Robert Parks, 57
  resignation of, 63
Jepsen, Roger, 139
Jischke, Martin C., Preface by, xiii–xiv
John, Maurice, 272
John Deere, 66
Johnson, Lyndon B., 19, 117,
    121–122, 128, 152
Jordan, Becky, xvii

Kehlenbeck, Alfred, 54
Kehlenbeck, Dorothy, 289n, 290n
Kellogg Foundation, 56, 61, 63
Kennedy, John F., 19, 44, 118–121
Kennedy, Robert, 151
Kent State University, 130–131, 133,
    137
Kerner, Otto, 152
Kerner Commission, 152
Kerr, Clark, 252, 295n
Khrushchev, Nikita, 65–70

Khrushchev, Nina, 69
Kildee, H. H., 51, 265
Kildee Hall, 265
King, Leslie L., 19
King, Martin Luther Jr., 150, 151, 152
Kirkham, Don, 62
Kissinger, Henry, 147
Kitchell, Ralph L., 95
Knapp, Seaman A., 175–176
Knoll, the
  history of, 86
  Parks family moves to, 85, 87
  renovations, 86–87, 267
Knox, Charles, 162–163, 167
Korean War, 118

LaFollette, Robert M., 37
Lagomarcino, Virgil, 53–54, 63,
    288n–289n
Land-Grant Act, 6, 175
Land-grant colleges, 6
Lange, Bill, 73
Larch Hall, 269, 271
Layton, Gloria, 171
Layton, Wilbur (Bill)
  appointment as vice president for
      student affairs, 95
  racial unrest, 170–171, 292n
  reliance upon, Parks's, 258
  student protests and, 134, 142, 143
Lease, Mary B., 181
LeBaron, Helen, 12, 68, 233–234
Lefka, Mary Lou, 125
Legislature, Iowa
  board of trustees creation, 8
  chartering of Iowa Agricultural College, 4, 8
  Extension Act of 1906, 182–183
  funding for Iowa State University,
      230, 231, 235
  Iowa Experimental Station established, 179
  Iowa State University name change,
      13
  student protests and, 232–233
Leningrad Philharmonic, 275

INDEX

Liberty Bowl, 274
Library
  dedication as the William Robert Parks and Ellen Sorge Parks Library, 283
  Ellen Parks's fondness for, 44–45
  funding for, 214–242, 248–249, 257–258, 266, 268
  millionth book acquired, 277
  Parks's commitment to, 249, 263
  Parks's office in, 261
  sculptures, 246
Lincoln, Abraham, 3, 5, 175
Lindbergh, Charles A., 28
Linton, Albert, 170–171
Living History Farms, 280
Lodge, Henry Cabot, 66, 70
London Symphony Orchestra, 275
Los Angeles Philharmonic, 281
Lusitania, 18
Lyle, Mary S., 62

Madden, Beverly, xvi
Madden, Warren, xvi, 234
Madison, James, 23
Majors, Johnny, 222–224, 273
Malcom X, 150–151
Manatt, Charles T., xvii
March of Concern, 134, 137
Marshall, Thurgood, 152, 158
Mashek, John, 51
Mason, James M., 5
Massachusetts Agricultural College, 175
Massachusetts Institute of Technology, 129
Matterson, Matty, 54, 55, 56, 85, 206
Maucker, J. W., 132–133, 237
McCarthyism, 38
McClellan, General George, 6
McConico, Fred, 170–171
McConico, Tony, 170–171
McGovern, George, 147
McJimsey, George and Sandra, 87
McKay Hall, 283
McKinney, John L., 162, 163, 164–168, 292n

McNamara, Robert, 119
McNee, John C., 44–45, 288n
Meat Laboratory, 276
Memorial Union
  construction projects, 243, 268
  Hamilton, Carl and, 94
  Nook, the, 54–55, 57
  Trophy Tavern, 273–274
Merchant (Dean of Veterinary Medicine), 12
Meredith, James, 151
Messerly, Francis, 164
Middle Tennessee College, 25
Middletown study, 16
Milton, John, 153, 292n
Montgomery, Alabama, 149–150
Moore, Wayne, xvii
  appointment as vice president for business and finance, 95, 266
  budget process, 234–235
  funding for building projects, 244, 295n
  student protests and, 134, 136, 141, 143–144, 232–233, 291n, 294n
Morrill, Justin Smith, 5, 6, 175
Morrill Act. *See* Land-Grant Act
Mosher, M. L., 183
Mueller, Joan, xvii
Mulberry, Tennessee, 17, 25–27, 31
Munger, Larry, 162
Murfreesboro, Tennessee, 17, 22, 25
Murray, William G., 51, 56
  Human Relations Committee, 157
Murray, William G. (*continued*)
  Living History Farms, 280
Music, Department of, 272

NAACP Legal Defense Fund, 158
Nagurski, Bronco, 207
National Aeronautics and Space Administration (NASA), 266, 268
National Association of State Universities and Land-Grant Colleges (NASULGC), 159, 225, 226, 231, 274
National Collegiate Athletic Association (NCAA), 202, 203, 206, 221, 294

National Council for Accreditation of Teacher Education, 232, 273
National Farmers' Alliance, 180
National Grange of the Patrons of Husbandry, 179–180
National Guard, 130, 131, 132, 135, 139, 145, 151, 252
National Industrial Recovery Act, 31
National Merit Scholars, 60–61
National Soil Tilth Center, 283
Newark, New Jersey, 152
New Deal, 31
New Hampshire, 46
New Philadelphia, 5
Newspaper, student, 76–77
Nichols, Harold, 208
Nixon, Richard M., 19, 44, 70, 118, 128, 140, 146–148
Nolan, Betty, 136
Nook, the, 54–55, 57
Norfolk, Virginia, 48
North Carolina A&T College, 150, 160
Northeastern University, 129
Nutritional programs, 193–194

Oberlin College, 32
O'Mara, Joe, 54, 57
Orangeburg, South Carolina, 152
Oratorical contests, 202
Order of the Knoll, 269
Oregon State University, 63, 130
Orr, Johnny, 225
Otopalik, Hugo, 208
The Owl, the Elephant, and the Other Side of the Mountain, 288n

Pace, John W., 244, 245, 295n
Page, J. Boyd, 63, 188
Parks, Aaron, 20
Parks, Ambrose, 20
Parks, Andrea, 43, 44, 53, 288n, 289n
  on father's public school years, 26
  graduate work, 85, 103

student curfews, 77–78
Parks, Benjamin Newton, 17, 22, 25, 26, 27
Parks, Benjamin Thurston, 20–21
Parks, Cindy, 44, 85, 87, 165–166
Parks, Claude Alexander, 24
Parks, Elisha Taylor, 24
Parks, Elisha Thomison, 22
Parks, Ellen, 262
  on administration, 58
  book club, 87
  career *versus* home, 42–45
  faculty receptions, 84
  first meeting of Robert, 40
  library, fondness for, 44–45
  marriage to Robert, 41–42
  news of Robert's appointment to presidency, 74
  pastimes, 44–45
  political orientation, 38, 43, 44
  race relations and, 156, 165–166
  Robert's inaugural address and, 99
  at University of Wisconsin, 39–41
  in Washington, D.C., 45–46, 48
Parks, Horace Newton, 24–25, 26, 30, 32
Parks, John, 20
Parks, Joseph Howard, 21, 24, 29, 30, 32, 287n
Parks, Louis and Rose, 21
Parks, Martha (nee Thomison), 21
Parks, Mary Badgett, 24
Parks, Mary (nee Thurston), 20
Parks, Minnie Angeline (nee Taylor), 17, 22, 23, 27, 33, 154–155
Parks, Minnie Lorraine, 25, 26
Parks, Oney, 20
Parks, Reuben, 20
Parks, Rosa, 150
Parks, Taylor, 32
Parks, Thomas, 19–20
Parks, Thomas, Jr, 20
Parks, William, 20
Parks, William Robert. *See also* Chronology of the Parks presidency

INDEX

ancestry, 19–24
birth of, 17
book club, 87
Bureau of Agricultural Economics, 45–46, 49–50
early years, 24–33
education of
   Berea College, 32–33, 35, 155–156
   public school, 25–32
   University of Kentucky, 35–36
   University of Wisconsin, 36, 40–41
Ellen (wife) (*See also* Parks, Ellen)
   first meeting, 40
   wedding, 41–42
humanism and, 100–103
humor, 96–97
Iowa State University
   as administrator, 57–58
   administrators, choice of, 92–95, 258–259
   appointment to president, 72–74, 76–77, 265
   athletics and, 206, 207, 209–214, 217–227
   curriculum expansion, 62–64, 89–92, 263
   dean of instruction, 59–63
   early opinion of, 50–51
   extension service, 94–95, 187–197
   faculty positions, 51–56
   faculty receptions, 84
   fine arts and, 247–248
   funding
      budget process, 233–235
      buildings, 243–249
      faculty salaries, 237–241
      growth and, 236
      library, 241–242, 248–249
   goals for, 82
   inaugural address, 98–103
   name change, 11–13
   student protests, 123, 134–146
   vice president, 61, 63–65
Khrushchev's visit to ISU, 68–69

Navy career, 47–49
political orientation, 38
race relations, 154–172
   childhood years, 153–155
   at Iowa State University, 156–172
   young-adult years, 155–156
religion, 27–28
retirement, 256–257, 261–262
on scholars, 79–80
on social conscience, 79–81
speeches of
   at Colorado State University (1963), 186–187, 197, 293n
   1986 convocation, 260
   1965 fall convocation, 81–82
   inaugural address, 98–103
   at Wartburg College (1963), 79–80
sports, participation in, 29–30, 33
style, 196, 253–255, 259
summary, 251–264
University of Wisconsin faculty, 56–57
Pass-fail grading system, 268
Peace Corps, 120, 186
Pearl Harbor, 117
Pearson, Raymond A., 86, 215
People's Party, 180
Pericles, 80
Pershing, General John (Blackjack), 18
Pesek, John, xvii
Petersen, Christian, 246
Peterson, Ben, 208, 274
Peterson, Elroy, 44, 288n, 290n
   book club, 87
   friendship with Robert Parks, 85, 206
   racial unrest and, 165–166, 292n
Peterson, Jean, 42–43, 44, 288n, 290n
   book club, 87
   racial unrest and, 165–166, 292n
Peterson, Peter A. and Sara R., xvii
Philadelphia Orchestra, 273
Philosophy, Department of, 270
Physical Education, Department of, 218–220, 276

Physics building, 269
Point Four, 186
Political Science, Department of, 270
Politics in Wisconsin, 37–38
Populism, 180–182
Port Huron, Michigan, 121
Poverty, 193
Prairie View University, 159
Princeton University, 129, 201
Privacy Act of 1974, 126
Progressive Farmer, 176
Project 400, 275
Psychology, Department of, 89

Race relations, 149–172
  in Ames, Iowa, 162–168
  at Iowa State University, 156–162, 168–172
  nationally, 149–153
Radio stations, ISU, 93–94
Ramsay, Frank, 72
Rasmussen, Diane, 69
Ray, Robert D., xvii, 279
  Foreword by, xi–xii
  student protests and, 132, 139
Reagan, Ronald W., 19
Redeker, Stanley, xvii, 131–132, 136, 145, 291n
Reedsburg, Wisconsin, 39, 41
Reedy, George, 121
Regents Rules of Conduct, 138–139
Religion, 27
Richardson, Lily Mae, 27
Rickenbacker, Eddie, 18
Roberts Hall, 271
Roby, Roosevelt, 162–163, 164, 166, 167
Roosevelt, Franklin, 29, 31, 41, 47
Roosevelt, Theodore, 18, 202
Ross, Earle D., xv, 56, 248, 275, 287n–289n, 292n–293n
Ross Hall, 248, 275
ROTC, 130, 131, 134, 142, 255
Sandage, Duane and Alpha, xvii
Sandeen, Arthur
  reliance upon, Parks's, 258

on Veisha 1970, 145, 291n
SANE (Committee for a Sane Nuclear Policy), 121
Sargent, Warren and Velma, xvii
Scheman Continuing Education Building, 211, 247, 276
Schilletter, J. C. "Shorty"
  reliance upon, Parks's, 258–259
  Schilletter Village, 276
  student unrest and, 144
Schilletter Village, 276
Schlenker, Ralph, xvii
Schlunz, Fred, 292n
  athlete eligibility and, 221, 294n
  reliance upon, Parks's, 258–259
Schnoor, Jerry, 255
Schwartz, James W., 95
Schwieder, Dorothy, 292n–293n
Scopes, John T., 28
Semester system, 279
Sharp, Paul, 55
Short Course Office, 95, 187, 188
Short courses, 94, 95, 176–177, 265
Siedelmann, Arnie, 139, 171
Simpson, Jerry, 181
Simpson College, 156
Slaves, 20, 21
Smith, Al, 29
Smith, Don, 123–128
Smith, Stuart, 139
Smith-Lever Act of 1914, 6, 175
Snedecor, George W., 271
Snedecor Hall, 271
Sociology and Anthropology, Department of, 90
Sorge, Ellen. *See* Parks, Ellen
Southern Christian Leadership Conference, 150
Special Events Committee, 216, 217, 272
Spedding, Frank H., 60
Speech, Department of, 91, 270
Speeches of Robert Parks
  at Colorado State University (1963), 186–187, 197, 293n
  1986 convocation, 260
  1965 fall convocation, 81–82

INDEX 315

inaugural address, 98–103
  at Wartburg College (1963), 79–80
Speth, Linda, xvii
Sports. *See* Athletics
Stanford University, 129
State Agricultural College and Model Farm, 4, 8, 9. *See also* Iowa State University
State appropriations, 230, 231, 232–233, 235, 239
State University, 7–8. *See also* University of Iowa
Statistics, Department of, 272
Steil, Arch, 221
Stephens, C. Y., 210
Stephens Auditorium, C. Y., 211, 246–247, 270
Stones River National Military Park, 17
Storms, Albert B., 86
Student Nonviolent Coordinating Committee (SNCC), 121, 150
Student Peace Union (SPU), 121
Students
  costs of education, 230, 233
  curfews, 77, 268
  financial aid, 61, 63–64, 230
  protests, 121–146, 162, 232–233, 252, 255–256
  reaction to Parks's appointment, 77
  Regents Rules of Conduct, 138–139
  university in loco parentis, 120
  Vietnam and, 120–123
Student's Bill of Rights, 124–126
Students for a Democratic Society (SDS), 121, 122, 124, 151
Sullivan, Lenore, 69
Sun Bowl, 273
Susskind, David, 134, 137

Taylor, Chris, 208, 274
Taylor, James, 22–23
Taylor, William Blanton, 23
Taylor, Zachary, 23
Teacher education program, 63–64, 194
Teachers Insurance and Annuity Association of America (TIAA), 64
Technical Institute in Agriculture, 268, 272
Television
  athletics and, 226
  course presentations via, 52–53, 267
  Iowa State University stations, 93–94
TENCO, 192
Tennessee
  extension programs, 185
  Parks, Robert and, 17, 24–31
  Parks ancestry and, 20–22
  race relations, 153–155
Tennessee Valley Authority, 31
Texas, 46
Texas State Alliance, 180
The Iowa Stater, 281, 287n
Thomas, Al, 159
Thompson, Gary, 207
Tillman, Ben, 181
Timm, Leroy C. "Cap," 206–207
Timm, Tippy, 206
Timmons, John, 50
Towers, 243, 266, 268
Town, George R., 275
Trice, Jack, 214–218
Trophy Tavern, 273–274
Truman, Harry, 85
Tufts University, 129
Tuition, 230, 231, 233
Turner, Richard, 136
Tuskegee Institute, 156
Twain, Mark, 16

Ulmer, Martin and Helen, 87
University of California (Berkeley), 122
University of Iowa. *See also* Boyd, Willard "Sandy"
  athletics, 203–204, 211–212
  Hancher, Virgil, 10–11, 12, 63
  poverty and welfare extension programs, 193
  race relations, 157
  student unrest, 128, 131–132
University of Kentucky, 35–36
University of Maryland, 55–56

University of Minnesota, 207, 214
University of Mississippi, 151
University of North Carolina at Chapel Hill, 55
University of Northern Iowa, 73
  poverty and welfare extension programs, 193
  student protests, 132–133
University of Oklahoma, 55
University of Virginia, 55
University of Wisconsin
  Parks, Robert and, 36, 40–41, 56–57
  race relations, 156
  student protests, 140
University Research Association, 266
University Village, 243, 266, 269, 275

Van Allen, James, 131
Van Houweling, Andrea Parks. *See* Parks, Andrea
Van Houweling, Robert Parks, 262, 295n
Van Pilsum, Joyce, 96, 124, 169–171
Veishea (1970), 133–138, 141, 145
Veterinary Medical Research Institute, 244, 266, 267
Veterinary Medicine
  Central Building, 244
  100th anniversary of college, 281
  relocation of college, 277
Vietnam, 119–123, 128–148, 252, 255
Vines, C. Austin, 292n
Vinograde, Bernard and Ann, 87
Voter registration, 150, 152

Waite, Davis H., 181
Wallace, Henry, 183
Warner, Glenn "Pop," 203
Wartburg College, 78–80
Watergate, 147

Weaver, James B., 181
Wedding of Robert and Ellen Parks, 41–42
Welch, Adonijah Strong, 8–9, 75, 176
Welch Hall, 271
Wellesley, Arthur, 201
Western Stock Journal and Farmer, 176
Whitman, Bill and Toni, xvii
Wickenden, Arthur C., 295n
Wiggins, Charles, 123
Wilhelm, Harley, 284
Wilhelm Hall, 284
Williams, Clyde, 209
Wilson, David and Julie, 87
Wilson, William Duane, 7
Wilson, Woodrow, 17–18
Wisconsin. *See also* University of Wisconsin
  cultural diversity, 38
  liberalism, political, 37–38
  Robert Parks's opinion of, 39
WOI-TV, 52, 93, 284
Wood, Grant, 246
Woodward, Al, 48
Woodward, Bob, 48
Woodward, Jane, 48
Woolworth, 150
World War I, 17–19
World War II, 41, 46–49, 156
Wrestling, 208, 271, 272

Yale University, 129, 201
Yemelyanov, V. S., 60
York, Alvin, 18–19
Young Peoples Socialist League (YPSL), 121

Zaffarano, Daniel and Suzanne, xvii
Zaring, Jane, xvii
Zumbach, Steven E., xvii